# INSURRECTION

# INSURRECTION

Five Schools of Revolutionary Thought

MILOS MARTIC

Foreword by A. James Gregor

## DUNELLEN

**New York • London**

International Standard Book Number 0-8046-7099-4

Library of Congress Catalogue Card Number 73-92088

Printed in the United States of America

UNIVERSITY PRESS OF CAMBRIDGE, MASS. SERIES
CONSULTING EDITOR: EUGENE H. NELLEN


**Distributed by**
Kennikat Press Corp.
90 So. Bayles Avenue
Port Washington, N.Y. 11050

**UK Distributions**
Martin Robertson & Company Ltd.

# Foreword

The preoccupation with irregular warfare, partisan or guerrilla combat, is perhaps as old as recorded history. In our own time the operation of irregulars or underground combatants, has had considerable influence upon the outcome of modern conflict. Memories of the second world war are still fresh in the minds of most analysts. Most students will have read of the hundreds of thousands of European "civilians" who were engaged in one or another form of irregular warfare against the military forces of the Third Reich and of Fascist Italy. They will remember the hundreds of thousands of partisans on the Eastern Front and in the Balkan countries. In Great Britain the Home Guard was being trained specifically for guerrilla warfare in anticipation of German landings. Even in the United States bands of civilians, armed with hunting rifles, shotguns, and hand guns, were organized into irregular units in anticipation of Japanese occupation.[1]

Throughout Asia, on the Malay peninsula, Java and the Chinese mainland, armed civilians struggled against the Japanese armed forces. Nor were the Axis forces loathe to invoke irregulars. Fascists led bands of Ascari irregulars against the British in Ethiopia. The Japanese population was armed to resist the Allied landings on the home islands and the Germans organized the ill-fated *Volkssturm* during the last days of the conflict.

As early as the eighteenth century, the revolutionary colonists of North America had invoked irregular warfare against the British. The Spanish, during the Napoleonic wars, employed guerrilla warfare to drive out the French armies. The French, in their turn, fell back upon irregular warfare after their effective defeat at the battle of Sedan in the Franco-Prussian war. The Chinese had utilized guerrilla tactics against the English during the Opium Wars—and the Philippine Insurrection against the United States at the turn of the century involved irregular combatants. Cuban nationalists, mobilized by the moral exhortation of José Martí, employed guerrilla tactics against the Spanish in the Cuban wars of liberation before the end of the nineteenth century.

In the years between the two great wars of the twentieth century, there were guerrilla activities in Latin America, Indochina and the Philippines. The roster of names that might be listed among the guerrilla leaders of the twentieth century is long and would include representatives from almost every political persuasion—some without any particular political conviction—and others whose activities are hard to distinguish from simple banditry.

After the end of the second world war, guerrilla warfare became more and more frequently identified, somehow, as a singularly Marxist revolutionary tactic. The victory of Mao Tse-tung's Red Army on the Chinese mainland signaled, to many analysts, the development of a special form of revolutionary warfare characteristic of Marxists.

It is at least doubtful whether guerrilla warfare, as a particular form of insurgency, has any intrinsic connection with the Marxism of Marx and Engels. There is, on the other hand, a historic, if not a theoretic, connection with the circumstances surrounding the Bolshevik revolution in Russia. But we also know that Lenin had serious reservations about the invocation of "guerrillaism," the "arbitrary actions," and the "unruly guerrilla spirit" that characterized "revolutionary romanticism."[2] In the case of Mao Tse-tung we have reasonably compelling evidence that he knew nothing of the writings of Friedrich Engels on military matters and probably knew of Lenin's opinions only indirectly. Most of Mao's notions about irregular warfare probably come from traditional Chinese sources, with the writings of Sun Tzu, more than two thousand years old, perhaps exercising the most influence.[3]

There is no doubt that both Marx and Engels were familiar with irregular warfare. They both specifically refer to instances of partisan or guerrilla warfare in Spain against the French, in China against the British, and in the Civil War in the United States. Marx carefully studied the revolutionary activities of the Spanish guerrillas against the Napoleonic armies—and described their tactics in a fashion that reads like a synoptic handbook of irregular warfare.[4] Engels's account of the guerrilla resistance of the Chinese against the "barbarians" is equally illuminating. Engels argued that irregular warfare, when it involves the fanatic participation of the masses, renders orthodox military response totally ineffectual and counterproductive.[5] Fifteen years later, in November 1870, he was to illustrate the same thesis—employing the irregular warfare of the French resistance against the victorious German army after the defeat at Sedan.[6]

What is equally clear, for all that, is that neither Marx nor Engels identified irregular warfare as a particularly Marxist tactic. It was but one form of struggle among many in the revolutionary's repertoire. Neither Marx nor Engels ever considered guerrilla warfare as anything other than a revolutionary weapon to be employed in very singular circumstances. This is evident when one considers that both Marx and Engels conceived "their" revolution, the revolution of the sophisticated urban proletariat, to be a function of advanced industrial society. While neither Marx nor Engels precluded the recourse to violence in making revolution, both conceived the revolution possible without violence.[7] It is equally clear that neither conceived all irregular wars, undertaken by "fanaticized masses," to be "progressive."

For Engels the warfare of Italian irregulars in their efforts to unify the Italian peninsula was progressive, because contemporary economic conditions required the development of viable demographic and resource units; and wars of liberation, in certain circumstances, serve to create such national entities. Italy and Germany were just such viable entities. On the other hand, Engels deplored the irregular warfare and insurrectionary activities of "non-viable" nationalist movements. He spoke of most of the "Slav nations" as "having no future," and any insurrectionary activity on their part, whether it involved regular or irregular warfare, as "counter-revolutionary."[8] For Engels it was not a question of "suppressed nationalities," but of "completely different levels of civilization," of the "level of social development," of the "basic historic, geographic, political and industrial prerequisites for independence and vitality,"[9] that determined the revolutionary or counterrevolutionary character of irregular warfare. It was a question of "the interests of civilization."[10]  Thus even though the irregular warfare of the Bedouins in Algeria was "heroic," Engels insisted that the victory of the French "imperialists" was to be welcomed, since it brought in its train the "civilisation, industry" and "order" of the bourgeoisie.[11]

For China, Marx anticipated that revolutionary activity would culminate in a bourgeois revolution characterized in the slogan, "Liberty, Equality and Fraternity." When Engels addressed himself to the possibilities of revolution in Russia, he insisted that all kinds of violence were possible under the impostures of Czarist restraints. But he rejected the suggestion that insurrectionary violence under the primitive economic conditions that prevailed in Russia could produce a socialism with which he would identify Marxism. A socialist revolution, Engels insisted, is only possible where the "productive forces have developed sufficiently to make the abolition of classes a real possibility."[12]  Anyone, Engels argued, who could assert that "revolution is easier to undertake in a land in which there is neither a proletariat nor a bourgeoisie, has not learned the ABC of socialism."[13]

For both Marx and Engels guerrilla warfare was recognized as an effective means of struggle, particularly against foreign invaders, but they both conceived socialism as the product of *class*, not international, warfare. National liberation movements that invoked irregular warfare won their support only if such movements were "in the interests of civilization," and were, in effect, conducted to provide a geopolitical space which was economically viable—or which could, alternatively, be construed as weakening capitalism. It is clear that they did not conceive guerrilla warfare in countries like China or Russia as capable of delivering any recognizable form of socialism. In countries where socialism was possible, that is to say, in the advanced industrial countries of the West, Engels argued explicitly against urban guerrilla warfare; and while he alluded to the necessity of obtaining peasant support for the socialist revolution, he nowhere suggested that that support would manifest itself in the form of rural guerrilla warfare.[14]

Only Lenin, who "creatively developed" Marxism, could speak of revolutions in underdeveloped countries, in which but precious few proletarians could be found, as *universally* serving the interests of socialism. Lenin anticipated such revolutions as "sparking" revolutions in the advanced industrial countries—revolutions which would provide the necessary economic base for socialism. Where revolutions were anticipated in such "primitive" conditions, Engels's injunctions against urgan guerrilla warfare would have to be modified.[15] During the Civil War in Russia that followed the Bolshevik seizure of political power, Lenin embraced irregular warfare, but he had clear reservations about its indiscriminate employment.

Whatever the case, it is clear that such activities could not be conceived as fostering socialism unless they constituted a preamble to revolution in the advanced industrial countries. There is no evidence that Lenin anticipated building socialism in one country. While his strategy did welcome insurrection in any country, it seems fairly obvious that the strategy was more calculated to serve the survival of the Bolsheviks than usher in the millenium.

When Mao invoked peasant guerrilla warfare to serve the communist revolution in China, it became clear that little survived of the Marxism of Marx and Engels. A mass of restive peasants, invoked by a call to resist a foreign invader, in this case the Japanese, undertook irregular warfare to bring a leadership of "declassed bourgeois intellectuals" to power in order to industrialize backward China. Whatever socialism such a movement delivers, it has precious little affinity with the socialism of Marx and Engels.

Unhappily, this has only been belatedly recognized by the Soviets. The Marxists of the Soviet Union now identify Maoism as a "petty bourgeois, nationalist and chauvinist, anti-Marxist movement" addicted to "military romanticism."[16] In a country innocent not only of proletarians, but of a bourgeoisie as well, Maoism employed irregular warfare to mobilize all recruitable population elements into a political struggle clearly committed to national interests and rapid industrialization.[17] Whatever socialism is to be found in China is the "socialism of poverty"—the provision of minimal subsistence to a population employed, by and large, in agricultural pursuits. Marxism has devolved into the rationale for movements devoted to national liberation and the rapid modernization of countries suffering colonialism and thwarted or delayed industrialization. All of Marxism collapses into a cry for revolutionary warfare—guerrilla wars directed essentially against foreign troops or a regime conceived as the tool of imperialism. If such a call for revolutionary war comes from a party that is clearly committed to "foreign interests," whether Marxist or not, the enterprise is faulted. When it became clear that the guerrilla forces in the Malay states did not represent "national" aspirations, the movement was suppressed. When the Huks of the Philippines could not make the case that the government represented only American imperialism, the movement was defeated. When the Greek guerrillas, after the end of the second world war, appeared to be extensions of Soviet policy, the movement collapsed. For four years, from 1945 until 1949, the communist party in Franco Spain undertook hundreds of guerrilla assaults against the government only to be suppressed.

Even Castro's adventure in Cuba won much of its support by employing the slogan, "The Fatherland or Earth!" and by invoking the resistance of Cubans against the depredations of the "imperialism from the North." Where the peculiar conditions which made successful guerrilla warfare possible in Cuba have not obtained, guerrilla warfare has been suppressed. There have been at least fifteen ill-fated guerrilla efforts in Latin America inspired by the Cuban model. All have been singular failures.

Strange things have befallen "Marxism" during the second half of the twentieth century. All of Marxism seems to have been telescoped into the strategy and tactics of guerrilla warfare. Nothing much survives of the social, political and military conceptions of the founders of classical Marxism. Certainly little is to be found in the writings of Debray and Cabral. There is precious little Marxism in the writings of Ché Guevara or Carlos Marighella. The mystique of guerrilla warfare has clouded all the subtleties and theoretic niceties of the founders of Marxism. In some cases all that remains are simplistic and sometimes simple-minded convictions that guerrilla warfare of have-not nations against the "rich" nations must inevitably succeed.[18] In its most degenerate form, this kind of guerrilla romanticism provokes student and black radicals to undertake barbarous and criminal acts that have scant political significance and no hope of revolutionary success.[19]

For at least these reasons Dr. Martic's book is welcome. We are afforded the occasion of reviewing a diverse and pluriform body of thought on a kind of warfare that will probably be of significance throughout the remainder of this century. There are a number of places in the contemporary world where one may expect irregular or guerrilla warfare to break out—and Dr. Martic's volume suggests where some of those places might be—and how much success the proponents of guerrilla warfare might enjoy in such circumstances. It is abundantly clear that the environment in advanced industrial societies is most inhospitable, at the moment, to guerrilla adventurers. The evidence for that is, at least in part, to be found in the tortured rationale offered in the theoretical writings of the guerrillas in our midst.

But more than that, Dr. Martic's book poses a number of problems to which professional political scientists and students of politics are compelled to address themselves. We know very little, in fact, about the conditions which foster successful revolutionary warfare. (Why did Cabral enjoy some significant success while the black revolutionaries in the Republic of South Africa have been incapable of mounting a single effective guerrilla band?) We know little about the individual and collective motivations of guerrilla combatants. (Is a nationalist passion the necessary and/or sufficient condition for precipitating guerrilla commitment?) At least in part because of our ignorance, we have no clear sense of what can be effective in suppressing guerrilla activity. Because of the very nature of irregular warfare we have little hard data, few defensible empirical generalizations, and no comprehensive strategy of interpretation.

We are compelled nonetheless to begin somewhere. And Dr. Martic's book is one of the better places to begin.

A. James Gregor
Berkeley, California

# Notes

1. "To Arms!" *Time*, 39: 13 (March 30, 1942); cf. B. Levy, *Guerrilla Warfare* (Boulder, Colo.: Panther, 1964).

2. V. I. Lenin, "The Present Situation and the Immediate Tasks of Soviet Power," *Collected Works* (Moscow: Progress, 1965), 29: 462; and "letter to the Workers and Peasants a propos of the Victory over Kolchak," *Ibid.*, p. 553.

3. Cf. J. L. Wallach, *Die Kriegslehr von Friedrich Engels* (Hamburg: Europaeische Verlagsanstalt, 1968), pp. 69-71.

4. Cf. K. Marx, "Revolutionary Spain," in K. Marx and F. Engels, *Revolution in Spain* (New York: International, 1939), pp. 50-55.

5. F. Engels, "Persien-China," in K. Marx and F. Engels, *Werke* (Berlin: Dietz, 1961), 12: 213 f.

6. K. Marx, "Rede ueber den Haager Kongress," *Werke*, 18: 160.

7. Engels, "Po und Rhein," *Werke*, 13: 267f.

8. Engels, "Democratic Panslavism," in P. W. Blackstock and B. F. Hoselitz, eds., *The Russian Menace to Europe* (Glencoe: Free Press, 1952), pp. 67-84.

9. *Ibid.*, pp. 68, 69, 71, 72.

10. Engels, "French Rule in Algeria," in S. Avineri, ed., *Karl Marx on Colonialism and Modernization* (Garden City, N.Y.: Doubleday, 1968), p. 43.

11. Marx, "Revue," *Werke*, 7: 221f.

12. Engels, "Soziales aus Russland," *Werke*, 18: 556.

13. *Ibid.*, p. 557.

14. Engels, "Introduction to the Class Struggles in France," in K. Marx and F. Engels, *Selected Works* (Moscow: Foreign Languages, 1955), 1: 124, 130-38.

15. Cf. V. I. Lenin, "Lessons of the Moscow Uprising," *Collected Works*, 11: 176 f. Lenin speaks of "practice [marching] ahead of theory" (*Ibid.*, p. 173).

16. Cf., for example, F. V. Konstantinov, M. I. Sladkovsky, and V. G. Georgiyev, eds., *A Critique of Mao Tse-tung's Theoretical Conceptions* (Moscow: Progress, 1972); V. I. Krivtsov, ed., *Maoism through the Eyes of Communists* (Moscow: Progress, 1970).

17. Cf. J. H. Kautsky, "Neo-Maoism, Marxism and Leninism," in *Communism and the Politics of Development* (New York: Wiley, 1968).

18. Cf. R. Taber, *The War of the Flea* (New York: Stuart, 1965).

19. In this regard, cf. M. Oppenheimer, *The Urban Guerrilla* (Chicago: Quadrangle, 1969).

# Contents

# INSURRECTION

# Introduction

During the past twenty or thirty years guerrilla warfare has become the central theme in the daily life of a number of countries in Asia, Africa, South America, and the Middle East. In some of them it has preempted the use of all other political weapons; in others it serves as the principal incubator of unrest, threatening to burst forth at any moment and embroil an entire population. Regardless of the underlying causes for the development of a guerrilla movement in a given country, that country is almost invariably forced upon an irreversible course. This puzzling form of warfare puts violence on a pedestal and nurtures generations geared to settle all disputes with brute force. Waged with utter disregard for ultimate cost, it leaves in its wake an insidious backlash of intolerance and utter chaos. The question of who is likely to emerge victorious from this frustrating muddle—the fittest, the glibbest, or the meanest— is largely a matter of conjecture.

The existence of a guerrilla movement in any one area is almost sure to be felt the world over. The hijacking and destruction of planes in Jordan in 1970, for instance, became overnight a major concern of all states that use air transport, and instilled misgivings in the heart of every airline passenger. The outcome of a guerrilla engagement in Laos or in Vietnam today may be of vital concern not only to the immediate theater but to Saigon, Washington, Moscow, Peking, Pnompenh, Hanoi, and others as well. If the leaders of urban guerrilla movements remain the sole means of communication between an incumbent regime and dissident segments of the population in the Middle East, the intricate machinery of supplying the world with oil may be thrown out of gear. Such incidents as the onslaughts against libraries or the burning of institutes on American campuses, student demonstrations in Sofia or Belgrade, Paris or Tokyo, Mexico City or Berlin, the "bourgeois counterrevolution in Czechoslovakia" of 1968, the December insurrection of Polish workers in 1970, the tragedy of the Munich Olympics, or the kidnapping and killing of diplomats—all pose a problem not only to the governments involved but to the world at large.

Guerrilla warfare through the ages has inspired author, poet, and painter. It has frequently thrust into prominence a humble human being. A peasant may become a leader of a guerrilla detachment, a village woman a member of the regional committee, an ex-librarian the chief military theoretician, a school drop-out or teacher the commander-in-chief. A professional soldier, on the other hand, may find overnight that his knowledge and training come to naught. As a form of warfare the guerrilla movement invariably fires the imagination of youth. In our age, for instance, the bookshelf of almost any student reasonably attuned to his times would surely contain at least one or two representative works on this subject. Thus it would seem that the concept of guerrilla warfare has become so much an integral part of the lives and thoughts of the old and the young, of statesmen, politicians, soldiers, agitators, journalists, professors and students, parents and offspring, that if the world is not interested in guerilla warfare, guerrilla warfare is interested in the world.

The number of universities currently delving into the theory and practical implications of guerrilla is also on the increase. By including the subject in their curriculum, these institutions contribute to the expansion of the body of knowledge on the subject and negate the theory fashionable in the West toward the end of the forties that concentration upon issues such as dictatorship, violence, terror, and guerrilla activities was almost equivalent to endorsement of all of them. The student will find authors of all political leanings as well as many who defy classification. If, for purposes of study, we were to single out the Marxist writers, who are statistically the most numerous on the subject of guerrilla, we would find them divided into classical Marxists, Marxist-Leninists, belated adherents to Stalinism, Maoists, Titoists, Castroists, Revisionists, and neo-Marxists, Trotsky-ites, New Leftists, Anarcho-Communists, African Marxists, and the representatives of the Latin American Marxist school, as well as a number of followers bogged down by a bewildering array of choices. Each of these groups, in attempting to express its subservience to that particle of infallibility of the Marxist doctrine it cherishes, tends to formulate on its own a unique conception of guerrilla warfare and to write its own *What Is To Be Done.**

On the other hand, because of the absence of comprehensive textbooks on the subject, the student may for instance regard guerrilla activity as a product of Marxist thought. But in order to avoid oversimplification and to interpret fairly the material he examines, the student should be reasonably informed on the times, on the author's ideology, and on considerations of tactics and policy that have impelled some authors to write history one chapter at a time without relating one chapter to another. Ideally, in other words, before he can thrust himself into the study of an author's elementary facts and conclusions, a student must possess the competence of an expert and the maturity of a political sage. The principal goals of this study, therefore, are to minimize these difficulties by assisting the serious student to secure some semblance of solid background and to supply some orientation in the voluminous material on insurrection.

In embarking on this project, I have started out with

*Reference to Lenin's work of the same title, published in 1902.

certain perceived similarities in the works of some contemporary authors on insurrection. These identifying traits, I believe, permit the grouping of such authors into an individual school of thought as separate and distinct from other fraternities of authors bound, again, by their own, original methodologies and their unique outlook. With this in mind, I have concentrated on five such groups of authors or schools of thought: the Marxist hard liners, the Latin American, the African, the New Leftist revolutionaries, and finally, the works of Western analysts. Within the compass of a single, brief explanation, I have attempted wherever possible to set forth the principal elements that serve to identify each of the schools in the light of certain criteria—ideology, political organization, political activity, military organization, military activity, and external influences—and then to evaluate them.

From a purely technical standpoint, the Marxist authors lend themselves most easily to this treatment. The Marxist literature, designed to serve a dual purpose, holds fast to the party-line in assuming the inevitable collapse of all social orders outside the Sino-Soviet bloc and the diminishing capacity of the bourgeois society to withstand any completely organized guerrilla onslaught.

But the present study makes a distinction between two writing patterns of the Marxists: one representing the countries where the communist guerrilla movements triumphed in the first part of this century (the U.S.S.R., China, Yugoslavia, and Albania), and the other coming from the pens of Marxists outside the communist bloc. Though the purpose of both is identical, these two subgroups of authors, if one may label them as such, manifest in their writing technique differing degrees of skill in processing data on insurrection and guerrilla warfare, as well as varying levels of flexibility in making compromises between the original Marxist thought and reality.

From the middle sixties on, the foundations of the hard

liner teachings on insurrection have been seriously challenged by the Latin American revolutionaries. Though they have no quarrel with the hard-liner dogma that history runs on rails according to a predictable schedule, they do reject the first postulates of the hard liners on the party cadre as the infallible "pointsman of history," along with a number of classical Bolshevik theses that concern the time, the place, and the instruments of revolutionary warfare. In essence, this is a protest school, one whose voice and latent push for destruction of the Bolshevik manual are strong—but not quite strong enough to cause a new manual to be produced. Since its principal concepts are still in the process of formulation, our treatment of its strategy and tactics, as well as of its ideology and doctrine, is necessarily more imprecise than is the case with the hard liners. Regrettably, the same may hold true of sections dealing with African and New Leftist writers. Moreover, some of the leading representatives of these schools have done a much more thorough job on some areas of their subject than on others, thus putting additional difficulties in the way of an objective assessment or survey.

The summary of views of authors from Western Europe and the United States has presented a particular problem because they do not appear to constitute a separate school of thought in the same sense as the other four. Rather, they are grouped in this study into what, for lack of a better term, may be called a school on the basis of their common methodological and research practices. In my opinion, the pioneering work of such Western authors, their specific research techniques, and some common traits in their presentation of material on insurrection more than justify their being classified as a school of thought *manqué*.

A most perplexing problem in a study of this sort concerns the criteria for selection of certain writers or situations and the exclusion of others. And the reader may question the very limited coverage on Mao Tse-tung, who is no doubt the most prominent expert today on application of guerrilla methods. Nor has much space been devoted to Ho Chi Minh, to the Viet Cong, or to the Pathet Lao. Some authors of guerrilla manuals, such as George Grivas, or movements such as the Black September or the Argentine Revolutionary Party of the People (ERP), are either mentioned in passing or the serious student may refer to the bibliography. The list is long and applies equally to all five schools of thought. In analyzing each of the schools of thought, I concentrate on those writers who because of the originality of their thinking may be said to constitute the focal point of their respective schools. For the same reason, I also limit myself to discussion of those events that I consider best illustrate the application of the teachings of a school to a given reality. In the case of Mao Tse-tung, for instance, innovative as his writings may be, he has proven himself first and foremost a grand practitioner of hard-liner thought on guerrilla warfare. Though his contribution in distilling and tightening the postulates of the Bolshevik manual and their application to the Chinese theater is significant, it has not essentially altered the philosophical base of that manual. His formula specifying the peasant as the basic cadre of the proletarian detachment, an innovation that many authors have considered to be Mao's chief alteration of the doctrine, was actually instituted as early as the Bolshevik revolution of 1917.

Partly in an effort to cushion the impact of the realtive neglect of some authors and overemphasis on others, as well as on events and insurrectionary activities, it has been my plan from the outset of this survey to follow the present volume with a separate reader on insurrection, guerrilla warfare, and political violence. Such a companion volume I am now preparing in collaboration with Professor A. James Gregor of the Political Science Department of the University of California at Berkeley. This collection of excerpts from works of both leading and lesser-known representatives of the five schools may aid the student in his quest for source material and for further data presented in capsule form.

In the course of this work, I have enjoyed the generous and constant advice of Professor Gregor and of Mrs. Edna Halperin. With their suggestions and comments, their reading and verification of the text, and their arguments and encouragement, they greatly helped me to cope with the not inconsiderable problems posed in the making of this study.

# 1    Marxist Hard Liners

Whether discussing the success or the failure of the communist guerrilla in a given country, Marxist authors from the East are faithful, on the whole, to certain set patterns of presentation. Here, in capsule form, is a typical picture of a successful guerrilla action. First of all, a power vacuum has developed as the result of an intolerable situation, and the old society has been reduced to an overripe plum ready to fall into anybody's open apron. This condition in turn supplies the prerequisites for initiation of a revolution. The local communist party, always seeing reason before anyone else and refusing to wait for what historically has to come anyway, then initiates a policy of guerrilla confrontation, transferring the responsibility for maintenance of contact with the class enemy, to paraphrase Clausewitz, from the street agitator to the partisan, from the leaflet to the sword. The beginning of guerrilla warfare is always characterized by birthpangs, with the party easing the pains as time elapses. The party lends strength to the revolutionary guerrilla movement and imparts to it a sense of direction and immediacy. With history on their side, the communists, as Lenin argues,[1] though they may commit tactical mistakes, must ultimately triumph, in the process attracting the majority to their camp. As one cornerstone of the old structure after another is dislodged, the party, symbolically speaking, brings the bourgeoisie to the battlefield, with the outcome determined in advance.[2]

This method of presentation of history results in even wider schematism in the treatment of the political and combat behavior of the class enemy. Be he Chiang Kai-shek in China, Kolchak in Siberia, Draza Mihailović in Yugoslavia, or the French in Indochina, the foe is unfailingly bound to place the noose around his own neck. Unresourceful and reactionary, he loses battles politically even when he wins military victories.[3] Because he is from the very outset on the strategic defensive, none of his estimates prove out in the long run. The military feats of the class antagonist, if any, these authors insist, enjoy only a short-range advantage. To add to this, the anti-guerrilla forces commit despicable atrocities because, in the final analysis, their main foe must be the general population. With one blunder following another, their ranks thin out and their men are caught on the horns of a dilemma, whether to die for nothing or to avoid destruction at any cost. Gradually but irreversibly, even their most natural external and internal class allies are forced to abandon them.[4]

Marxist-Leninist doctrine, that "has revealed . . . the magnificent future of humanity freed from the yoke of capitalism,"[5] enables the partisan leadership to synchronize the dynamic unity between theory and practice, i.e., strategy and tactics. For the total success of the venture, it is essential that neither outrun the other. Sound strategy must inspire tactics; tactics, in turn, must enrich strategy with realities that could not have been envisioned. Strategy is thus definitely saved from being sterile and rough. tactics from transforming itself into opportunism.[6]

However, these sources allege, in cases where communist guerrilla has collapsed, as occurred in Malaya, in the Philippines, or in Greece,[7] it is virtually certain that the basic dogmas of Marxist-Leninist teaching on revolution and guerrilla warfare have been violated. A defeated party may, for example, have trespassed upon doctrine with respect to the timing of the outbreak of guerrilla warfare, to strategy and tactics, to its cadre and recruiting policies. It may have erred in its treatment of the population, may have misjudged the advantages and weaknesses of the class enemy, or may have adopted an ill-advised policy toward those borderline groups which in any revolution vacillate between the two principal camps. It may have mis-guessed the reaction of the imperialist bloc, or, on the other hand, may have over or underestimated the aid that would be forthcoming from the socialist countries.

This doctrinary disorder is most likely to be found at the inception of guerrilla warfare, though it persists in the later stages as well. As the Marxist authors make all too clear, this theoretical anarchy may affect only certain features of the guerrilla action, but it may also appear in combination with other circumstances, in the process laying the groundwork for further deviations. Thus the author may assign priority to what is politically explicable according to his doctrine over what actually appears to have taken place; that is, he may acknowledge actual happenings only when they become explicable in terms of policy. Also, he constantly takes refuge in repetitions, casual comments and evasions, exaggerations and euphemisms.

Take, for example, the defeat of the Huks in the Philippines in the early fifties. In May 1954 the Huk movement, to all intents and purposes, appeared defeated. Its leader, Luis Taruc, fell into enemy hands, while the remaining guerrillas were scattered throughout the archipelago. The Filipino farmer, until that time the ally of the Huks, refused to support them further and began to treat the guerrilla first as a nuisance and then as an outright enemy. Minister of Defense Ramon Magsaysay, in charge of anti-Huk operations, dealt the final blow by pulling the rug out from under the Huks. He took from their hands in the 1951-54 period and espoused as his own the principal issues that had attracted popular support to their cause in the first place. At his insistence some of the chronic maladies of Philippine administration were treated, among them the awkward bureaucratic apparatus, corruption, nepotism, and rigged elections. "Land for the landless," one of the most effective slogans of the guerrillas, now became Magsaysay's battle cry. He reorganized the government's regular troops, placing the emphasis on initiative, surprise, mobility, pursuit, and constant offensive. Against the Huk guerrillas he employed guerrilla methods, giving the insurgents a dose of their own medicine and profiting more than Taruc from Mao Tse-tung's writings on guerrilla.[8]

Faced with such a dismal series of defeats, the Marxist author must indeed walk a tightrope. If he fails to analyze all the reasons for the defeat of the Huks, his account is incomplete and he runs the risk of being accused of "bourgeois professorial formalism." Again, if he dwells on the reasons, he cannot escape a certain amount of speculation, which may involve him in a series of doctrinary sins. To absolve the Huk leadership of guilt on the grounds that their forces were outnumbered[9] exposes the author to charges of defeatism. On the other hand, if he convicts Taruc for letting Magsaysay beat him at his own game, he exposes himself to charges of revisionism, for, as we are constantly reminded, it is simply unthinkable that a reactionary politician can under any circumstances successfuly employ guerrilla methods. Finally, if our Marxist writer admits that Mao Tse-tung's China was not able to aid the Huks directly and therefore condemned the movement to defeat, he is guilty of opportunism.

From this delicate situation the author's only out is to place all his reliance on proven slogans, discussing Huk problems in diagrams and reasoning in quotations. The Huks, "having severed the umbilical cord to the large masses of people, defeated themselves"; "misplacing the accent on secondary issues, they allowed the Manila government to take the upper hand"; "overly relying on help from the outside, the Huk leadership failed to develop inner resources of the

Philippine proletariat." These are only a few of the Marxist embellishments that the author may fall back on to avoid becoming the accused rather than the accuser.

From this point on the reader is told repeatedly that such estimates must serve as the sole basis for viewing the defeat of the Huks. Exposed as he is to this unceasing barrage of doctrinal jargon, the reader comes to accept it as almost factual. Later Marxist authors who discuss the Huks are then perfectly free to quote the first author. Party activists acknowledge these later works and repeat the findings of these authors, while communist theoreticians, in treating Huk practices, find a readily available supply of reliable source materials.

If skillfully executed, this procedure is not likely to create problems insofar as the already indoctrinated domestic reader is concerned. Having no access to controversial materials, he accepts the author's arguments at face value. But when this same line of argument is presented to a reader outside the communist bloc, it is found to be full of inaccuracies and *non sequiturs*. The bulk of Eastern texts, because they are stilted and repetitive, in effect diminish the reader's capacity to understand what actually happened in the development of a given guerrilla movement. The reader is constantly led to believe that all historical processes may be presented in black and white distinctions. The Marxist author appears here as a psychiatrist flashing Rorschach cards at a reader-patient; instead of awaiting responses from the patient, he provides the answers himself. As the interview proceeds the patient is expected to raise only those questions the doctor has already answered, all other matters being irrelevant. Unfortunately for the communist author, not every reader—certainly not the curious student—is a patient. He is likely to ask countless questions, to weigh one answer against another in the attempt to make the pieces fall into place. If one author fails to satisfy him, he naturally turns to other sources.

In the case of guerrilla warfare and its relation to Marxist doctrine, the number of questions the student may raise is almost endless. First of all, this type of warfare is frequently based on reverse logic. Precisely because they are weak, the Marxists insist, the guerrillas have a solid chance to win. If they succeed in playing their cards judiciously, they may operate with strength they do not actually possess. Allegedly, anti-guerrilla forces are bound to lose the contest not because of lack of military strength but for want of political astuteness. All in all, Marxist doctrine is the factor that determines the character of guerrilla action. It lays out a rigidly fixed course for the partisan. At the same time, the immediate needs of insurrectionists furnish a sort of rationale for the doctrine, for without a provision for direct action the Marxist catechism would be a Holy Bible read by nobody.

The reader who has just become aware that historical happenings are guided by the Marxist-Leninist manual on insurrection is now redirected to understand that guerrilla warfare bears no resemblance to a pleasure trip in which the chief concern is to work out the itinerary. Which of these elements deserves priority? Are we confronted with a combination of two policies neither of which can be effective without the other? Or, on the other hand, should the entire problem of the relationship of the two be bypassed because guerrilla warfare is but the accomplishment of the possible? How is it possible in this warfare, which by its very nature rejects any firm manual, that according to Marxist theory the altogether unprecedented may be handled with precedents? For these and other questions the student is unprepared because the Marxist author as a rule presents him with a limited number of facts and schemes in which those facts can be correlated.[10]

Out of each guerrilla victory is born a bewildering array of new isms: Maoism in China, Titoism in Yugoslavia, Castroism in Cuba, African Marxism in some African states. Specifically, in order to dislodge Kerensky in 1917, what Lenin found indispensable was a party composed of revolutionary elite, rather than of the amorphous proletarian class prescribed by Marx. Mao Tse-tung and Tito discovered their principal allies in the "vacillating" Chinese and Yugoslav peasants. Theoretically, both the Chinese Communist Party (CCP) and the Communist Party of Yugoslavia (CPY), now League of Communists of Yugoslavia (LCY), acted in the name of the working class; but in both cases their victories were achieved ostensibly without its support. Castro defeated Batista by relying neither on the Cuban farmer nor on the Cuban worker. In addition, at least officially, the entire Cuban guerrilla action was carried out without resort to Marxist ideology and even, for that matter, without the presence of a Marxist party. It sufficed, in this case, to have a handful of devoted followers, trained, imaginative, and never asking why. Again, Carlos Marighella left the Communist Party of Brazil believing that this outmoded and ossified organization could only be a deterrent to victory in urban guerrilla.

From these few examples the contemporary Western student may deduce that what the communists intend to achieve in revolutionary insurrection amounts to setting in motion a trembler that would completely overturn human society. As soon as the "bayonet is put on the order of the day" (Lenin), the communists are faced with innumerable difficulties. Be they trifling in nature or urgent, these "frictions in war"[11] restrict the rebel's maneuvering space. Though in theory one new element does not necessarily alter the picture, in practice it tends to combine with others, confronting a Marxist rebel with a situation he could not have anticipated.

Consider, for instance, the Second Sumadija Partisan Detachment, which operated in Central Serbia in the summer of 1941. The majority of the partisans were "politically unenlightened peasants." Except for the prewar members of the CPY, who had to go underground as soon as Germany declared war on the U.S.S.R. (June 12, 1941), workers employed in the only significant industrial complex in the area, a freight-car factory in Smederevska Palanka, continued for the most part to work for the German occupation forces.

In addition, well-to-do inhabitants of some of the richest villages in Serbia, such as Azanja and Kusiljevo, joined the partisans, while the poorest peasants from villages like Gradac and Crni Kal rallied to anti-communist forces. Thus, the rich peasant-partisan became "the principal fighter for the rights of the proletarian class," while members of that very class in Smederevska Palanka paid little heed to the struggle. Besides, this same rich peasant-landowner, petty bourgeois, and, according to the Marxist beliefs, most natural enemy of the proletarian cause, began to exterminate his poor peasant brother.

As pragmatic soldiers, Bogosav Marković, commander of the detachment, and his political commissar, Tanasije Mladenović, had to cater to these rich peasants because they were the prime source of cadres. As ideologues in uniform, however, they had to view these same peasants with suspicion and to regard them as class enemies. To put it another way, these guerrilla leaders could no more abandon doctrine than they could ignore the demands of reality. They took the only possible course: they continued to pay lip service to Marxist doctrine while acting as though the greater part of it did not exist.[12]

The moment the first bullet is fired, it becomes crystal-clear to the communist leaders that the principal strength is "on the street" (Lenin). In the concept of the "street," as Lenin viewed it, there is no tolerance for complexities. The street cannot be expected to have any awareness of "refined impeccability of doctrinal prognostications," nor, once action has begun, can the street's tribunes be expected to thumb through the pages of their manuals seeking the most appropriate quotations for the situation at hand. Instead they are forced to play it by ear; and to a considerable extent the fate of the revolution will rest upon the flexibility and imagination of the activists and upon a readiness to suppress party dogma of yesterday and come to terms with reality. According to Marx, it is at this juncture that a rebel becomes an artist of revolution definitely freed of the fear that his improvised moves may do violence to his ideology.

Of all the present-day representatives of hard-liner teaching on insurrection, Mao Tse-tung is the most influential. But would it be accurate to classify him as a follower of the Bolshevik manual on guerrilla? He has actually updated the manual and has opened new avenues of research that may readily serve the practical Marxist revolutionist. His contributions cover in depth almost every aspect of insurrection, from analysis of the character of the various phases, and of the instruments of this warfare, the strategy and tactics of partisan detachments, and the role of the peasantry in communist revolution, to the mechanism of mass indoctrination and thought reform. But at a certain point, as I propose to show, he departs from the Bolshevik rule-book to draw up his own guidelines for the New China.

Since the thirties Mao's main contention has been that in China, a semi-colonial and semi-feudal country oppressed internally by domestic exploiters and externally by imperialists, the principal form of liberation struggle must be war and the form of organization an army.[13] Other forms of struggle, such as strikes, boycotts, mass and class organizations, indispensable as they may be, cannot and should not be overlooked; but from no matter what point of view they are to be assessed, "they are all for the sake of war." In China before World War II, the people had no legislative body to serve them, nor did they have the legal right to organize or to exert pressure upon their rulers by peaceful means. Since all avenues of protest were closed, there was no need for the Chinese communists to undergo a long period of legal clashes before launching an insurrection.[14]

The type of war Mao discusses in his works is of purely class-revolutionary character, and relies for its direction on whatever methods the time, the place, and the instruments dictate. A continuation of politics, war is politics, political action to be exact, and, he writes, paraphrasing Clausewitz, "there has not been a single war since ancient times that does not bear a political character." The struggle against the Japanese, for instance, was inseparable from its chief political aim—the defeat of Japanese imperialism and the building of a new China. This aim ultimately determined the type of political and material weapons to be used.

Mao Tse-tung devotes considerable space, especially in the works written in the thirties, to the relationship between war and politics. He either quotes Clausewitz directly or cites portions of Lenin's theses in which Lenin himself relies on the thoughts of the Prussian general. Thus Chairman Mao repeatedly calls attention to two ill-founded concepts: one that tends to belittle the role of politics and to separate it from war, and the other that confounds war and politics. Both, he says, are utterly wrong.[15] Reliance on the axiom that political power grows out of the barrel of a gun and that the Party commands the gun is the hallmark of the political literacy of every true communist.[16] If it were the other way around, i.e., the gun commanding the Party, then little would remain of the Party's role as the revolutionary brain guiding the freedom fighter. What must be clearly understood, Mao insists, is that politics often reaches a stage beyond which it cannot proceed by relying on traditional means of struggle. To clear the path of solidly entrenched obstacles, a shift to different, now bloody means is called for.

The basic objectives of long-term politics still remain the same. What is changed is the manner of approach to and the methods for destroying all obstructions confronting the Party. The specific techniques must be mastered by the revolutionist; but here again, he must understand clearly that the goals dictated by politics are the *ultima ratio* of his whole endeavor. The history of the Chinese Communist Party (CCP) affords ample illustrations that a revolutionary party may shift its method of struggle in different periods of a revolutionary war without losing sight of its long-term objectives. For example, in the First Revolutionary Civil War, 1924-27, conventional methods of warfare prevailed under the banner of the Kuomintang-Communist United Front. In the Second Revolutionary Civil War or the War of Agrarian Revolution, 1927-37, conventional means were supplanted by a form of guerrilla warfare. Although high-level mobility warfare with larger contingents of troops was adopted at a still later period, operations continued to be waged in guerrilla fashion. During the anti-Japanese war, 1937-45, a return to the earlier form of irregular warfare was deemed expedient; while in the Third Revolutionary Civil War, 1945-49, regular warfare resurfaced as the characteristic form of struggle. Throughout all these shifts in means and methods, Mao argues, the Party remained steadfast in its principal aim: to liberate the country and to create a New China.

As Mao sees it, the victory of the Chinese people in their twenty-two-year war may be credited largely to the ability of the CCP leadership to harmonize Marxist-Leninist theory on people's war with the specific conditions in China. Since 1927, this leadership has insisted that the Chinese Revoltuion is a continuation of the great October Revolution, that the road of the October Revolution is the common road for all people's revolutions. The Chinese and the Russian revolutions had the following characteristics in common: at the head of both stood a monolithic communist party, the avant-garde of the working class; both were based on a worker-peasant alliance; in both instances, state power was seized by violent means and a dictatorship of the proletariat was subsequently established; in the aftermath of the victory, both the Russian and Chinese parties began to build socialism; and both were inseparable from the proletarian world revolution.[17]

The advantages of such a political orientation were inestimable, Mao assures us, because Chinese communists, directed by Marxist theory and benefiting from the Bolshevik experience, were not too preoccupied with the central problems of any insurrection: in the name of what cause is the insurrection initiated and how is the goal to be achieved? At least as far as basic problems of ideology and doctrine

were concerned, there was no necessity to rediscover what
had already been discovered, to prove what had already been
proved by the Bolsheviks. This enabled the Chinese to avoid
the miscalculations and oversights that had proved costly to
many a revolution in the past. They were thus able to
conserve their energies for specifically Chinese problems, as
well as to maintain their own ideological consistency.

China of the twenties and thirties, according to Mao
Tse-tung, was a heaven-sent ground for the new vehicle of
revolution—a politically mature communist party. The Chinese masses traditionally had had more than their share of
reasons to take to arms and to rebel. Some of their uprisings
were spontaneous, others organized. But despite individual
acts of heroism that on occasion had forced the oppressor to
retreat temporarily, no lasting success was scored until the
CCP, led by the scientific Marxist-Leninist theory on revolution, came into its own. Leaders of this party taught the
masses that "the Marxist-Leninist principle of revolution
holds universally true for China and for all other countries,"
and that no other guiding compass could therefore have been
relied on.[18] Marxist teaching insisted that seizure of power
must be accomplished by an armed force, and that settlement
of the issue by war—the highest form of revolution—was the
central task of the rebels. As in the Russia of 1917, the
oppressors could be defeated only with naked force employed within the framework of those patterns that Lenin
and Stalin had so carefully spelled out. Yet, in Chairman
Mao's opinion, this did not mean that the Soviet experience
could be applied mechanically to Chinese conditions, since
China differed essentially in four ways.

First of all, in the period between the two world wars
China was a vast, semi-colonial country unevenly developed
politically and economically. A frail capitalist economy
coexisted with a semi-feudal mode of production. Along with
the few modern industrial and commercial centers were to be
found "boundless expanses of stagnant rural districts." On
the one hand, there were several million industrial proletar-

ians, and on the other, hundreds of millions of peasants and artisans. Great warlords controlled the central government; lesser warlords held sway in the countryside. Two types of armed forces existed: a central army under Chiang Kai-shek and the troops of a motley array of brigands under the warlords. Roads and transportation networks were underdeveloped. People were politically disunited but rebellious nevertheless.[19]

The second essential difference between the Russia of 1917 and the Chinese position in 1936 lay in the great material strength of the CCP's enemy, the Kuomintang. Chiang Kai-shek held the reins of power over a considerable portion of the country. He had "gained the support of the principal counterrevolutionary countries of the world." In technical training the army of the Kuomintang was more or less on a par with the armies of modern states; and it was better equipped than the Chinese Red Army and numerically superior. Its power was nationwide in scope. It controlled the key positions in politics, in the economy, and in cultural life.

In the third place, the Red Army was weak and small. It was dispersed for the most part throughout remote regions and deprived of any outside help. Besides this, the small revolutionary bases established by the communists were located in rural districts and were constantly shifting from one area to another. In all, its arms were insufficient in number and firepower, its supplies extremely limited, and its supply lines far from adequate.

The nature and the quality of the CCP leadership and the agrarian revolution provided the fourth difference from the Soviet experience. The Red partisan, in sharp contrast to the Kuomintang soldier, was fighting to acquire his own piece of land, for his own interests. Since his leaders were striving for the same goal, this unity of aims laid the ground for a unity of political goals among the partisans and for a self-imposed discipline. Thus the Party was able to secure the support of the peasantry and to generate as well an admirable degree of fighting spirit. The Kuomintang soldier, on the other hand, fought to preserve the status quo; that is to say, he was defending the rights of the landlords in a country desperately in need of agrarian reform, a cause contrary to his own interests. This soldier and his officers thus invariably found themselves disunited, their will to fight greatly weakened.[20]

The first and fourth characteristics, the semi-colonial, unevenly developed country and the agrarian revolution, pointed to a real possibility for growth of the Red Army and its eventual victory over the enemy; the second and the third, the well-equipped enemy and the small, weak Red Army, to the impossibility of swift growth for the communist forces and a speedy victory. The combination of these favorable and unfavorable condtions, according to Mao, required the adoption of guerrilla methods against the Kuomintang and the acceptance of protracted war. This course determined in essence the entire military and political strategy of the Party. It forced the Chinese revolutionaries to take a firm stand along the following lines:

1. against adventurism on the attack
2. against conservatism on the defense
3. against flight-ism in deploying forces
4. against guerrilla-ism in the Red Army, but for its guerrilla character
5. against protracted campaigns and a strategy of quick decision, for a strategy of protracted war and campaigns of quick decision
7. against the mere routing of the enemy, for a war of annihilation
8. against the principle of striking with both fists at the same time
9. against a large rear area
10. against an absolutely centralized command, for a relatively centralized command
11. against a purely military viewpoint and the concept of roving insurgents
12. against banditry

13. against warlordism

14. against a sectarian cadre policy

15. against isolationism and the antagonizing of possible allies

16. against keeping the Red Army at its old stage of development, for striving to improve and upgrade it.[21]

These thoughts of Mao Tse-tung derived from concepts formulated by Lenin on revolutionary insurrection and guerrilla warfare. At first glance, in the works written between 1927 and 1937, it would seem that Mao was accepting without qualification all the definitions and recommendations of Lenin concerning the nature of insurrection and guerrilla, strategy, tactics and logistics, the type and scope of maximal and minimal objectives of the Party, the treatment of population, the selection and tempering of Party cadres, and the development of all the potentials of the underground army.[22]

Mao's propensity to quote freely from Lenin is reflected in a peculiar blend of dry Bolshevik jargon combined with fresh illustrations, popular legends, and events from Chinese history. Like the Bolshevik leaders, Mao masterfully reduces the phenomenon of guerrilla to the simplest form, appearing to leave no loose ends. Guerrilla operations, he says, are necessary and natural tools of the oppressed; they do not constitute an independent form of warfare. These concepts Mao takes almost verbatim from Lenin.[23]

With qualities and objectives peculiar to itself, guerrilla warfare, he continues, is the weapon of the weaker adversary. Only the life force of the enemy, not his real estate, is the guerrilla's principal target. It goes without saying that guerrilla success is contingent upon several favorable preconditions. The list of these, which Chairman Mao borrows in altered form from Karl von Clausewitz, includes an invader piercing deep into the heart of the weaker country; a cruel and oppressive occupation policy; favorable terrain, climate, and national psychology; and support of the people.[24]

During the war against the Japanese all these preconditions, according to Mao, were ideally represented. The control of enormous geographical areas and of urban industrial mining centers, the maintenance of a network of strong points and supply lines, mop-up operations against the rebels and operations along a jagged front thousands of miles long—all these required a far larger army than Japan could commit. In additon, the Japanese were enraged by the behavior of the population and confused by a war "unlike other wars." In order to economize their forces, they had to apply brutal measures against the Chinese people, pushing even normally passive and apolitical peasants to take up arms.

As for these millions of Chinese, however, in order to become militarily effective they had first to be organized, their hatred channeled, and some sort of order of priorities established for short-term and long-term goals. Only a politically mature Marxist-Leninist party could feel equal to the challenge. Characteristically, the Party established from the outset the correct relationship between guerrilla warfare and national politics, making the armed struggle subservient to general politics. The communists insisted on two basic goals for the struggle: liberation from the Japanese and emancipation of the country from its previous semi-colonial and semi-feudal status. To achieve their aims, the Party leadership set up the following fundamental steps: to arouse and organize the people; to achieve internal political unity; to establish bases; to equip the forces; to recover the national strength; to destroy the enemy's national strength; and to regain the lost territory.[25]

With the exception of the first two tasks, the political mobilization and unification of the people, the remaining five in the opinion of many are military in nature. It is said by militarists, according to Mao, that guerrilla hostilities presuppose a highly specialized type of warfare and "only regular troops can carry on guerrilla operations." The misfits in society, they tell us, cannot call forth the sustained will and skill necessary to see the war through.[26]

Mao contends that the military fail to ask two basic

questions: How is it possible to wage a mass war against the Japanese without participation of the masses; and from what other reservoir may the underground army be drawn? In addition, they fail to take into consideration the ties between guerrilla warfare and a revolutionary cause that moves the people to take up arms. Basically, this war derives from the masses. It is their product and in order to succeed it must be supported by them.

The Party cadres, themselves the product of ideological guidance along Marxist-Leninist lines and of long training in the submission of military to political goals, are ideally suited for the leadership posts. During peacetime they have passed through the hard school of the class struggle waged by unorthodox, quasi-guerrilla methods, though without arms. To survive this training, a cadre has had to show courage, resourcefulness, and initiative. What he now faces is a type of warfare whose strategy is based on alertness, mobility, and readiness for attack. The advantages of his earlier training will naturally surface. Mao's writings are full of tributes to the cadre. He considers him at one and the same time a tiger and a fox, and recalls Stalin's principle that cadres solve everything.

In guerrilla warfare, Mao Tse-tung says, the gods are on the side of the fighter who seems to come from the east while attacking from the west; who avoids the solid and attacks the hollow; who attacks only to withdraw, always delivering a lightning blow and seeking a lightning decision. When a stronger enemy advances, the guerrilla must pull back. When the enemy stops, the guerrilla goads him, striking him when he is weary, pursuing him when he withdraws. The rear flanks and other vulnerable spots are the enemy's vital points, and who is better able to take advantage of these weaknesses than the trained cadre, who is accustomed to living in the midst of the class enemy, to being harassed and persecuted himself?[27]

This cadre can easily adapt himself to the requirements of both types of guerrilla warfare, revolutionary and counterrevolutionary. The first type Mao defines as warfare carried on in the interests of the whole people, or the greater part of them. It has a broad base in the national manpower and, in accord with the laws of historical development, is a just war. As long as the guerrillas' policies are not contrary to national policy, their struggle is likely to flourish. The counterrevolutionary is typified by the White Russian guerrilla or by the group trained by the Italians in Abyssinia or by the puppet government in Manchuria and Mongolia. These guerrillas represent and fight for the oppressor. They are reactionary and enjoy no broad base of support from the people. Hence they are an easy target, losing the battle before it begins.[28] In the revolutionary guerrilla struggle the trained cadre represents the natural catalyst who enlightens and mobilizes the people; in the counterrevolutionary battle, whether he is armed, an infiltrator, or a rear political worker, he undermines the spirit of the enemy guerrilla and creates confusion in the ranks.

The cadre's role is further enhanced in both general revolutionary wars and in purely "class wars," a distinction that frequently seems to be tenuous at best. Without regard to class or party, in the first instance a nation as a whole resorts to guerrilla methods as an instrument of the struggle for liberation. In the face of an invader, the previous clashes and bickering among citizens are temporarily suppressed. The people become sympathetic to one another, and are often inclined to bend over backward to achieve national unity. In a "class war," on the contrary, the foe is not normally of foreign origin. One class fights another, frequently making use of guerrilla methods similar to those employed in a general revolutionary war but with other objectives. Though in the class war "internal purity" and spiritual bonds are achieved with greater ease in view of the similar class origins of the revolutionists, the success of the venture depends largely, too, on "powerful political leaders who work unceasingly to bring about internal unification." In the struggle against the Japanese, these powerful leaders came from the ranks of the CCP, a party determined to expel the invader and to reform China.[29]

This peculiar situation of the party's men, i.e., their involvement in a protracted struggle for general internal harmony and in an even more protracted effort for the future class war against domestic exploiters, forced them to cast about for new patterns. Such patterns concerned their theory and practice on insurrection, their recruiting policy, and their teaching on the tempo and the stages of revolution.

Though composed historically of the same elements, national guerrilla warfare, says Mao, has employed varying implements as times, peoples, and conditions change. Methods employed by the guerrillas in the Opium War or by those fighting in Manchuria after the Mukden Incident differed as much from those practiced in sections of China occupied by the Japanese, as they did, for instance, from those employed by the Moroccans in their battles against the French and Spanish colonialists. Such differences are quite natural, expressing as they do characteristics of different people in different periods; "and therefore," quoting from Clausewitz, Mao says, "every period must have its independent theory of war."[30]

To discover the origin of the *sui generis* forms of fighting specific for each society involved in insurrection, Mao explores many avenues: the history of a nation; its tradition in the struggle against the oppressor; its terrain, climate, and national psychology; its economic condition and its class and political structure; the aspirations of its people; the politics and the stamina of the enemy; the international situation; and the ideological maturity and organizational preparedness of the cadres that lead the masses. By assimilating these particulars the local rebel learns which tactics to use, and the learning process is likely to be costly both in time and in blood. Mao says of this experience, "For a hundred years the best sons and daughters of the woe-stricken Chinese nation have waged struggles and sacrificed themselves in quest of the truth that would save our country and our people." Some of them were quickly defeated. Others triumphed temporarily. But no sooner had one fallen than others stepped into the breach. Under the influence of these rebels, the people acquired some basic knowledge of war and formed certain opinions about particular forms of fighting. Some of their conclusions had already been reached by other nations and had been tailored to suit local conditions; others applied specifically to China. After the First World War and the October Revolution, when the masses suddenly discovered that "the truth of truths, Marxism-Leninism," was the best weapon to liberate the nation, the Chinese rebels reached a new stage. The CCP became the sole advocate and organizer of the use of this weapon. It integrated the universal truths of Marxism-Leninism with the concrete practices within the Chinese struggle and lent a new aspect to the popular revolt. Especially after the outbreak of hostilities against the Japanese, the Party went even a step farther and rendered a valuable contribution to the practice of the war of resistance and especially to the study of China in her relations with the rest of the world.[31] Moreover, this qualitative leap produced two significant results: the experiences of the international revolutionary movement were closely tied with Chinese practices, and the Marxist-Leninist theory on war and warfare was greatly enriched.

Since this doctrine, as Mao wrote in 1941, rests on an indissoluble bond between theory and practice, it stimulates a communist to study all aspects of the daily struggle and to weigh conflicting evidence with an open mind. Ideally, such an orientation would in time rule out any inclination on his part to formalism, or subjectivism, or to the misguided course of bypassing unwelcome realities. In many instances, serious research was abandoned and material was collected in haphazard fashion. Marxism-Leninism was retained at best as a weapon of the critics of the old, but for all practical purposes it was abandoned as a guide for action.

Mao finds that many of "our Marxist-Leninist scholars"

seemed obsessed with a sort of floating Marxian radicalism, sustained neither by correct understanding of the true spirit of the doctrine nor by activist ardor. These sterile Marxists resembled nothing more than a blind man groping for a fish.

This group was later joined by young people who had been studying in Europe, in America, and in Japan. Full of contempt for the common folk, many of this élitist minority seemed but a senseless "talking machine," boastful and noisy. They, too, were armed with clichés. Their jargon was "fleshy without substance, brittle without solidity." They made speeches, taught others what they did not know themselves, and wrote articles in which all arguments were neatly structured under A,B,C, and D, or 1, 2, 3, and 4.[32]

The theoretical incompetence of both the wooden local scholar of Marxism-Leninism and the shallow cosmopolitan was particularly evident in the failure of both to relate the main problem of their time, revolutionary warfare in China and in Asia, with the Marxist-Leninist teaching on that warfare. This failure, Mao tells us repeatedly, was a direct result of their failure to relate book learning to action in the field, or, to be more precise, of their utter inability to focus simultaneously on the laws of war in general, on the laws of revolutionary warfare as formulated by the Marxist-Leninist classics, and on the laws of the present Chinese revolutionary war.[33] This short-sightedness laid the groundwork for the appearance of three schools of thought, all, in Mao's opinion, as theoretically untenable as they were inimical to the success of the liberation front.

The first group of these unspecified heretics maintained that for victory in war it was sufficient to subscribe to the technical rules of war published by the reactionary Chinese government and the reactionary military academies of China. Mao's answer is that these heretics forget that the eintire body of knowledge on the military trade espoused by these reactionary institutions is copied from abroad. True, some of the more flexible of these heretics point out that in the past, combat technique was learned at the cost of blood when people asked, "Why are they of no use?" Of course, they are of use, and we must cherish such experiences, Mao assures us, but "we must also cherish experiences acquired at the cost of our own blood."[34]

Another group held the view that it was quite enough to study and apply the Bolshevik experiences. Their logic was rather simple: Our war, like the war in the Soviet Union, is a revolutionary war. Since the Bolsheviks were victorious, how can there be any alternative but to follow their example? That the Bolsheviks won precisely because they had avoided robot-like application of the rules of warfare, the protagonists of this concept obviously failed to take into consideration. Lenin and Stalin wrote their own manual of warfare, never attempting to whittle the feet down to fit the shoes.

The third troup declared that the experiences of the Northern Expedition of 1926-27 were of lasting value and therefore should serve as the most reliable compass in future operations. Driving straight to the heart of the big cities was the Chinese recipe for certain victory. Chairman Mao's answer to this argument is that one should adopt only those measures of the Northern Expedition that are still suitable under present conditions.[35]

Chairman Mao points out that a rebel may learn from military science how to preserve himself and to annihilate the foe; from Marxist-Leninist doctrine how to wage a class war; and from Chinese tradition how to succeed in revolutionary class war in China. But the communists, in Mao's opinion, seem to have come closest to the truth. True enough, from the military angle the party's agitators taught a patriot all there was to know about the use of the rifle, even when not to use it. As for political indoctrination, they taught him who was the enemy in each period of the struggle, how to hold the secondary enemy in check until the opportune moment, and how to adapt their fighting technique to circumstances. For instance, in the Second Revolutionary War, the prime target of the rebel was the domestic oppressor and his arm, the Kuomintang pretorians. In the anti-Japanese war the Kuomintang became temporarily an indispensable ally only to reassume its role as the principal class enemy once the Japanese had been expelled.

In additon, the CCP and the masses under its tutelage had to struggle against a number of secondary enemies. The odds against them and the problems the Chinese communists faced were far different from those faced by the Bolsheviks at the time of the Russian Revolution. Mao regards this as quite natural, since the politico-administrative structure of the two countries differed, as did the international situation at the time. Wide differences existed, too, in the revolutionary consciousness of the masses and in the relative strength of the communist party in each case. If differences in geography climate, psychology, national traditions, and the level of development of military science are added to these, the conclusion is inescapable that despite the great contributions of the Bolsheviks, the rebellious Chinese masses had no choice but to write their own manual.

Unlike their Russian brothers, the big landlords in China were divided into two categories. The first, following the lead of one wing of the big bourgeoisie, the capitulators, immediately surrendered to the Japanese and turned collaborator. The second, under the influence of the other wing of the big bourgeoisie, the diehards, vacillated between its own class interests and the liberation struggle of the people.[36]

The Chinese bourgeoisie, the class enemy without whose "non-communist hands communism in China could not be built," is divided by Mao into the bourgeoisie of comprador character and the national bourgeoisie.[37] Tied in the countryside to feudal lords, the first serves foreign capitalists as well, and consequently owes its allegiance to various imperialist powers. This wing of the bourgeoisie is definitely reactionary and represents a perennial target for the local revolutionist. In the war against the Japanese, however, the position of the compradors was somewhat more complex, since some of them, the capitulators, served the Japanese, and others the pro-Westerners, the Anglo-Americans. Under controlled conditions the communists would use the pro-Westerners in the struggle against the Japanese as well as in undermining the position of the capitulators. But by the same token the Party dared not forget that as soon as their English and American masters undertook to oppose the Chinese revolution, the pro-Westerners would follow suit.

The national bourgeoisie, consisting mainly of small capitalists, had its own peculiar dual character. Oppressed by imperialists and fettered by feudalism, its members were at odds with both, thus in effect constituting a revolutionary force—not necessarily reliable, but helpful nevertheless. These bourgeois lacked the courage and the incentive to fight imperialism and feudalism openly because their ties to either or both had never been completely severed. When coerced by the oppressor, they were inclined to join the revolutionists, but the alliance with them would immediately be broken once the imperialists and feudal lords agreed to make the desired concessions. To such an unreliable ally, the CCP could turn only during certain periods, always keeping a watchful eye for a knife in the back.

Treatment of the petty bourgeois (intellectuals, students, small merchants, artisans, and professional men), as well as of the peasantry, also required of the communists a higher degree of elasticity and imaginativeness than could have been learned from the Bolshevik manual.[38] Chinese intellectuals, for example, were divided into groups: those whose livelihood depended on the oppressors and those fearful of losing either their jobs or the opportunity to study. These elements, though they opposed feudalism and imperialism and the big warlords, were not vociferous. The first group the Party treated as open enemies; the second, as a potential revolutionary force that might even spearhead an insurrection if properly handled. In particular, those among them who were sufficiently impoverished and who had little or no hope of ever becoming insiders were more likely to switch sides and identify themselves with the people's cause.[39]

Small merchants were threatened with bankruptcy by the

oppressors and with confiscation of property in the event of a communist victory. The camp they would ultimately choose depended to a large extent on the ability of the party agitators to shatter the shopkeepers' abiding fear of revolution and to involve them in the mass struggle. In the case of the professional men, such as doctors, who were looked upon more favorably by the rulers and who were given some opportunity to exploit the masses, the party faced a more difficult challenge.

Though the party leaders were faithful believers in Lenin's and Stalin's golden rules concerning the peasantry, Mao implies that the CCP might be inclined to bend the rules much more than any contemporary Marxists, not excluding the Bolsheviks.[40] Like their counterparts in pre-1917 Russia, the rich peasants in China (with landlords, constituting about 10 percent of the rural population) practiced usury and ruthlessly exploited the village poor. Unlike their counterparts in Russia, however, most of them cultivated the land themselves, and "their productive activities will remain useful for some time to come." Therefore, as a class they should not be confounded with the landlords nor should they be prematurely liquidated.[41]

The middle peasants, who constituted 20 percent of the rural population, were themselves exploited and enjoyed no political rights to speak of. They, in Mao's opinion, would be inclined to join the revolutionary forces readily and to fight for the communist cause. They vacillated less than the Russian middle peasants and should be considered a reliable ally of the party and an important motive force of the revolution. In fact, the attitude of this segment Mao regarded as the possible determining factor of victory or defeat. Together with the poor peasants, the remaining 70 percent of the rural population, who were "the biggest motive force of the Chinese revolution," the middle peasants would form the bulk of partisan units and would determine to a large extent tactics, type of political work among soldiers, and treatment of population.

Marxist doctrine, of course, specifies that the industrial proletariat should be the main cadre of the revolutionary army. In a country as populous as China, however, where the proletarian class is small, (2.5 to 3 million workers and about 12 million hired laborers in small-scale industries and handicrafts), the communists, as did the Bolsheviks in the 1917-21 period, had to seek out the soldier of the revolution primarily from among the landless and the rural petty bourgeois, the middle peasants. To form proletarian units in sections of China where there were no proletarians was no easy task. While the epicenter of the struggle was in the countryside, most of the proletarians lived in the cities, where they were employed in factories and enterprises that belonged to the Japanese or to the big capitalists. In principle, Mao argues, this class has the highest political consciousness and sense for organization; but in China it is inferior numerically, it lacks experience, as compared with the proletariat of capitalist countries, its cultural level is low as compared with the bourgeoisie, and "it cannot win victory by virtue of its own strength alone."[42]

Such a complex social structure was not the only factor that forced the party to formulate the specifically Chinese conception of guerrilla warfare. Other considerations, such as the nature of the enemy, the dual character of their Kuomintang allies, and the international situation made their influence felt. Japanese fascists, for instance, considered a communist revolutionist in China both a national and a class enemy. The Kuomintang soldier, on the other hand, was for the Japanese primarily a political foe but a class brother when the Chinese revolutionists were in question. Forced to combine its struggle for the revolution with the struggle for national liberation, from 1937 to 1945 the CCP had to cultivate an alliance with the bourgeois Kuomintang. The foreign supporters of the Kuomintang, the United States and England, impressed by the fighting qualities of the Red partisan and by his contribution to the Allied cause, were making friendly gestures to the communists from 1941 to 1945. Mao issued instructions that for the duration the suspicion of these essentially lethal foes of the Chinese communists should not be aroused. Thus the Party faced conflicting demands: in order to extract aid from the imperialists it had to appear to emply its military arm exclusively against the fascists; but in order to carry on the revolution it had to sap Kuomintang strength and whenever possible to liquidate its cadres without attracting suspicion.

To enable the Red army to "grow out of nothing and expand from a small force into a big one," the Party based its strategy against the Japanese on the following principles: to carry out offensives in a defensive war, battles of quick decision in a protracted war, and exterior-line operations within interior-line operations; to coordinate irregular with regular warfare, to establish base areas; to emphasize both the strategic defensive and strategic offensive; to accelerate the mobile war; and to establish a correct chain of command. The implementation of these directives would serve to preserve and expand the Red forces, to annihilate or rout the foreign and domestic enemy, and to create a mass Red Army by coordinating partisan and regular warfare.[43]

Writing in May 1938, Mao points out that Japan was militarily strong and on the offensive; China, weak and on the defensive.[44] Japanese troops were operating on the exterior line of the theater, Chinese on the interior. The Japanese fascists were numerically weak, the Chinese revolutionaries numerically strong. The more time that elapsed the greater the Chinese advantage. In additon, the Japanese were invaders unfamiliar with China and with the psychology of the people. They dealt brutally with the population, making new enemies every step of the way. The situation afforded the Chinese the opportunity to carry on offensive campaigns in a strategically defensive war, to score quick decisions in many small battles, to wage a protracted war "on the exterior line within the strategic interior line." Even before the anti-Japanese struggle, Mao insisted that the two forms of fighting–offensive and defensive–must be combined. When the enemy advances, he wrote in December 1936,[45] the Red forces must make an orderly withdrawal, meeting the enemy's offensive with a stubborn defensive. This is the first stage of the counter-campaign. When the enemy comes to a standstill, the rebels attack, meeting the enemy defensive with a rebel offensive. This is the second stage of the counter-campaign, and ideally these two forms should be harmonized in any operation whether involving the Red regulars or the Red guerrillas.

It is the guerrilla's goal to isolate and annihilate small segments of the enemy's forces, to disrupt communications, to give them no rest. These efforts of the guerrilla should enable the Red regulars, for their part, to withstand enemy pressure, to gain time to strengthen their own positions. In having to transfer his men to counter the new menace from the Chinese regular, many a Japanese turns his back on the Red guerrilla only to find himself caught in the middle. In this manner the Red forces can stack up many minor victories while sapping the strength of the Japanese army.

From the political angle, the Party's cause receives ever-growing publicity on a world scale. Marxists in other countries hasten to their aid, as do the imperialist Western states in their eagerness to find an effective ally in the struggle against Japan. Finally, in the countryside, many hitherto neutral or undecided join the revolutionary forces, swelling the ranks of both the regulars and the guerrillas.[46] Initiative, flexibility, and the planning of actions are in this context the principal tools of the revolutionist. They enable him to mold reality politically and militarily and to impose his will over his adversaries. Taking advantage of the principal Japanese weaknesses–insufficient forces fighting on a foreign soil, the inflexibility of the Japanese military command, and barbarous treatment of the Chinese people–the guerrillas could allow "free play to their resourcefulness" as well as having a free hand in winning the support of millions upon millions of people.[47]

The Tokyo militarists, underestimating China's strength, were guilty of many errors in judgment. They supplied piecemeal reinforcements, for example. Their strategic co-ordination left much to be desired. They dispersed their main forces before the task had been accomplished, and their troops failed to wipe out the rebels the Japanese army managed to encircle. Moreover, obsessed with the notion "that China could be swallowed in one gulp," they misjudged the stamina of the Chinese soldiers. They simply treated all armed patriots as faceless bandits. Of the CCP, of its policy, its organization, and its cadres, these militarists knew suprisingly little.

Commanders of units in the unorthodox war, "directors of guerrilla," to use Mao's term, early realized that a politically unenlightened military technician could normally be ex-pected to show initiative only in tactical matters. The guerrilla fighters attempted routinely to force the Japanese to do battle on guerrilla terms. If a guerrilla refused a contact, the Japanese troops were likely to advance into the vacuum and then halt to wait for new directives from distant headquarters. By default, then, initiative was shifted to the guerrilla commander, who did not have to depend on directives.[48] If he made an error, he could instantly rectify it. If an unexpected opportunity presented itself, he had the authority to exploit it.

Under such leadership it became quite impossible to carry on guerrilla warfare in haphazard fashion or to make a game of it. Any action undertaken by the insurrectionists usually coincided with the needs of the Red regulars. These forces in turn were headed by another, identically trained and politi-cally seasoned commander who was also a Party member. The coordinated efforts in strategy or in campaigns or in battles (in Mao's opinion, the second basic problem of the liberation war) were rarely accompanied with disagreements. All members of the same team, the commander of the Red regulars and the director of the Red guerrilla offered one another a helping hand in all operations. This became especially important later, when the Japanese were expelled. Now the task of the Chinese revolutionists to win the ensuing class war against the domestic foe was greatly facilitated.[49]

The establishment of guerrilla bases, the third strategic problem of the liberation war, Mao treats as both a political and a military project.[50] Established in the mountains, on the plains, or in the river-lake-estuary regions, the bases were to serve as supply depots, training, recuperation, and medical centers for guerrilla; and, of more significance for the success of the revolution, as mini-models of the type of life that should prevail when the communist revolution has ended in victory.

Throughout Mao's works all aspects of revolutionary activity are treated in the best hard-liner tradition. His writings, too, present state power as the *ultima ratio* of class insurrection. But the peasant instead of the classical Marxian proletarian is the principal cadre of revolution. In addition, Mao believes firmly that an important segment of revolutionary cadres is recruited from among the intellectuals or student youth. Here he agrees with Lenin, that these ex-petty bourgeois are likely to be highly endowed with political acumen and capable of rendering valuable service to the cause.

The most perplexing problem—how to start the insurrection—is ideally resolved by the Party, according to Mao, when the struggle must be carried on against a foreign invader. The Party then enjoys a heaven-sent opportunity to identify itself with the masses. It can recruit from among them new members or sympathizers, and ultimately assume the leadership of the entire struggle.

To the Bolshevik experience Mao devotes special attention. The Russian communists, he points out, took over more than one-sixth of the globe, and organized the first international fortress of Marxist socialism. Since one cannot quarrel with such a victor, his ideological and doctrinal patterns must have been correct. Besides, the Bolshevik example taught the foreign insurrectionist that he must exercise resourcefulness and imagination to tailor the prerequisites for victory in his own country. And he must above all not permit himself to be the slave of theory. Moreover, the Chinese communists were greatly indebted to the Bolsheviks, for the Bolsheviks were operating in one of the largest countries of the world preparing foundations for the key role the Soviet Union was to play on the world scene. A great power in her own right, China had to prepare herself for a similar role. The precepts that applied to specifically Russian problems were of no more than academic interest to the Chinese. But the Bolshevik example of how to grasp the reins of power was one that the Chinese communist might well follow.

## Notes

1. "Our people may commit stupidities (provided, of course, that they are not too serious and are rectified in time) and yet in the long run come out the victors" (V. I. Lenin, *"Left-Wing" Communism: An Infantile Disorder* (New York: International Publishers, 1940), p. 64.

2. From the speeches and writings of Stalin are drawn many of the oft-quoted clichés used in describing the role of the communist party, such as "a militant party," "a revolutionary party," "one bold enough to lead the proletarians in the struggle for power." Such a party is variously described as the vanguard of the working class, the instrument of the proletariat, and as a party strengthened by purging itself of opportunistic elements. (See Iosif Stalin, "The Party," in *Iosif Stalin, Problems of Leninism* (Moscow: Foreign Languages Publishing House, 1953), pp. 96-110.)

Mao Tse-tung viewed a party member as playing the exemplary role in "all spheres of work." He must "set an example in fighting valiantly performing political work and upholding internal unity and solidarity." An organized communist must be an indefatigable preacher of the people. (See Mao Tse-tung, "The Role of the Chinese Communist Party in the National War," *Collected Works* (New York: International Publishers, 1954), 2: 244-48.)

Set on such a foundation, members of the communist party are presumably capable of carrying out any task and deserve all the credit for success. The party member, said Tito in discussing the leading role of the CPY in the 1941-45 Civil War in Yugoslavia, "selflessly remained with the people in the most agonizing days of their history. He was the first to take up arms and go into combat, to offer heroic examples of loyalty to the people." (See *Komunist*, No. 1 Oct. 1946.)

"Under the Party's glorious banner," says Vo Nguyen Giap, the Vietnamese people "have heightened their stalwart and unsubmissive spirit of resistance and their thoroughly revolutionary spirit in firmly maintaining and developing the offensive position of the revolution, and in making worthy contributions to the world revolution" (*Banner of People's War: The Party's Military Line* (New York: Praeger, 1970), p. 15.)

Any obstacle, according to Marxist authors, can easily be overcome by such human material. "Five days after the entry of the Germans into Salonika (April 9, 1941) the district committee of the CP met in secret and decided on armed struggle against the invader. The EAM (Ethniko Apeleftherotiko Metopo; National Liberation Front) was then formed under the leadership of the CPG, attracting to its ranks other parties and organizations. Though "the struggle against the German power was not easy," under the guidance of the communists, problems were solved; and "by the beginning of 1942 EAM was a force to be reckoned with." (See E. Joannides, "Bloody But Unbowed: The Story of the Greek People's Struggle for Freedom," quoted from *Guerrilla Warfare and Marxism* . . . William J. Pomeroy, ed. (New York: International Publishers, 1968, pp. 158-60.)

3. This line of reasoning gave rise to numerous communist slogans relating to guerrilla action, such as "We are winning even while losing!"; "The bandit lost just because he won!"; "We can afford to lose a thousand times; it is sufficient to win but once!" Régis Debray, in *Revolution in the Revolution? Armed Struggle and Political Struggle in Latin America*, trans. by Bobbye Ortez (New York: Grove Press, Inc., 1967) p. 23, asserts that "for a revolutionary, failure is a springboard. As a source of theory it is richer than victory: it accumulates experience and knowledge." In the same work (p. 24) Ché Guevara is quoted as saying, "As far as the final result is concerned, it does not matter whether one movement or another is temporarily defeated."

4. This writing pattern comes in especially handy in cases when a Marxist author must give reasonable answers to evident paradoxes of history, as in the case of the generous, unrestricted aid to Tito by the capitalist West from 1943 on, or the efforts of some U.S. generals to bend over backward in their dealings with Mao Tse-tung, 1945-49.

5. Clemens P. Dutt, ed., *Fundamentals of Marxism-Leninism*, 2nd rev. ed. (Moscow: Foreign Languages Publishing House, 1963), p. 17.

6. For a broader discussion of the unity between the two, see

Gabriel A. Almond, *The Appeals of Communism* (Princeton, N.J.: Princeton University Press, 1954), pp. 32-41.

7. An orthodox Marxist might, for instance, accuse the leaders of the Communist Party of Greece, 1941-49, at one and the same time of opportunism and excessive dogmatism; of sectarianism in cadre policy and of "bourgeois laxity." In other words, the CPG could be labeled opportunistic because in forming its partisan detachments it placed undue reliance on the peasant rather than on the urban proletarian. That Greece of the time was overwhelmingly an agricultural country might be of no consequence to such an author. Or the fact that Mao Tse-tung, Tito, and Enver Hoxha organized partisan shock brigades precisely drawing recruits from "vacillating, floundering peasants," he would also sidestep or gloss over. Purportedly, the CPG was sectarian because it was only after a laborious procedure that party ranks were opened to a peasant-partisan manifesting a sufficient level of class-consciousness, while workers, even though employed part-time in factories run by the German occupation, were readily admitted. The leaders of the party, blindly anti-fascist and found wanting in militant anti-imperialist sentiments, were alleged to have behaved as "petty bourgeois country politicians." Thus, every conceivable doctrinary sin could be ascribed to them. For a broader understanding of variations of these accusations see the suggested bibliography on the Civil War in Greece.

8. The defeat of the Huks and the policies of Magsaysay have been competently discussed in Napoleon D. Valeriano and Charles T. R. Bohannan, *Counter-Guerrilla Operations: The Philippine Experience* (New York: Praeger, 1962); Alvin H. Scaff, *The Philippine Answer to Communism* (Stanford, Calif.: Stanford University Press, 1955); and Charles W. Thayer, *Guerrilla* (New York: Harper and Row, 1963), pp. 26-45.

9. The Huks had been estimated to have 12,000 armed guerrillas enjoying the support of at least 1,000,000 local inhabitants. The 30,000 government troops, according to Thayer, "could count on hardly more than 1,000,000 active supporters." (*Guerrilla*, p. 33)

10. On this count Mao Tse-tung alone may be considered free of guilt. Because of the freshness of his approach and the depth of his comprehension of the subject, Mao Tse-tung's treatises on guerrilla are the only Eastern texts distinguished by any degree of substantive and methodological originality. With only a few rare exceptions the researcher is met on all other fronts with monotonous, unimaginative sameness.

11. Clausewitzian term. See Karl von Clausewitz, "Friction in War," in *On War*, trans. by O. J. Matthÿs Jolles (New York: Modern Library, 1943), pp. 53-55.

12. For a discussion of the difficulties, both doctrinal and actual, faced by this Partisan Detachment, see the work of party activist Vita

Cvetković, *Izvestaj Pise Ko Prezivi*: . . .(A survivor's account), 2 vols. Vol. I (Belgrade: Nolit, 1960); Vol. II (Belgrade: Nolit, 1962).

13. Mao Tse-tung, "Problems of War and Strategy," in Mao Tse-tung, *Selected Works* (New York: International Publishers, 1954), 2:268.

14. *Ibid.*, p. 267.

15. Mao Tse-tung, "On the Protracted War," *Selected Works*, 2:203. See also, Mao Tse-tung, "On the Rectification of Incorrect Ideas in the Party," *Selected Works*, 1:106-8.

16. Mao Tse-tung, "Problems of War," p. 272.

17. See Lin Piao, "International Significance of Comrade Mao Tse-tung's Theory of People's War," in Pomeroy, *Guerrilla Warfare and Marxism*, p. 194.

18. See Mao Tse-tung, "Problems of China's Revolutionary War," *Selected Works*, 1:192-3.

19. *Ibid.*, pp. 193-5.

20. For Mao Tse-tung's summary of these characteristics, see "Problems of China's Revolutionary War," pp. 193-6.

21. *Ibid.*, pp. 197-8.

22. The disciples of Mao still appear to find it a thorny problem to reconcile two aspects of Mao's heritage on guerrilla. On the one hand, they see Mao, the imaginative practitioner of Lenin's teaching, but in no case a theoretical innovator. On the other, there is Mao, the father of a new concept on guerrilla, one that makes claims to having "universal significance" for all contemporary revolutionists, whether Leninist or not. A study of Lin Piao's panegyric on the international significance of Mao's teachings might give the impression that Mao assumes multiple roles—iron Leninist, Chinese Lenin, and brilliant Leninist disciple who has outgrown his teacher and laid the groundwork for a new manual on insurrection. See also William Pomeroy's views on Mao's "universality" in *Guerrilla Warfare and Marxism*, pp. 25-28 and 167-68; and Chalmers Johnson, *Autopsy on People's War* (Berkeley: University of California Press, 1973.)

23. Unless otherwise indicated, Mao's definitions of and reflections on guerrilla warfare are taken from Mao Tse-tung, "What is Guerrilla Warfare," *On Guerrilla Warfare*, trans. by S. B. Griffith. (New York: Praeger, 1961), pp. 41-50.

24. Compare Mao's thoughts with those of Clausewitz as they appear in Chap. 26, Bk. VI "Arming the Nation," *On War*, pp. 457-62.

25. Mao Tse-tung, *On Guerrilla Warfare*, p. 43.

26. For Mao's discussion with Jen Ch'i Shan and Yeh Ch'ing, see *Ibid.*, pp. 44-45.

27. *Ibid.*, p. 46.

28. *Ibid.*, pp. 47-48. Compare these thoughts on the reactionary guerrilla with previous statements to the effect that in a war of a counterrevolutionary nature "there is no place for guerrilla hostilities" (*Ibid.*, pp. 43-44).

29. *Ibid.*, pp. 63-64.

30. Mao refers in several instances in *On Protracted War* and in *On Guerrilla Warfare* directly to Clausewitz, *On War*. The Clausewitz work had at that time not been translated into Chinese; but Mao is apparently borrowing Lenin's interpretation of Clausewitzian theory, especially as it appears in Lenin's works, *Socialism and War* and *Collapse of the Second International*.

31. See Mao Tse-tung, "Reform Our Study," *Selected Works*, 4:12-22.

32. See *Ibid.*, pp. 13-18.

33. Mao Tse-tung, "Problems of China's Revolutionary War," p. 176.

34. *Ibid.*, pp. 176-77.

35. *Ibid.*, pp. 177-78.

36. Mao Tse-tung, "The Chinese Revolution and the Chinese Communist Party," *Selected Works*, 3:88.

37. *Ibid.*, pp. 88-90.

38. See *Ibid.*, pp. 90-91.

39. As striking proof of the role of such intellectuals, Mao refers to students sent to study abroad before the revolution of 1911, to the May 4th Movement of 1919, to the May 30th Movement of 1925, and to the December 9th Movement of 1935. Upon their return many of these dépaysé or déraciné students joined the communist movement and supported its cause.

40. Mao Tse-tung, "The Chinese Revolution and the Chinese Communist Party," pp. 92-93.

41. For Mao's arguments on the peasantry, see *Ibid.*, pp. 92-93.

42. How to be victorious in a proletarian revolution without a proletariat, or to be more exact, with the minimal help that class in China can render is a question faced by Lenin in Russia and by Tito in Yugoslavia. Mao answers briefly, in rather imprecise terms and in a jargon replete with trite slogans (*Ibid.*, pp. 92-95). He considers the theoretical problem of proletarian leadership automatically resolved by the fact that a majority of the leaders of the CCP were officially proletarians, if not by vocation, at least according to their official biographies.

43. Mao Tse-tung, "Strategic Problems in the Anti-Japanese Guerrilla War," *Selected Works*, 2:122-23.

44. See Chap. IV, "On Our Own Initiative, With Flexibility and According to Plan, Carry Out Offensives in a Defensive War, Battles of Quick Decision in a Protracted War, and Exterior-Line Operations within Interior-Line Operations," in Mao Tse-tung, *Ibid.*, pp. 123-32.

45. Mao Tse-tung, "Problems of China's Revolutionary War," 1:198-99.

46. Mao Tse-tung, "Strategic Problems," 2:125.

47. For Mao's discussion on initiative in guerrilla warfare, see *Ibid.*, pp. 127-28.

48. *Ibid.*, pp. 129-31.

49. *Ibid.*, pp. 132-34.

50. For a broader discussion of the establishment of base areas, see *Ibid.*, Chap. VI, pp. 134-45.

# 2 Contemporary Latin American Marxists

Never has a clash between reality and dogma in which dogma has ended up a casualty received full treatment in the writings of the old school of Marxists. The task of portraying such a phenomenon has fallen primarily to contemporary Marxist authors from South America. In their studies these writers attempt to bring down to earth the Marxist-Leninist teachings on insurrection. They treat its elements more elastically than the old-line writers and seem more willing to adopt a commonsense attitude toward guerrilla practices. This shift may be accounted for in two ways. First comes the impressive weight of historical experience, which apparently convinced authors like Che Guevara, Carlos Marighella, Régis Debray, and others that the capacity of Marxist doctrine to command men and revolutionary upheavals has never progressed beyond a certain level. This is a fact of life that has become abundantly clear since the termination of the Civil War in Russia, 1917-21. A second explanation is the desire on the part of these authors to reach a broader public. The first situation pointed up the need to sift through and resurrect a number of classical Marxist theoretical patterns; and the second, the advisability of abandoning traditional Marxist methodology in order to get through to the modern-day student of guerrilla.

One constantly recurring theme is to be found in the works of most of these authors: Marxist doctrine cannot meet the essential requirement of all revolutionary situations—that the possible must prevail over what is theoretically correct. Few of these writers have yet dared to question openly the overall value of the Marxist manual on insurrection. Most of them grant that it is an extraordinary analytical weapon that aids the rebel to reduce all participants in a revolution to two principal antagonists, the proletariat and the bourgeoisie, and to adopt whatever policies seem best suited to attracting to his camp any wavering or reluctant or uncommitted segments of the populace. In addition, these writers regard the manual as a unique and indispensable organizational tool. Following its direction, the leaders of a revolution may assemble on a moment's notice and keep under their thumb the most valuable cadres in any civil war, the seasoned communists. Maintaining a balance between the value commitments and the methods for their implementation, the manual suggests the basic framework for political and propaganda work, for security and intelligence efforts, for a full-scale military apparatus, and for ties with communists abroad.

On the other hand, as already mentioned, the manual does present problems. It is true that without it the communist organizers may lose "the general staff of the revolution," the party cadres; but if they follow it literally, they are in danger of losing the "army of revolution," or all those who may join the struggle without having the vaguest notion of what it is all about. Examples of successful guerrilla lead the communist to believe that the manual in its technical detail guarantees the most certain road to success; but then he is reminded by the records of actual experience that the road to success is not identical in any two places. To find the middle ground between these two extremes poses a critical problem that each revolutionary leader must solve for himself. It goes almost without saying that many have failed dismally.

## Che Guevara in Bolivia: the Controversial Marxist Guerrilla

The example of Ernesto "Che" Guevara's stay in Bolivia in the middle sixties is a case in point. Che arrived in that country as the undisputed Marxist authority on guerrilla warfare. Internationally known as the author of a widely popular manual and as a lecturer who had something new to offer on the subject, he enjoyed the reputation of a legendary hero.[1] It was this imaginative guerrilla leader from the Sierra Maestra Mountains, Camaguey, and Las Villas, "cougar of Santa Clara," El Che as he was called by many Latin American revolutionaries, who was now making blunders, both political and military. His politics in Bolivia were unrealistic, his military conduct dated. As for his political actions, it can only be said that he never seemed quite aware of what country he was in; and his military experience had made of him a leftist mercenary, whose strength lay in the bayonet and who kept uppermost in his mind what he had learned in boot camp.

Without preparing the ground, Guevara pushed the concept of "export of revolution" very prematurely from Cuba to Latin America. One of Guevara's admirers, Ciro Roberto Bustos, an Argentinian painter, makes what appears to be a very perceptive analysis of the Cuban leader's political mistakes. Bustos faults Che for choosing Bolivia in the first place and for underestimating the strength and fighting spirit of the army and the intense nationalism of the people.[2] Not only was his choice of country ill-advised, but his knowledge of it scanty and characterized by wishful thinking. As matters developed, everything Che met in Bolivia was contrary to what he had expected. Farmers and miners regarded his partisans as nothing more than foreign intruders, and flatly refused to play the Cuban game. Che ignored the Bolivian communists, too; and they, in turn, ignored him. He pinned his hopes on help from Castro, and when this failed to materialize Che found himself alone.

On the military level, he was unwilling to admit that his "three golden rules of guerrilla" would not apply in Bolivia. His guiding principles were these:

1. Popular forces can win a war against the enemy.

2. It is not necessary to wait until all conditions for making a revolution exist; the insurrection can create them.

3. In underdeveloped America the countryside is the basic area for armed fighting.[3]

To his great dismay he discovered that the Bolivian regulars were not as "emasculated" as he had believed, and that in order to overcome them a good deal more was needed than sheer revolutionary will. That the insurrectionist cannot create all the conditions for insurrection he also learned much too late. As for this third dictum, that the countryside was to figure as the only scene of action, this policy cost him most dearly. Flying in the face of reason, he cut all ties with the cities. Thus he cut himself off from nearly all political, propaganda, cadre, medical, and other help that would have been readily available from urban centers.

As if these errors in judgment were not serious enough, the additional mistakes that led him and his forces to disaster appear even more astonishing if one accepts Guevara as the guru of Latin American theory on guerrilla warfare. Guevara's last previous visit to Bolivia, before his return there in 1966, was in 1953 when he was twenty-five years old.[4] At that time he was still impetuous and far from being what the Marxists would call a mature revolutionary. He was completely aware that for long years Bolivian national dignity had been trampled underfoot, and quite correctly viewed the history of the country as a succession of rebellions against intruders, against the La Paz government, against misery, oppression, corruption, and city politicos. The image of the country as a powder keg waiting for an arsonist became stamped upon the memory of the young man. For these people to take to arms periodically, to fight valiantly, and to pay dearly for their heroism was in their very blood. It was this heroism and readiness to sacrifice that Guevara considered the only catalyst binding together this country which in modern times had been a nation in name only.[5] As a result of this 1953 visit, revolution in Bolivia became Guevara's *idée fixe*.[6] In the beginning of the sixties, therefore, when he and Fidel began to consider the most fertile soil for starting the "continental revolution," the choice quite naturally zeroed in on Bolivia. All the ideal conditions for the inception of guerrilla were present here. A number of Bolivian revolutionaries he had met over the years in Cuba kept reaffirming his belief that Bolivia was still "the place," that no change in the country had significantly altered the picture Guevara had formed in 1953.[7]

Only this obsession with Bolivia could explain Guevara's refusal to take into account the events that had shaped the character of the nation with which he thought he was acquainted. He clung stubbornly to those phenomena of recent Bolivian political history that had impressed him: the sporadic outbursts of the people (such as the uprising of miners in May 1965) and the weak army, which he judged quite incapable of suppressing any revolution organized according to the Cuban model. Failure of the 1965 uprising, for instance, he regarded solely as a natural result of the system of "workers' self-defense zones," which aimed at organizing quasi-partisan units to defend by arms the revolutionary acts of the miners.[8] It was this primitive and self-defeating technique alone, according to Guevara, that was responsible for failure. The military strength of the Bolivian regulars, he believed, had contributed in no way to the defeat.[9]

Under Che's tutelage, as he had originally planned, the Bolivian guerrillas were to reject the zones, as well as to establish a clear-cut policy toward the Bolivian communists. It was Guevara's contention that the communists, who were splintered into three antagonistic groups (pro-Soviet hard liners, Maoists, and Trotskyites), had consistently left the rebels dangling. They had done amazingly little to help the cause. Instead, their only contribution had been to put forth scores of political obstacles at the most inopportune moments and at every step of the way.[10] They either did not or could not recognize the value of Fidel Castro's motto, "The duty of a revolutionary is to make revolution!" and endlessly quarreled over who was to start the gargantuan project of national liberation, the people or the revolutionaries, and with or without the party.[11] What Guevara saw in them was a gallery of faceless organization men, frittering away their time passing resolutions. The Bolivian communists he was certain could never raise anyone to power.[12] What would alleviate all these problems, he figured, was a new type of "nucleus of subversion," a small number of knowledgeable, hardened, and, if necessary, imported revolutionaries who could make any gamble pay off. In 1966, therefore, he selected a handful of *barbudos*[13] and departed for Bolivia, fully expecting an almost effortless triumph.

At this juncture, his plan was simple. The Cubans were to start matters off by carrying out armed actions, and by recruiting and tempering a handful of Bolivian *barbudos*. These in turn, following the example of the Castro pattern in Cuba, would gradually activate the entire nation, thus destroying the foreign and domestic oppressor, and once and for all would "sever the chain that binds Bolivia to the Yankee imperialists." Bolivia, once enflamed, was to provide the spark that would ignite first Argentina and Peru, and then other Latin American nations. But once liberated completely, she would inevitably become the epicenter from which the domino theory would become operative on the whole continent. Bolivia would become the "general staff of continental revolution," the center for the coordination of activities of the different national liberation armies. The stream of supplies and matériel that would be forthcoming from the countries of the socialist bloc—and this was a thought that Guevara never abandoned[14] —could then be cached on this enormous supply base. In addition, a headquarters for diplomatic and propaganda efforts could be established here to support Latin American guerrillas in their battle to win over international public opinion and to protect themselves from the intrigues of the imperialist bloc. Also, it would be an impregnable sanctuary for the wounded, for the training of specialists, for security check of neophytes, for political schooling of cadres and future people's authorities.

To crown the project, Guevara assigned to Bolivia the role of setting a trap for the United States. It was to be another Vietnam, to drag Washington into a war which it could not win and would not dare to lose. And "once additional guerrilla movements emerged in Peru and Argentina, he believed the United States would rapidly exhaust itself trying to suppress them,"[15] until it reached the point where it would no longer have the strength to suppress anybody.[16]

However, the actual situation Guevara found in Bolivia in 1966 fell far short of being ideal for the Marxist insurrectionist. In 1953 land had been ceded to Bolivian peasants, often far larger plots than "they could hope to work even with the help of their children." In the southeast, a part of the country where Guevara planned to establish his first *foco*,[17] a peasant could have land just for the price of asking. As Daniel James pointed out, Bolivian Indians, who made up two-thirds of the country's 4,250,000 inhabitants, now experienced the pride of possession for the first time, and were passing through all the stages characteristic of newly established landowners.[18] They had lost the hostility Guevara remembered from his past visit. They were preoccupied rather with the natural concerns of all farmers, such as how to improve their plots; how to acquire livestock, seed, and farm implements; what new methods to adopt, and above all how to hang onto what they had. Perhaps for the first time in the history of Bolivia, the peasantry and the government had found a sort of modus vivendi. This process of rapprochement had been given a big boost following the overthrow of Victor Pas Estenssoro and his Movimento Nacionalista Revolucionario on November 4, 1964. The last thing the

Bolivian peasant needed at this moment was an "agrarian revolutionary" and his rosy promises to redistribute, at the cost of peasant bloodshed, land that had already been distributed.

To all these considerations Che was apparently oblivious.[19] Seeing himself presented with an opportunity that comes to a man once in a lifetime, he proceeded as though Bolivians were still living in wretched conditions, and assumed that following their class instincts they would not fail to side with the guerrilla whether indigenous or imported. He appeared not in the least interested in the political moods of the Bolivian peasantry in general, but focused only on those he intended to recruit. Even here he was completely undiscriminating: he actuall failed to secure even one guerrilla who spoke the dialect of the area in which he operated.[20]

Still living in the past, he further defeated his own cause by remembering the Cuban farmers' resistance to cooperatives in the early sixties. Again, contrary to his own teachings, he began to accept cooperation from and recruited only those rare inhabitants who in his judgment would pose no threat to the future Marxist regime in Bolivia. Already suspicious, the villagers became even more so. To this Che reacted by slackening political and propaganda work in the countryside, ultimately bringing it to a complete standstill. Such a winding down of activity among the villagers left even those few with whom Guevara did cooperate completely in the dark as to the guerrilla's true goals. The vast majority of the populace considered Che and his followers as armed wanderers at best, a group of political bandits who might strike anyone at any time. For this reason it was charged that the Bolivian peasant was the last to understand why Che had come to his country.

In his monthly analyses, Guevara notes the peasants' ignoring of guerrillas as well as their increasing willingness to support the government troops. The following selected entries occur in his *Diaries*:

*December 1966*: "The formation of the Cuban team has been successfully accomplished, the people's morale is good, and there are only small problems. The Bolivians are good although there are few of them."

*January 1967*: "Of all the things foreseen, the one that is going slowest is the recruitment of Bolivian combatants."

*April 1967*: "The isolation continues to be complete ... The peasant base has not yet been developed, althought it appears that through planned terror we can neutralize some of them: support will come later. Not one enlistment has been obtained."

*May 1967*: "The most important characteristics are ... complete lack of peasant recruitment, although they are losing their fear of us and we are beginning to win their admiration. It is a slow and patient task ... The army issued a communique announcing the arrest of all the peasants who collaborated with us in the Masicuri zone. Now comes the stage in which terror will be used against the peasants by both sides, with different objectives."

*June 1967*: "The most important items are ... the lack of peasant recruits continues. It is a vicious circle: to get this enlistment we need to settle in a populated area, and for this we need men ... All the Cubans are excellent in combat, and we have only two or three lazy Bolivians."

*July 1967*: "The peasantry still is not joining us, although there were some encouraging signs from some peasants we know."

*August 1967*: "We still have not incorporated the peasants. The most urgent tasks continue to be the same as last month, that is: reestablish contact, enroll combatants, supply ourselves with medicine and equipment."

*September 1967*: "The situation is the same as last month except that now the Army appears to be more effective ... and the peasants ... are turning into informers."[21]

The ill effects of his obsession with the Cuban model were most marked here. Not unlike a high communist functionary accustomed to legislate into existence changes of mind and customs, Guevara acted as though he expected any peasant sympathetic to the guerrilla cause to become a perfect *barbudo* overnight if properly coerced. As if they were conscripts and not volunteers, he treated them harshly. Whatever the peasant did and regardless of the dangers to which he might expose himself and his family in order to help the guerrillas, he was clearly given to understand that he was still "a lazy Bolivian" whom nobody trusted. Kept completely in the dark as to the rationale of the great risk he was undertaking, the peasant began to view Guevara as another edition of a foreign intruder using him for ulterior motives.

Then came "the planned terror" and pressure on the peasants by both sides that Guevara mentions in his analyses of April and May 1967. The government regulars terrorized those who cooperated with Guevara; Guevara in turn terrorized both those who cooperated with the army and the neutrals. Only partly trusting his own collaborators, he forced the majority of peasants in his area to make a clear choice between camps: that of the bearded and strangely dressed foreigners who did not speak their language, or that of the army units, which were composed for the most part of their own conscripted sons. In order not to be bothered by the army, the peasant needed only to remain neutral. But he risked attack from Guevara whether he collaborated or not.

Beginning roughly from May 1967, the rapprochement of the peasant and the regulars became evident to everybody except Guevara. The peasant now was increasingly willing to help the troops, acting as informer, scout, or intelligence spotter. And because the army accepted his services with gratitude, the peasant now entrusted his fate to an army victory. This mass change of mood was not lost on Guevara's supporters, who gradually began to desert him.

For some unaccountable reason, Guevara failed to draw the proper conclusions from two highly significant events of this period: the June 1967 unrest in the mining area of Siglo

II and Oruro, and the Fourth Peasant National Congress in July of the same year. In the first instance, army troops sent to keep order among the miners collided with them, leaving twenty-one dead and seventy wounded. On June 24, a forty-eight hour strike was declared protesting the army intervention. The miners carried on the entire action by themselves, making it perfectly clear that they wanted no part of Guevara's aid. In their view he was a foreigner who could not share nor understand the grievances of Bolivians. One month later, delegates assembled at the Fourth Peasant National Congress made these sentiments even clearer. They decided overwhelmingly to oppose Guevara and "back the government against the guerrillas, with arms if necessary," concluding to this end the Pacto-Campesino Militar, a military alliance with the government troops.[22]

The unsettled relations with the Bolivian communists were also greatly responsible for Guevara's death. The help he did receive from the Communist Party of Bolivia (PCB), the pro-Moscow wing, was minimal. It took the form of empty promises made by the secretary of the party, Mario Monje Molina, that ultimately forced Guevara to assert that the "Bolivian communists are pigs."[23] On the other hand, they rendered lukewarm applause to the *barbudos*, especially after Guevara's first successful ambush against the government troops at Nancahuazú on March 23, 1967. His stay in Bolivia then became the *cause célébre* of the leftist international press. Save for their common conviction that the La Paz government must be overthrown at all costs, the PCB and Guevara were continuously at loggerheads. Monje and other officials of the party first criticized Guevara's basic plan that guerrilla warfare should be carried on exclusively in the countryside rather than in the cities as well. They attacked also the premature character of the uprising, Guevara's impetuosity, and his ambitions to put all leftist forces in Bolivia under his command. In particular they resented his deep-seated lack of faith in the revolutionary firmness of the PCB.[24]

Be that as it may, Guevara is not without blame for having failed to settle the problem of relations with Bolivian communists while he was still in Cuba. Apparently neither he nor Castro fully understood the awkward position of the pro-Moscow PCB, which, at least in words, wished to aid Guevara's venture, but could not do so without the go-ahead from Moscow. Such a signal was not so easy to obtain because Fidel and Che, by their initiation of the insurrection, clearly demonstrated their desire to transfer the political leadership of Latin American affairs from Moscow to Havana.

In December 1966 Monje arrived in Havana to settle this ticklish situation with Castro, and after a number of discussions left for Bolivia still confused as to how to proceed. Indeed, on New Year's Day 1967 he met Che at Nancahuazú, where, according to Ricardo Rojo, he proposed the following: "The Party cannot commit itself officially in the guerrilla war but it can be done in another way, for instance, if I resign my post first. Then, I could follow, with the guerrillas, a line parallel to the Party's, without being in the Party."[25] Though Guevara believed that no serious revolutionary should propose anything of the sort under conditions of combat, he was receptive to the ideas of Monje until Monje made two additional demands: first, that he (Monje) was to supervise all negotiations with other groups that might help (Primarily the pro-Maoists and the Trotsky-ites); and second, that he would assume the post of chief military and political leader. This proposal Guevara violently rejected: "Certainly not, I am the leader;" and from that moment the war between the two was on.

Guevara's chief difficulty in dealing with the Bolivian communists, as well as with other leftist elements, arose from his treating all of them as though he were Castro of the 1956-59 period. It is known, of course, that the help rendered Castro by the Cuban communists, at least officially, was negligible, while the leftists and liberals from the island rushed forward of their own volition to offer their services to the cause. Still spellbound by these memories, Guevara acted as though he fully expected history to repeat itself. He appears to have seen little point in courting any of these groups in Bolivia, and seemingly set his course as though they did not exist. He therefore ended up by alienating most of them, particularly the PCB.

Harris mentions five ways in which PCB leaders betrayed Che and his cause: by transmitting to Havana false information about the political situation and about the party's determination to launch a guerrilla operation; by preventing Cuba-trained Bolivians from joining Che; by promising support to Che that never materialized; by preventing their own party militants from fighting with Che; and providing important information about Che to the Bolivian authorities and the CIA.[26] In Harris's opinion, "each of these moves was an act of betrayal and together they insured the defeat of Che's operation."

Through PCB sources Guevara acquired a totally incorrect picture of his chances for a revolutionary take-over in Bolivia. Monje and other pro-Soviet hard liners promised him significant cadres, political, material, and other help; and on the basis of their promises Guevara formulated his first plans. However, immediately after Monje's conversation with Castro in Havana and his meeting with Guevara at Nancahuazú, it became clear that Che had his own show in mind and that the role he envisioned for the PCB was an auxiliary one. Not suprisingly, Monje and his followers decided to go back on their word and, by isolating him from militant cadres who could have joined the *barbudos*, to leave Guevara in mid-air. The last and most serious of Harris's accusations against the Bolivian communists—that "they provided the Bolivian authorities and the CIA with important information about Che," was a not unexpected outgrowth of this change of heart, because from the moment Guevara openly scorned Monje's demands for leadership, the pro-Muscovites had no course but to regard him if not as an open enemy then at best as an intolerable nuisance.[27]

Even if we accept Harris's analysis of PCB policy, Che, as

political-military leader of the uprising, can certainly not be absolved. For even if the PCB had misinformed Che and had led him to believe that the Bolivian peasants were friendly, it was up to him to doublecheck and to evaluate their advice. If he were following the procedure for a guerrilla leader as set forth in his own manual, Guevara should first of all have been unwilling to rely on one source exclusively whether his information came from the communists or not. As a man who had taken great pains to emphasize to the Latin American insurrectionists the importance of examining and reexamining the complexities of any revolutionary situation, he had gone to Bolivia with a highly generalized picture of the country, a picture which with only minor modifications could have been made to fit any nation on the continent.

Not only was his thinking very fuzzy with respect to detail, but he appeared to be quite oblivious of the general impression his Bolivian adventure might leave upon the socialist bloc. He was aware that the PCB wanted a revolution in Bolivia, but a revolution that unfolded in accord with Moscow's designs.[28] This lack of perception he then coupled with a mistaken assessment of pro-Maoists and Trotskyites in Bolivia. He seemed completely unaware of the intensity and the dimension of the ongoing Sino-Soviet dispute and of the protracted battle between the followers of Moscow, of Peking, and of Trotsky. He evidently believed that once guerrilla warfare was under way in Bolivia, all these groups would forget their past disagreements and of one accord flock to the *barbudo* camp.

That his experiment in Bolivia might put Castro in an unenviable situation appears not to have entered into Guevara's calculations. The Cuban premier, during the greater part of 1966 in agreement with Guevara, was now forced to make a painful decision. He could not abandon his friend, but at the same time as a practical politician he had to keep uppermost in his mind that the security and progress of Cuba depended on the Soviets. Early in 1967, therefore, Fidel, still officially espousing Guevara's cause, gradually began to wash his hands of Guevara. This he accomplished by renegging on his earlier promises of aid; and at the end, when Che needed him most, he virtually cut all contacts, even radio.[29]

Guevara's oversights at the political level were bound to reflect on his strategy. Wrapped up in his experience of the campaign against Batista, he completely overlooked the character of the new Bolivian army. He appeared to be almost unaware that facing him was no longer a poorly trained Batista regular. The Bolivian officer he now confronted was invariably better trained than his Cuban counterpart and increasingly able to use guerrilla methods himself. The element of surprise, on which Guevara had so strongly counted initially, was now equally a technique of the adversary. The Bolivian regulars were not only better armed than Batista's troops, but they were equipped with motor transport, helicopters, and a reliable system of communication and supply. Furthermore, Che seems to have ignored the presence in the country of a number of U.S. experts on guerrilla who had helped to train the Bolivian forces in counterinsurgency methods. The American advisers were recommending many sophisticated methods for dealing politically with insurrection, such as reforms in treatment of population and the popularizing of slogans that would have universal appeal.[30]

Under these conditions Guevara's military skill faltered. He regarded the handful of his followers not only as partisans in the usual sense of the term but also as a revolutionary symbol, as a sort of international revolutionary globetrotters. The first role assigned to the *barbudos* was that they be ready to sacrifice themselves for the military success of every concrete action in Bolivia. On the other hand, since Bolivia was but the springboard to other Latin American countries, their secondary role demanded that they conserve their life force. In order to synchronize the two roles, Guevara transferred the emphasis from the struggle of masses concentrated in cities to the rural population, and then organized self-sustained units tied to large segments of the village population only when an individual campaign required such action. His guerrilla could thus act on his own, without undue reliance on the population or on political parties that might be inclined to support him. In other words, Guevara's guerrilla would choose not only the time and the place for attack, but also the type and duration of help required. The first pattern would guarantee the military success of operations, saving the guerrilla from security leaks, infiltration, and two-faced collaborators; the other would enable Guevara to carry on "a people's war" in Bolivia with limited participation by Bolivians.

It is over this point—the city vs. the countryside—that Guevara's manual on continental insurrection clashed seriously with the Marxist manual. The direct, Bolshevik type of assault on the cities Guevara considered pure adventurism. In his view, a typical South American city represented a cage for the rebel as much as a fortress of the repressive forces. Here the best of the enemy's politico-military, administrative, police, and other personnel were quartered. Real possibilities for a rebel to engage governmental forces militarily on a mass scale or to perpetrate serious, lasting strikes would be severely limited. The urban activist would at best be forced to limit himself to such measures as passive resistance, propaganda against the establishment, sabotage, and the collection and dispatch of financial and medical aid to units in the countryside.

Though all these measures might in themselves constitute a significant contribution, no single instrument could decide the fate of a revolution. The dangers and the casualties suffered by activists in the destruction of buildings, for instance, or in the assassination of individual representatives of the enemy's apparatus, would be quite disproportionate to the tangible results. By his quick reaction and repressive measures the enemy would generate an image of impressive power. The people might be left so terrorized that they would be reluctant to give aid to the insurrectionist.

It was in the countryside, Guevara maintained, that

decisive battles were to be won, where the destruction of the enemy's life force was tactically within reach. On a continent such as South America, the enemy could not control every square mile of land no matter how well organized, mobile, or hardened he might be. It was in a situation such as this that the maneuvering space of the guerrilla would be unlimited. In that interspace left unguarded by enemy forces, the partisan might safely choose a target: an isolated enemy unit, a desolate outpost, or poorly defended communications. One three-man patrol, for instance, could harass an entire enemy batallion, then quickly shift to another position. Before the first unit could regain its balance, another would be attacked. Thus a mere handful of partisans could create the illusion of a crown fire exploding over a region.

Such actions would ordinarily be carried out at night. Fire contact as a rule is brief and massive, with the element of surprise ever-present. The local population, taken completely unawares, would at first be inclined to ascribe to the guerrillas strength they did not possess. As they observed the government losses, the people would gradually come to believe that numerical superiority of the govenment force might really not be overwhelming; and sooner or later their faith in the government would be undermined.

Another cogent argument of Guevara was that only in the countryside could guerrilla forces establish a *foco*. Here, never pressed for time, a guerrilla could calmly and systematically search for possible collaborators, check and recheck them. All others who could not be of direct service could safely be disregarded and spared unnecessary exposure to the brutality of the oppressor.[31]

In the beginning Guevara apparently considered all these principles reasonable and applicable to Bolivia; but, as it turned out, his entire plan could not have been more unsound. Having once started to sever ties with the city, he set himself on an irreversible course. His reluctance to seek support in the urban centers, the Bolivian communists welcomed, for it saved them the clashes with Moscow that would have been inevitable if the PCB had moved on a broad scale to help him. Monje and other leaders insisted that the PCB was eager to help, but for the reasons already given this help was rejected by Guevara. Therefore, the PCB held Guevara alone responsible for his isolation. Besides, the leftists and oppositionists to whom Guevara had made it clear that their help could be of use only when asked for directly, found themselves politically off balance. With their initial enthusiasm dampened, they volunteered fewer and fewer services; and in the end, as Ciro Bustos reports, "there was no support at all."[32]

Guevara's "planned terror" against the neutral villagers forced them to side with the government in self-defense. But since he and his men could not subsist without at least some help from the villagers, he selected supporters indiscriminately—at the expense of security. The army thus gained a long-sought opportunity to infiltrate the *barbudos*, and for the first time to become forewarned of their every step.

Guevara's breaches of security did not stop here, however. Basking in the glory of the international importance of his Bolivian adventure, he did his utmost to popularize it. He kept his journal and even encouraged others, such as Rolando (Eliseo Reyes Rodriguez), Pombo (Harry Villegas Tamayo), Braulio (Israel Reyes Zayas), to do the same.[33] He received journalists like Debray, and permitted Bustos free rein in sketching individual guerrillas. Later, when the government forces captured this material, identification of all of them was a simple matter.

For a legendary guerrilla, Che displayed an amazing degree of mediocrity as a commander. Contrary to the popular notion, he was unimaginative, unaggressive, and incapable of keeping his men together.[34] On April 17, 1967, for instance, his guerrilla force accidentally split into two groups, one led by himself, the other led by Joaquin Vilo (Juan Vitalio Acuna Nunez). Che unsuccessfully attempted to reestablish contact, but the army destroyed Joaquin's group on August 31 in Masicuri Bajo (Vado del Yeso). The desertion of some of his guerrillas, notably Chingolo (Hugo Choque Silva) and Eusebio (Eusebio Tapia Aruni), so enraged Che that he spent too much time lamenting the trust he had placed in the two and exposed those who remained to long tirades on the weaknesses a revolutionary must guard against. Chingolo and Eusebio joined army units as scouts, kept pinpointing the *focos* of guerrillas and, on August 8, guided the regulars to large caches of arms, ammunition, and drugs.

Guevara's lack of imagination led him to make haphazard choice of targets. Even his definitely successful moves, such as the ambushes against the army on March 23 at Nancahuazú, on April 10 in the zone of Iripiti, on May 8 at Pincal, and the July 6 take-over of the garrison at Samaipata, occurred more because of some inadequately trained Bolivian officers than because of Guevara's talent. He failed to sense how much the stupidity of the foe had contributed to his own successes, or to realize that no one could bank on that stupidity to continue. He attempted instead to employ the same tactical tricks, the known itineraries, the same travel folder, and the same set of orders.

With the help of the U.S. advisers, the Bolivian officers soon grasped the limits of Guevara's capabilities and in turn set their own snares. During the most critical period for the *barbudos*, August-October 1967, because of this inclination to repeat himself, Che became progressively more vulnerable. For example, after an encounter with the army that remains indelible in the mind of Ciro Bustos, Guevara ordered his men to remain in the same spot for twelve days. Here, of course, they became sitting ducks. The outcome of each of the three battles that resulted in the crushing of the Bolivian adventure—August 23 in Masicurí Bajo, September 26 at La Higuera, and October 8, the clash at Quebrada del Yuro—was thus predetermined. "It looked," the Bolivian officers boasted later, "as though we were attacking sleepwalkers on the edge of a cliff, the suicidal lemming."

Explain or analyze or try to justify as one may the oversights and outright blunders of Guevara, the contemporary reader is still at a loss to fathom how he could have bungled so badly. If he was in fact a leading Marxist authority on guerrilla, how did it happen that in Bolivia he acted like an irresponsible arsonist? He was ill-prepared for retreat and he exposed himself as a helpless, bumbling amateur. On what foundations, then, did the entire myth surrounding his stay in Bolivia rest? Why did the defeat and death of this man have a more important bearing on the long-term outlook of future guerrillas than any possible victory? What elements of his personality led to the creation of the legend built around him when we have here a typical case of an unsuccessful guerrilla leader who was easily defeated by a regular, poorly prepared Bolivian army? Above all, why does Guevara's name leap into prominence any time revolution is discussed today, and why does the mere mention of his name seem to be the last word on guerrilla?

Understandably, the answer to none of these questions is simple. First of all Guevara died young, and, according to rumor, without complaint. He had been oblivious to the material wealth offered him in Havana; he had left a position of preeminence there in order to go to Bolivia. He was incorruptible, unaffected by the privileges secured for the "new class" of Cuba. What he valued above all else was the notion of the battle itself. And in one of these engagements he simply disappeared.

Abandoned by the more practical Fidel, Che during the greater part of his stay in Bolivia was subject to severe attacks of asthma. Without medication, half-hungry most of the time, he enjoyed no real companionship in spite of the presence of his *barbudos*, who adored him as much as they feared him. Indeed, in evaluating the man the historian is faced with the problem of which aspects of Che's character during his last months deserve more emphasis: his senseless brutality toward the peasants or his compassionate wish to be their doctor, his severity toward his men or his ruthless demands on himself.

Such doubt as to his true role may be more readily

entertained by Che's lethal enemies—the bourgeois politician, the bourgeois political scientist, the soldier—than by Che's "lethal friend," the communist hard liner. For all the precepts he espoused—continental revolution, the imperative of separation from Moscow and its manual on insurrection, the deep suspicion of indigenous communists who imitate faithfully either the Russians or the Chinese, as well as his choice of the battlefield in the countryside rather than in the city—are in direct opposition to everything that, according to Che, the already ossified, half-dead "communist aristocrats" hold to be true. Besides, the myth of Guevara inspired such radical theoreticians on guerrilla as Debray. He indirectly stimulated rebels like Marighella, who helped to develop Che's half-formed idea that a Latin American guerrilla must first cut all ties with the communists and only then dare to commit himself to revolution. Finally, Guevara's entire philosophy made generations of rebels immune to anything hard liners had to say, and gave rise to self-styled pseudo- or anarco-revolutionaries, who, as we shall point out, reject any pattern and destroy merely for the sake of destruction.

From the Marxist point of view these were unforgivable sins; and had Che not been cut down in mid-career, he would in all probability have become the object of bitter attack, particularly by Moscow. But because it is rarely expedient to attack a legend, the burden of guilt for his heresy had to be passed on. And it landed squarely on the shoulders of Guevara's most faithful disciples, Régis Debray and Carlos Marighella.

## Régis Debray: The Guerrilla Versus the Party Bureaucracy

The French journalist Régis Debray sheds new light on much material with which we are already familiar. He clarifies the underlying reasons for the divergence between the classical Marxist manual on insurrection and Guevara's theory on continental revolution. More persistently than any other author who treats the subject, he criticizes the dangerously antiquated character of the hard liners' philosophy on guerrilla warfare. This disciple of Jean-Paul Sartre and "intellectual offspring of Fidel," as much doubting Thomas as classical Marxist, views a majority of Latin American communist leaders as "bourgeoisified" politicians, and strongly advises the future rebel to keep an eye on the communists.

Debray proves himself, in fact, to be a rather complicated writer. Although in principle he professes allegiance to Marxist teachings, he does permit himself some flexibility in the interpretation of leading Marxist dogmas when it suits his purpose. However, in the process of analyzing the actual role the communists play in the guerrilla venture, he is likely to lose his objectivity and to become brusque and overcritical. He acknowledges the past contributions of the hard-line communists, but also he pleads for these "dogmatic class fighters" to be put in their proper place. His inconsistency is so pronounced that it would appear as though two authors must have written *Revolution in the Revolution?* On the one hand, he comes through as a level-headed *presque* Marxist whose chief preoccupation is to find the road by which the communists may improve their guerrilla technique. On the other hand, he is an irritated, radical intellectual disturbed by the cynicism of the communist leaders, whom he attacks not only on ideological grounds, but for their two-faced practices as well.

Each time he is faced with the task of defining a typical Latin American communist party, he hesitates to pass judgment. He treats it as an avant-garde phenomenon inspired by progressive theory as well as an arrogant team of bureaucratic functionaries deathly afriad of the creative capacity of the people; as a domestic party and as the foreign field representative of the home office. He admits readily that at one time the Latin American parties were a breeding ground for revolutionaries prepared to die for their ideals and to destroy others; but he must recognize also that in our times these are parties capable only of destroying others. For what he witnessed, or thought he witnessed, was that the leaders of these parties rarely died for their cause. What they were doing instead was seeing to it that others made the supreme sacrifice.

In his interview with journalists who visited him in his Bolivian jail cell, Debray emphasized that such officials profess to believe in victorious revolution; but they feel that success will be achieved less because of the heroism of local insurrectionists than because all the pieces have fallen into place in the international power struggle. These professional politicos attend one international conference after another, constantly consulting with foreign communists. Instead of actually sparking a revolution at home, they prefer to speculate on what effects an insurrection in their own country might have on the socialist bloc as a whole. In the meantime, they cannot assess what is happening in the world about them. Are the conditions for insurrection already ripe or could they be accelerated? Should the city activists and guerrillas in the *foco* synchronize their plans and establish a uniform military doctrine? Regardless of what they say for public consumption, it is all too typical of their attitude, Debray points out, to consider indigenous guerrilla warfare as much too delicate an instrument to be left to the people.

The first clash between the party and the guerrillas occurs over how to designate the movement. Should it be called "the armed people" or "the armed fist," of a liberation front or of the party? This conflict boils down to a determination of the very nature of the movement and of the degree of responsibility assigned to the *foco*. If the guerrillas adopt Camilo Cienfuego's motto, "The rebel army is the people in uniform," they will be setting themselves on the right track and will provide a solemn safeguard against the dictates of the party. On the other hand, if they allow themselves to be called the "armed fist," they forfeit their independence to the city and, according to Debray, the battle is already half-lost. The party leadership keeps reminding them of successful models, of the Bolsheviks, of the Chinese communists, of the North Vietnamese. But the guerrillas may be ordered to exclude from their ranks all pro-Maoists, Trotskyites, and anarchists, precisely at a moment when all hands are most needed. Their contacts with the Party Central Committee must function flawlessly no matter what the odds nor what the extent to which security is jeopardized.

Any subordination of the guerrilla to the party may, and, in Debray's estimation, does, constitute a grave political error; and "since many military errors derive from a single political error," the total destruction of an incipient *foco* often follows as the night the day. It is only because history has heretofore been tolerant that the long series of false starts and gross misjudgments in Latin America have not doomed the armed struggle there. But the price of a single unsound theory can be a military defeat involving countless lives.[35]

Since one cannot count indefinitely on history's tolerance, a revolutionary must be clear in his own mind that all the models employed by others are essentially a part of the past, which cannot be repeated. The true revolutionary, as Debray sees him, should avoid being misled by the ghosts of history, or falling into the trap of superimposing the past as he remembers it on his present course.[36]

Lenin imitated some patterns of the Paris Commune. The Chinese communists in Canton of the twenties thought "in terms of repeating the Russian October . . . and the Vietnamese comrades, a year after the foundation of their party, in terms of organizing insurrections of peasant soviets in the northern part of their country."[37] Hence the Latin American communists are not the only ones afflicted with this malady. For this reason it was a "stroke of good luck that Fidel had not read the military writings of Mao Tse-tung before disembarking on the coast of Oriente." Had he been aware of them he could hardly have "invented, on the spot out of his own experience, principles of a military doctrine in conformity with the terrain."[38] Mao's writings had already taken on the aura of a dogma in the minds of many revolutionaries.

Therefore, the "highly special and profoundly distinct conditions of development" in Latin American presuppose such a limited degree of maneuverability as to make impossible a swift response to an emergency. For this reason, Debray concludes, "all the theoretical work on people's war does as much harm as good."[39]

The compulsion to copy others seems to be particularly acute in the case of the communist intellectual. Allegiance to dogma is his trademark, his justification for being, and his substitute for concrete revolutionary work. But it is the very essence of his nature that leads him to chart his course from books or from outworn theories. And it is one of the ironies of history that in much of Latin America the vanguard role in the revolution has been assigned to intellectuals and students.[40]

This paradoxical situation, that physically unfit, pedantic men from the city are able to "subordinate the guerrilla group strategically and tactically," arises both from the superb skill of the communists to impose their leadership upon all the militants and to the proverbial naïveté of the militants themselves, who, when it is already too late, discover that the party functionaries are the natural opponents of any group that would steal their show.

The most widely used type of trap a party sets for the guerrilla groups it intends to harness is the appointing of the guerrilla commander from among the party leadership. It is Debray's contention that this trap, viewed from any angle, is a lethal one. The guerrilla group, the "fist" of the party, becomes then fully dependent on the "head," the leadership, which is located in the city. Contacts between the city and the mountains cannot be maintained through an *ad hoc* emissary because of his lack of power to influence political decisions adopted by the Central Committee of the party; nor can they be maintained through a permanent liaison in the city, because the delegate tends to lose sight of his assigned role and soon becomes a city politico himself. The only reasonable solution, then, seems to call for the guerrilla commander himself to descend to the city every time " 'politics' are made and guided."

Because the commander is ordinarily a member of the Central Committee, he is bound to participate in discussions. "If he is not a member of the directing body, all the more reason for him to go, for he must be informed of the political positions." However, he is not long in discovering that the "head," more often than not, "knows nothing of the war and is immersed in the 'political life' of good times." What he comes up against is an empty, or incompetent, or dead "head," and much "time is needed in order to make it understand the facts of that world more remote than the moon which is guerrilla life."[41]

Thus, in order to achieve anything, the commander must either prolong his stay in the city or keep returning to it, in either case running the deadly risk of capture or assassination or of meeting a mysterious fate.[42] The whole matter thus has a disastrous effect on the morale of partisans left in the mountains. In the interval between their leader's departure and his return, they can do little but twiddle their thumbs.

This whole setup leads inevitably to the "deproletarianization" of the guerrillas. Of all the thoughts of Debray, contemporary Marxists consider this the most flagrantly heretic. The city, Debray admits, is indeed a jungle, but far less brutal than one is inclined to believe. True, "men garrote each other in order to assert their superiority, but they no longer fight to survive. Life is for all—unequally given, but given nonetheless."[43] In Debray's view, the average city-dweller ceased long ago to be a creator of values: he is only a consumer. Life is the daily art of figuring things out, of compromising, of abandonment of principles. If resources are inadequate, a man with minimal skill can still make do. "With the affluence of the Yankees and the corruption that follows in their wake," this can be accomplished without much difficulty.

In more ways than one the city is therefore a "cemetery of revolutionaries and resources" (Fidel Castro). It is, Debray adds, the sum of "lukewarm incubators" which inevitably "make one infantile and bourgeois." It is the place where the militant instincts of a class fighter tend to subside because in the city political infighting is often more effective than direct confrontation.

The insistence of communists in Latin America on the primordial character of urban areas is based on simple premises. It is here that "the organs of the central power"— political parties, the press, congress, the ministers, the hostile administration, and the army apparatus—are located. Also, this is where the "vital forces of population" reside: the industrial proletariat, the factories, the trade unions, the university, the sympathetic pressure groups. In a word, the head of the octopus is here; and, according to the bureaucratic logic of orthodox Marxists, this is where the headquarters of the octopus-hunters belong, too.

Debray disagrees fundamentally with such an interpretation of the battlefield, where the main showdown must take place. It is in the countryside, he contends, in the mountains, in "the seclusion of the so-called virgin forest," and in desolate areas where few have reason to enter, that the dedicated guerrilla is spawned. Here a man must daily solve the problems of being, trusting no one because his very survival is at stake. Under these conditions the law of survival of the fittest operates at the optimum: the fittest remain; the unfit "abandon the field, desert, or choose to return to the city to undertake other assignments." However strong his Marxist-Leninist convictions, an inhabitant of the city cannot "understand the vital importance of a square yard of cloth, a can of gun grease, a pound of salt or sugar, a pair of boots."[44]

More than all of the "hidden sabotage or indifference, or betrayal by the city apparatus," it is this "irreducible difference in living conditions, therefore in thought and behavior," that has recently imperiled many guerrilla *focos*. Even "the best of comrades from the capital or from abroad fall prey to this difference, which is tantamount to 'objective betrayal.' " In comparison with this physically soft, psychologically unprepared revolutionary apostle, well-oriented to more comfortable forms of class struggle, the guerrilla becomes the proletarian in the true sense of the word. Debray likens the relationship between the city leadership and the guerrilla *foco* to that between the bourgeoisie and the proletariat. The two do not breathe the same air. The *foco* needs the city leadership only to the extent that an artificial lung may be needed for temporary relief of asphyxia.[45]

This bourgeoisie is never at hand when most needed, warns Debray. It would rather spend "thousands of dollars on propaganda work at home and abroad, on the support of functionaries, on setting up publications, on convening amnesty congresses, etc.," than help the *foco*, despite the fact that "certain guerrilla fronts have survived on $200 sent them over a period of a year by the political organization on which they depend."

If Debray's assessment of the situation has merit, the safest course is not to count on any help from the city leadership. Help from the urban areas, if it ever does arrive, is likely to be too late and to consist largely of nonessentials. Moreover, it is usually sent by some awkward means over an ill-chosen route. For everything that a city politico undertakes, more people are involved than are technically required, and the enemy is thus given an opportunity to intercept the shipment or to discover the channels, the contacts, and the collaborators. To expose oneself to the "hazards of transportation, the difficulties caused by encirclement operations or other mobilizations of enemy forces" is self-defeating, for the city people, even if they are completely sincere in wishing to help the *foco*, can wreak havoc.

For a guerrilla group to be forced to rely on a city organization is politically hazardous, to say the least. If a Bolivian Indian, for instance, joined the *barbudos*, Guevara needed months of careful checking and screening before accepting him as a full-fledged partisan. In the course of the "probationary period," many newcomers were liquidated. Others, who had not yet passed the final test, were forced into combat situations with the La Paz regulars, with the gnawing suspicion that their own comrades-in-arms were at their rear. At the same time, the newcomer from the city was to be treated as a prima ballerina, all doors to be open to him, his party credentials unquestioned; and his top security clearance issued by the party general staff was to supersede any clearance issued under fire.

This "duality of security clearances," one issued by the comrade-in-arms, the other by "party civilians," irritated recruits and collaborators of the *foco* alike, and alienated a number of prospective sympathizers. But this alienation Debray considers a far less serious matter than the opening this practice affords to the class enemy to infiltrate and discover the exact location of the *foco*. Infiltration is "always done from the city to the mountains, from outside to inside, rather than the other way around." To be exact, this is the most certain way for an enemy agent to approach the *foco*: to become one of the guerrillas and to bring about the destruction of the *foco*.

Dependence of the guerrilla on the city in matters of logistics and security results in total subordination to the party in tactics and strategy as well. Here, in Debray's estimation, lies a gross violation of basic laws of revolutionary war, because the war is carried on in one part of the country while masterminded in another. In precisely the same position as a U.S. general commanding military operations in Vietnam while political decisions concerning his operations are made by civilians in Washington, the guerrilla commander who depends on the city soon understands that his function is a purely formalistic one. His hands are tied; he may order direct actions only if explicitly empowered to do so.

This amateur "bourgeois" leadership in the city essentially civilian in nature, and without any special competence in military or political matters, tends to play games with the guerrillas. It draws up elaborate plans for harassing the incumbent regime and passes them along to the military apparatus for instant action. Debray points up the ludicrous results of such a policy.[46]

To guerrillas themselves the question of who is ultimately to direct the production—some abstract commander, a collective body of distant civilians, or their own immediate flesh-and-blood leader—stems more from a wish for survival than from principle. The soldier senses instinctively that something is amiss in the general picture, because the distant commander pushes him in one direction and the one at hand very frequently gives opposite orders. He cannot help but feel either as "an artillery gunner who has not been told in what direction to fire," or, what is worse, as one ordered by two officers to shoot in different directions simultaneously. Hence these confused partisans inevitably become lost in the field, shoot at random, and die in vain.

If "such waste, such slaughter" are to be eliminated, a new type of "centralized executive leadership" must be set up in such a way that both arms of the revolution, the guerrilla front and the party in the city, will draw the greatest possible advantage. The central body must be solely responsible for overall, clear strategy and tactics because in the absence of these there is no sane plan of action. This leadership should not be located in the city, Debray advises, nor should it be permitted to suffer from "force of tradition, the deep-rooted adherence to forms of organization fixed and hallowed in time," that the hard-line communists champion.

It must consist of those who die for the revolution rather than of those who only talk of doing so, of partisans who are daily exposed to front-line danger, and not of accomplished political brawlers to whom abstract principles, sustained bargaining, and a sense of loyalty to the shifting interests of other socialist states are perhaps more important than their own man in the mountain. The basic weapon of the class struggle in the city is the leaflet; in the *foco*, the bullet. The *foco* is therefore the best "foundry of cadres," the only place from which a novice need not be sent back to the party school to become a revolutionary. "As we know," Debray repeats, "the mountain proletarianizes the bourgeois and peasant elements, and the city can bourgeoisify the proletarian." If this is not the case, how then is it possible to explain that urban proletarians are consistently among the missing in all open clashes with the regime?[47]

To recognize the guerrillas as "the directive wing and motive force of the movement" and subsequently to place the command exclusively in their hands, is as logical as it is imperative. "For the sake of its own salvation, this small group (*foco*) *cannot* remain quiescent and isolated. It stakes everything. *Patria o muerte*. It will either die—physically—or conquer, saving the country and itself."[48]

When a warrior under fire makes a decision about a campaign, he misses no opportunity "to combine and coordinate the available means and gear them to a main direction of action." Thus, the abstract policy of many a communist party, "reformist or disoriented," one which "converts the revolutionary movement into a disjointed marionette," will find the deadliest enemy in such a warrior."

In developing his argument, Debray lays stress on the fact that many party leaders refuse "to abandon the city and go to the mountains," even under threat of death. Meanwhile the situation becomes ever more critical until it is finally too late; the leaders are either thrown into jail or killed.[49] Then "a substitute, underground leadership is quickly set up," but it is cut off from the rank and file, from the front organizations, from sympathizers. "Lacking the qualifications of the former duly elected leaders, now imprisoned or annihilated," the new functionaries, still in a state of shock from the recent tragedy, hesitate to accept cooperation from new quarters, cancel recruitment of new members, and become "completely drawn into the underground routine." "The city terrorism" then emerges, followed by "banditry in the countryside."

Neither type of activity occurs because militants lack

morale, Debray is quick to remind us. In fact they possess morale to an admirable degree. In every instance when terrorism in the city and banditry in the countryside wreak havoc, "it is the comrades, the militant Communists, who have carried the principal burden of the war." Upon examining the casualty lists, Debray finds that "almost all the dead (as well as the imprisoned) were party members." But neither sacrifice nor martyrdom serves any really useful purpose. It is more to the point to seek to learn what has gone wrong.[50]

Probably the greatest danger to the survival of the *foco*, in Debray's eyes, lies in the outmoded concept of the People's Front. He calls it "a showy façade," that exists "at the expense of the party itself."[51] It is "composed essentially of members of the party that had formed it," and, not surprisingly, it is that party that lends to a front the necessary cadres and other help. But "since one party does not make a front," the communists are forced to secure and publicly register the assistance of "famous progressive 'independent personalities.' " The names of these "independent personalities" and their "magnificent programs are widely publicized abroad but remain unknown at home."[52]

Meanwhile, small groups of full-fledged party members get together and work out "tables of organization more complex and unintelligible than those of a ministry." They map out the future, insist that socialism is within reach, and consider themselves as though "they have squared accounts with history." Since they regard it as axiomatic that institutions must take priority over action, it is their opinion that forms of organization must "precede the content, while content itself remains unorganized." These party members, Debray laments, "are not yet liberated from the old obsession; they believe that revolutionary awareness and organization must and can in every case precede revolutionary action." They blueprint the future and make imaginary alliances, fully expecting that "all this beautiful artificial machinery" will somehow absorb the attention, thus providing the excuse "for not putting into operation the *instrument for achieving it*—the people's army, which alone can give historical significance and effectiveness to a political front."[53]

Underneath it all, there is in part "the same naïve idealism that inspires those who are addicted to the electoral opium, for whom socialism will come on the day when one-half plus one of the electorate vote for it." The picture is incomplete, however, because it omits a more dangerous sin of party leaders, their urge to be reformers. "The same hypotheses which govern the very peaceful activities of the reformists are unconsciously applied to the armed struggle;"[54] or to put it another way, every time they must make a choice between open, oft risky, military confrontation with the class enemy and political maneuvers, it is more than likely they will choose political maneuvers.

What Debray's analysis amounts to is that the *foco* must take over all former military-political functions of the "general staff," the central committee, and that the central committee now becomes an auxiliary fist of the *foco*. Numerically, the *foco* is a small but monolithic nucleus, the "small motor" that sets in motion the "big motor"—the entire nation. As its victories pile up, the *foco* generates a contagious example of how to squash the oppressor and inevitably awakens the masses. Each new action attracts new recruits, enabling the guerrilla leader to lay the groundwork for the creation, first, of the popular army, then of a much wider body, the national revolutionary front.

In guerrilla warfare, Debray argues, it is imperative to start with the possible, "to proceed from the small to the large," from the top of the pyramid down. "To attempt to proceed in the opposite way is pointless" because "it is not a front which will create this nucleus (the *foco*), but rather the nucleus which, as it develops, will permit the creation of a national revolutionary front."[55] The weaker that nucleus is "the more it must distrust alliances," particularly those with the city. In the very beginning, a lukewarm, reluctant ally is as much a menace as the class enemy. If on the other hand, his dedication and readiness to sacrifice are above suspicion, he ought to be saved for the future, for "in order to die with dignity, it is not necessary to be accompanied."[56]

However, once the *foco* is on a firm footing, a reliable ally is as imperative as a rifle. For instance, it is possible for a city activist to be so successful in his raids as to "keep busy as much as three-quarters of the army." Not only can he shift the brunt of the pressure of the enemy's army away from the *foco*, but he can enable the *foco* to stand its ground against much stronger forces. "In Cuba, for instance, Batista could never utilize more than 10,000 out of his 50,000 men against the guerrillas at one time. And the rebel army, its chief tells us, became invincible when it reached a ratio of 1 to 500."[57]

Before undertaking any action, the city activist must recognize two fundamental principles: his direction and purpose must come from the *foco*, and in a conflict of loyalty between the party and the *foco*, his allegiance must be to the *foco*.

"The revolutionary thing," wrote Fidel Castro, "is not the coup d'état but the incorporation of the military into the armed struggle."[58] "It is fundamental to recognize," Che Guevara wrote in 1960, "that a suburban guerrilla band can never spring up of its own accord." It should take no action on its own initiative, but should be subservient to the overall "strategic" plans.[59]

These overall "strategic plans" can be devised and coordinated only by a "technically capable executive group, centralized and united on the basis of identical class interests." "Political cadres," i.e., "those who counterpose political line to military strategy, political leadership to military leadership," live in a dual world, in which politics represents one side, the military the other. The people's war is a mere technique practiced in the countryside, just an arm of the political super-technique.[60]

It is these "purists" who "remain aloof from technical problems of war," preferring to concern themselves with "a thousand and one 'international democratic organizations' dedicated to their own survival rather than devote themselves to a serious and concrete study of military questions related to the war of their people."[61] A heterogeneous national revolutionary front is even less able to lead the armed struggle. An expedient mechanism for propaganda and unification of scattered leftist groups, it can at best assume the diplomatic conduct of war, but in no case its operational leadership.

Then "who will make the revolution in Latin America? Who? The people, the revolutionaries, with or without the party."[62] Where is one to seek an avant-garde without which no revolution can succeed: in a communist party that occupies the de jure place of the popular vanguard but not the de facto; in a People's Front that derives strength and cadres from such a party; or in the *foco* itself, the new party in embryo? Debray points out that when some of these facts appear to contradict a tradition, it takes courage to face them head on. In the party doctrine there is no metaphysical equation between the vanguard and Marxism-Leninism. But the dialectical implication is all too clear, and is fortified by a historical tradition. The only questions remaining concern the manner of reactivating the party apparatus and the form the vanguard should assume.[63]

To all these questions, of course, Debray has already given due consideration. Revolution is to be made by "the people," the "people in uniform," while the vanguard would appear in the form of the *foco*. Involved daily in guerrilla activities, a member of the *foco* confronts danger around the clock, and what he professes must be inseparable from what he does. His past, his class status become for the most part irrelevant; and experiences from Cuba, Venezuela, Guatemala, and other countries have amply demonstrated that "people—even petty bourgeois or peasants—are more quickly and more completely molded by the experience of guerrilla warfare than by an equal amount of time spent in a training-school for cadres.

Therefore, to the questions: Which should be strengthened today, the party or the guerrillas, embryo of the people's army? Which is the decisive link? Where should the principal efforts be made? the answer must be unequivocal: the guerrillas, and in no case the party. As conceived by Debray, it is only in the guerrillas that hope for a new style of leadership, a new organization, and new ideological reflexes, lies.

A new leadership, "united, if possible, in one person," will definitely remove from the historic scene "any duality of functions or powers" and will shatter the artificially created contradiction between the political and the military form of struggle against imperialism. A new organization will force "the reconstruction of the Party" and put an end to "the plethora of commissions, secretariats, congresses . . . and assemblies at all levels." Faced with the conditions of the death-bout constantly waged between the revolutionaries in the *foco* and the oppressive forces, the party would cease to be a discussion club. It would suspend temporarily the " 'internal' party democracy," as well as "the principles of democratic centralism which guarantees it." Its discipline would then become military discipline, eliminating in its course all patterns that could paralyze the war efforts. More significantly, for the first time after a long period, the party would be able to rid itself of useless administrative ballast, and, in the case of true militants, to set their readiness for sacrifice on the right course. The third element, new ideological reflexes, will draw revolutionary theory and revolutionary practice together, and in a sense establish a symbiosis between the two. This symbiosis in return would serve to break the vicious circle of bureaucratism and reformism.

Finally, the *foco* is the best testing-ground for separating the actor from the fighter; and it is here that the age of a revolutionary and the intensity of his militancy are critical factors. In support of this position Debray argues that a person advanced in years and accustomed to city living would have neither the flexibility to adjust to underground activity nor the physical stamina necessary for waging guerrilla war.[64]

## The Critics of Debray and the Latin American Scene

By calling attention to the generation gap among revolution-aries, Régis Debray, who has already delivered a number of punches below the belt at contemporary Latin American communist parties, naturally has invited sharp criticism from all quarters. His theses on guerrilla warfare are criticized most of all by the hard liners, because his essay, *Revolution in the Revolution?* whatever else it may represent, is primarily an ode to "hostility toward the Latin American communist parties."[65] He attacks the obsolete structure of these parties, their dogmatism and their white-collar attitudes toward the theory and practice of guerrilla warfare, their objective separation from and fear of the masses. Imitators of foreign models and nothing more, these ideological robots, he asserts, long ago relinquished the right to represent legitimately the interests of the revolution on the continent. Naturally, Marxist-Leninists cannot tolerate such attacks from anyone—not even from Debray.

His thoughts evoked a strong reaction also on the part of a great number of nonparty militants who viewed guerrilla methods as the countermedicine for all of today's problems. To them, in particular, *Revolution in the Revolution?* "was clearly not a nine-day journalistic wonder, but a reflection of a major turning point in the history of the Latin-American revolution."[66] Disqualifying the hard liners from the role of leadership in a guerrilla venture and asserting that they are a dangerous deterrent to any revolutionary metamorphosis, Debray has posed many thorny questions. The first concerns the vacuum of continental proportions that would surely be created if the traditional communist parties were to vacate the political scene. What other catalyst could assume their role? What is to guarantee that a new catalyst would not replace the dogmatism of the old parties with a new, perhaps more dangerous one? True, Debray assigns this role of the catalyst to the *foco*, again a minority, again a revolutionary élite, which should presumably achieve with military means what the communist parties could not have arrived at through political means. Would not both the working class and the downtrodden in the cities, who had little in common with one another, perhaps be left aside, this time to a much greater degree, because Debray thinks solely in terms of the countryside?

In addition, while giving disproportionate attention to the interests of the *foco*, Debray almost loses sight of the much larger project, the revolution. Moreover, he separates the guerrilla in the mountains from the activist in the cities, and in the cities sees nothing more than a revolutionary apprentice who dances only when the master of the mountain calls the tune. In much the same way, Debray neglects to examine other vital issues, too. For instance, he fails to point out that not all urban revolutionary groups can be treated as a uniform bloc. Nor is he apparently aware that under his recommended scheme of cooperation with the *foco*, the urban militarists cannot fully develop their revolutionary potential.

However, it is Debray's handling of his facts, his gross generalizations, his tendency to view the entire continent through the experience of one country, the sketchy character of his conclusions, and above all, his irritating trait of raising a question only to follow it with another question or a series of questions—it is all these characteristics that have stimulated theoreticians and practitioners of revolution alike to challenge his thoughts and to cite a lack of clarity in his theses.

The charge most frequently made against Debray is that he tends to assign too much importance to the military side of revolutionary take-over. All the South American states, whether Brazil or Bolivia, Peru or Paraguay, in his opinion are unquestionably ripe for revolution to the same degree, and have been so for some time. He embraces Lenin's formula: " 'The upper classes' cannot carry on in the old way, and 'the lower classes' do not want to live in the old way." What prevents the success of the revolution, then, is the presence of "armed forces of oligarchies in power, supported by United States imperialism," and these, as one may easily see, can be defeated only by military means. It is therefore the gun that will control politics, and not the other way around, as Mao Tse-tung contends. Hence, the *foco*, "the Party in embryo," must supersede and replace all other forms of organization, just as happened in Cuba.

In discussing the Cuban experience, which Debray cites in support of his *foco* theory, he does not stick too close to facts. He says, for instance, that "during the first two years of warfare, Fidel did not hold a single political rally in his zone of operations." According to this statement Fidel put the gun before political action, when in fact political action rated a high priority. Since the Sierra was to determine the entire historical process in Cuba, Castro was not dependent on the city except in rare, and clearly not in decisive, situations. Debray's contention was challenged even by like-minded revolutionaries such as Simón Torres and Julio Aronde, who said they had commented on Debray's works solely "as the expression of our solidarity toward one whom we consider not only an intellectual but a revolutionary fighter."[67]

In the opinion of Torres and Aronde, Régis Debray failed to recognize the contributions of the Federation of University Students (FEU), and their preparatory political work in the years 1955 and 1956. The students' opposition to Batista "attained incredible aggressiveness," later making possible "the survival and initial success of those revolutionaries in the July 26th Movement who had become guerrilleros." It was the same FEU which, in February 1956, created the Revolutionary Directorate. Debray also assesses superficially the real role of the PSP (Partido Socialista Popular), the pre-Castro communist party. He refers to them primarily in negative terms, i.e., as a force which "adopted the line of the armed struggle only in 1958," when the victor was already in sight. However, he fails to acknowledge that the PSP "influenced certain sectors of the working class," sponsored a number of actions, and promoted different forms of the class struggle "at the center of which stood the Rebel Army."[68]

Torres and Aronde find it particularly difficult to condone the limited attention Debray gives to the political conditions that paved the way for the initiation of the Sierra *foco*: "the intense political propaganda effort carried out by Fidel from exile and by the July 26th Movement (M-26-7) within Cuba, and the relatively virgin state of the Cuban countryside, which had not been won over to the positons of the bourgeoisie."[69]  Castro's innumerable contacts with activists at home and abroad, his efforts to prepare a climate conducive to revolutionary war and to win over the city populations, as well as the series of campaigns that the July 26th Movement had organized much before a single guerrilla departed for the Sierra, Debray for curious reasons does not list as political actions. He cannot allow himself to admit that before Fidel disembarked, "the military line had to be subordinated to the political;" otherwise there would have been no revoltuion. Debray fails to mention that "Fidel, against all military considerations, announces that his expedition will arrive in Cuba in 1956 and no later, expressing this in a specific political slogan: to be heroes or martyrs that year."

Finally, on the matter of confrontations between peasants and the army, or between peasants and the landowners, or between peasants and the *guardia rural*, Debray is completely silent. It was only when all other means of settling the crisis had proved ineffective that armed struggle became the order of the day. Thus, with the transfer of the campaign against Batista from political to purely military means, the *foco* came into being when Castro had all but reached the end of his rope.

Having failed to assess political conditions that preceded the Cuban revolution, Debray blunders even more seriously in summing up political conditions in other Latin American countries. To him the atmosphere on the entire continent seemed charged with revolutionary overtones. What was lacking was leadership and correct military doctrine. Debray's critics note, however, that he "offers no supporting evidence or arguments" for all these generalizations; and his essays fail to provide a broad analysis of that specific constellation of sociopolitical, economic, historical, or military conditons that bring revolutionary enthusiasm to the surface. If an individual country did threaten to violate Debray's rule, as was the case with Peru in 1965, he might mention it in passing but would not elaborate on it.

According to another pair of critics, Professors A. G. Frank and S. A. Shah,[70] Debray shows no interest in the class structure of individual countries, or in the dynamic in which a Latin American revolutionary must work. No economic and social analyses of Latin America are to be found in Debray's three essays, not even in "Problems of Revolutionary Strategy in Latin America,"[71] which Frank and Shah find to be the most analytical of the three. Thus, Debray consistently separates theory from practice, long-term goals from immediate ones, leaving revolutionary movements stripped of any political program. Is the Latin American revolution bourgeois or socialist? Is the prime enemy U.S. imperialism, local oligarchy, or government troops; corrupted segments of the bourgeoisie or rich peasants? What political weapons are at the rebel's disposal to suppress the reformist zeal among his own men? Who are those men, and what political motives will move them? These are but a few of the questions he leaves open.

"Does he really understand so little of Marxism," ask Leo Huberman and Paul M. Sweezy, "as to assume that anyone who takes to the hills can, by doing a good enough job of fighting, create a political vanguard, activate a mass movement, and lead a socialist revolution?" Emiliano Zapata,

Pancho Villa, and Augusto Caesar Sandino did precisely that:
they went to the hills and performed miracles of valor, but
the repressive forces remained nevertheless. What Huberman
and Sweezy evidently intend is to pinpoint exactly which
part of Debray's theory is reconcilable with Marxist teaching
on revolution and which clearly departs from it. Alleging
"that in Latin America today all the necessary *political*
conditions for successful revolution already exist just below
the surface of social life," Debray, to their way of thinking,
does not answer the critically important question as to how
these conditions were created in the first place. If the
development was spontaneous, then in Debray's case one
meets with a sharp departure from Marxism-Leninism. If,
again, the conditions came about as a result of long-term,
carefully planned activities of revolutionaries, then Debray's
*foco* theory could to a limited extent be reconciled with
Marxist teachings. Debray does persistently play down the
political phase preceding the *foco* phase, and in so doing
almost inevitably distorts the character and underestimates
the complexity of the political-military relation within the
*foco* phase.[72]

Huberman and Sweezy relate this objection to Debray's
argument that during the whole period—"between the initiation of the *foco* and the winning of final victory"—it is the
military activity that incorporates all other forms of activity,
including the political. The people in the *foco* achieve this in
two ways: "first, by attracting young people who already
have the necessary political understanding, and molding them
into a disciplined vanguard; and second, by dispelling the fear
which has been the main if not the only force holding the
masses in check." Thus, once the *foco* is established, "there is
no place in Debray's theory for an agency of political activity
as such until *after* a new party has developed out of the
*foco*." The traditional communist parties, unrelated as they
are to the revolutionary process, ought to drop out of sight
just as would any other organization that might take it upon

itself to play an independent role during the period of actual fighting.

In Debray's theory, they continue, "those not directly involved in the guerrilla struggle can acquire political experience and education only vicariously." With their tolerance for Debray's heresy completely exhausted, they point out: "To say that this is a caricature of a real revolutionary process such as took place in Cuba or is likely to take place anywhere else, is to put it mildly."[73]

Huberman and Sweezy are evidently not overcritical of Debray's specific errors and omissions, because they do grant that there is much more to a theory on revolution than mere factual correctness. None of the fifteen authors whose critical essays they include in *Régis Debray and the Latin American Revolution* are openly hostile to Debray or excessively harsh. On the contrary, all of them recognize some merit in his contribution. They merely express doubts about those premises that they consider likely to generate unnecessary confusion in the minds of rebels. Their apparent fairness toward him is all the more understandable because their assignment was to criticize theses of a revolutionary sentenced to long-term imprisonment—not an enviable task for a militant. However, their attempt to be fair prevents them from fully exposing Debray's cardinal sin—attacks on the communists. Instead of taking him to task on this point, they limit themselves to protracted discussion of technical inconsistencies of Debray's *foco* theory.

In his essay "Questions on the Debray Thesis,"[74] William J. Pomeroy, probably the most competent Marxist authority on guerrilla warfare among these critics, points out that Debray, in essence an armchair strategist, based his doctrine "on much too little in the way of tactical experience." He charges that Debray ignored the role of the communists in political education of the people and overlooked the significance of the preparatory organizational work carried on by activists. For instance, Debray quotes Castro's letter to Frank

País of July 21, 1957, in which Fidel emphasizes his surprise at the overwhelming help the Cuban peasants rendered to the *barbudos*. "Who has organized them so wonderfully? Where did they acquire so much ability, astuteness, courage, self-sacrifice? No one knows! It is almost a mystery! They organize themselves all alone, spontaneously!"[75] As Pomeroy sees it, there is no mystery in this, because people in Oriente Province, the center of Fidel's activities, and in its capital city, Santiago de Cuba, had wide experience in opposing the government and were quite familiar with the fundamentals of revolutionary technique.

Pomeroy, who had been active in the Huk movement in the early fifties, offers also a number of reflections that should nullify Debray's findings on a party-led guerrilla movement. The Philippine Liberation Army was not identical with the party, but "the two were interconnected, with the directives coming from a party source." The Huks drew their basic cadres from the pre-World War II peasant unions in central Luzon and from among the Philippine communists. They established armed groups of from thirty to sixty men, carried on what Che Guevara and Debray called "the propaganda of action," and threatened by their mere presence the stability of the Manila government. True, in given areas they were effective in rallying mass support for an insurrectionary movement, but in additon they forced the government to dispatch new contingents of troops to those very areas. Thus in the long run they canceled out the effect of their actions.

Only in cases where the people did have some degree of organizational experience, as happened in Laguna Province, were the Huks able to establish themselves for any length of time. Here the Sakdal Movement ("a messianic nationalist movement that staged an abortive revolt in 1935") was active, as were those trade unions that had struggled against the coconut-processing industries. In every area where political preparatory work had not preceded guerrilla activities, the Huk movement "was wiped out as soon as it was formed." In other areas, *lumpen* elements, primitive social rebels "of a semi-bandit type," joined the guerrillas. Some of them became true revolutionaries; others did more harm than good.[76]

All in all, it was not the Huk nucleus that organized the people, according to Pomeroy. Rather it was the party cadres that took over the organization of the nucleus, that set up party schools and study courses, and that gave the whole movement its political direction. In Pomeroy's critique of the *foco* theory, however, it is not these objections that are the most significant. This is in spite of the fact that the case of the Huks offers a concrete illustration that a handful of "pure revolutionaries" cannot, as Debray believes, set an entire country afire under all conditons. What is more significant in this critique is Pomeroy's reference to Debray's undue emphasis on the point that young revolutionaries are the only human material that a revolutionary guerrilla movement ought to count on.

In the Philippines, for instance, the situation was quite the opposite. The young fighters, while militarily competent and full of vigor, were by and large politically unsophisticated and unmotivated. As is normal for young people, they were more attracted by the spirit of adventure and by the physical challenges of guerrilla warfare than by theory, party books, or manuals. At the same time, many Huks in their fifties, and even a few in their sixties, because of the strength of their convictions and their revolutionary determinism, "stood up to the rigors of Huk guerrilla life much better than many young and politically immature members."[77]

Correct as he may be in evaluating the vital statistics and combat behavior of both the young members and the old, Pomeroy seems to overlook the fact that at this point he is discussing a movement that was defeated and whose record, therefore, can hardly be cited as a model of theoretical or tactical correctness. What Debray wants to underline in arguing that only the young can play the dominant role in guerrilla warfare should not be reduced to the simplistic statement: "don't trust anyone over thirty." In fact, Debray rarely misses the opportunity to pay tribute to the wisdom and the usefulness of the old cadres. What he finds lacking in them, however, is the political and tactical elasticity biologically impossible for an old revolutionary.

Partly coherent, partly formless, Debray's delicate allusion to the generation gap between the old revolutionary and the young is definitely a sin of which he is yet to be accused, especially if at some future time he gives it a more definite form. In this context he seems to speak as the unofficial representative of all the young rebels of today with unformulated doubts concerning the old generations of professional Marxists, be they pro-Soviet or pro-Chinese or conventional Trotskyites.

As Debray indicates, the young guerrilla who tends to put his entire being on the line for the benefit of the cause is completely oblivious of the consequences. He is an idealist, impetuous and unsparing of himself as well as of others. He is willing to sacrifice himself for a change, even a change for the worse, because in the struggle he has only his life to lose. His fanaticism has no basis in reason. It seems rather to have more in common with religious frenzy than with sober political reasoning. In guerrilla warfare, therefore, as in any warfare, he is best suited to serve as cannon fodder. While many at party headquarters, where tomorrow's policies are being made, profess that the future of revolution belongs to the young, our youthful fighter sees the older generation determining the future.

In this context Debray is sympathetic with the fears of the young, wary of the future, and apprehensive over the possibility that a successful revolution may be followed by a new system again composed of elderly people, all burdened with prejudices, tired of fighting, and therefore the natural prey of bureaucracy and corruption. We are then right back where we started.

In common with many who have advanced new thoughts and presented them in synopsis form, Régis Debray expends too little effort in testing his conclusions and leaves many of his arguments hanging in mid-air. He attacks the dogmatism of the hard liners as damaging and obsolete only to end with his own, perhaps even more pronounced, dogmatism. On the one hand, he states that the model of Cuba should by no means be copied; on the other hand, the only model he recommends or with which he is familiar is that of the Cuban experience.

A typical intellectual who takes it upon himself to teach others the techniques of warfare, he is often guilty of elementary errors. He never questions how it would be possible to organize a revolutionary war around one *foco* nucleus in a country of continental proportions such as Brazil.[78] Would not a venture on that scale, in order to function at all, normally require several *focos*, which in their turn must be embraced by another super*foco*? Would not such a super*foco* amount to a new edition of the old set-up, in effect spawning an administrative apparatus removed again from direct combat? Nor does he deem it necessary to reexamine the particular conditions in countries such as Argentina,[79] where a majority of the population lives in and around urban centers and where the *foco* would be ineffectual. Or why is it more difficult to be an armed partisan roaming about the mountains than an armed illegal activist in the city?[80]

Strangely, this man who adheres to the categorical imperative proclaimed in Havana, that "the duty of every revolutionary is to make the revolution," is not always certain what kind of a revolution he is to make in a given country. He seems to vacillate between bourgeois-democratic and socialist. On rare occasions, when it appears that Debray will at long last arrive at a decision, the essayist is off on another tack, embarking upon a revolution somewhere else on the continent.

Furthermore, Debray attacks all communist parties in Latin America indiscriminately, despite the fact that he has foremost in mind the PCB. The earlier role of the communists in insurrection he now transfers to the uniform, political-military leadership of the *foco*, usually combined in one leader. Since in the course of this discussion Debray has in mind Fidel and his example from the 1956-59 period, he unwittingly exaggerates to the point where it seems that in Cuba "the germs of the revolutionary party were already present at Fidel's birth."[81] In other words, Debray seems to imply that in any country where revolutionaries of Fidel's and Raúl's stamp happen not to have been born, a revolution is either impractical or over-difficult to achieve.

In addition, his choice of Marxian terms is not always well-advised. For instance, he confounds revolutionary ethics and revolutionary politics. When he discusses ideology, it turns out that he is referring to the doctrine. Throughout his works, strategy and tactics are often used interchangeably, while the maximal and minimal goals of a guerilla movement are never clearly defined. He does acknowledge that "without revolutionary theory there is no revolutionary movement," but at the same time he assures us of the dubious role of theory in general because "all the theoretical works on people's war do as much harm as good." The terms "The proletarian cause" and "a proletarian" mean one thing at one point and another somewhere else. Since "revolution revolutionizes the counterrevolution," and the *foco* may bourgeoisify a proletarian and proletarianize the bourgeois, it remains quite unclear who is finally a proletarian—a member of the working class, an active militant, a participant in the *foco*, or yesterday's counterrevolutionary who has joined the *foco* today.[82]

In the present limited discussion, attention is directed only to some of the most inconsistent of Debray's theses. Yet these inconsistencies may not be nearly so significant as his critics would have us believe. When Debray published his essays, he was only in his middle twenties. During this period he was involved in practical revolutionary activities, and his writings show the effects of the pressure under which he worked and of his inability to research his findings more carefully. The two dominant figures from whom he drew inspiration, Jean-Paul Sartre and Fidel Castro left Debray with a compulsion to copy—a condition not too uncommon in the case of a gifted disciple. In addition, he was overimpressed with the revolution in Cuba. He should not, however, be held solely responsible for this attitude because many other, more experienced, revolutionaries and direct participants are still intoxicated with the outcome of this event. Nor should he be unduly criticized for his failure to break out single-handedly from the entire theoretical impasse into which the Latin American hard liners had backed themselves. Except, of course, in the case of Fidel Castro and Che Guevara, the theory of these leaders suffered serious neglect, and consisted, as has been repeatedly pointed out, of the copying of models from the U.S.S.R. and Asia. The development of their theory over the past few decades, when it has been discussed at all, is reduced either to sporadic contributions of individual party members or to meaningless comments of high officials. Many of these functionaries have been ready at the drop of a hat to indicate to the victims fallen in uprisings in Peru, in Bolivia, in Colombia, or in Guatemala, just where they have erred.

In this respect *Revolution in the Revolution?* marks a turning point, because Debray put his hand to solving some of the thorniest problems in the area of guerrilla warfare. That he did not succeed is not surprising, because the task was a little more than he had bargained for. Knowing better what he did not want than what he did, Debray advanced a number of untested novelties, and volunteered a manual on revolutionary war that he had failed to proofread. He relied more on his revolutionary instincts than on the realities of the continent he was out to incite; and as a result, he substituted one theoretical impasse for another, one untenable dogmatism for another.

## Notes

1. Reference to Guevara's speeches during his visits to China and Russia in the fall of 1960.

2. See Georgie Ann Geyer, "An Interview with Régis Debray," *Saturday Review*, 5 (Aug. 24, 1968): 16. Ciro Bustos shared a cell with Debray and was interviewed at the same time.

3. For a broader analysis of these fundamental lessons, see Ernesto Guevara, *Guerrilla Warfare*, (New York: Monthly Review Press, 1961), pp. 1-2.

4. Ricardo Rojo, in *My Friend Ché*, trans. by Julian Casart (New York: Dial Press, 1968), pp. 15-41, describes Che's first stay in Bolivia, his eagerness to ignite the flame of insurrection in Latin America, and his essentially meager awareness of the minimum conditions for starting a rebellion.

5. *The Complete Bolivian Diaries of Ché Guevara and Other Captured Documents*, ed. and with an introd. by Daniel James (New York: Stein and Day, 1968), p.59.

6. Luis J. Gonzalez and Gustavo A. Sánchez Salazar, *The Great Rebel—Ché Guevara in Bolivia*, trans. by Helen R. Lane (New York: Grove Press, 1969(, p. 45.

7. For an analysis of reasons why Che chose Bolivia, see Richard Harris, *Death of a Revolutionary: Ché Guevara's Last Mission*, (New York: Norton, 1970), pp. 61-70.

8. In summarizing his philosophy regarding the self-defense zones, in his preface to Giap, *Guerre du peuple, armee du peuple* (quoted from Debray, *Revolution in the Revolution?* p. 31, Guevara describes self-defense as merely a small part of a whole, and a self-defense zone as complete in itself, with the surrounding area kept free of disturbance. The *foco* could thus be isolated and trapped unless there were possible recourse to the first phase of the people's war: guerrilla warfare.

9. In keeping with the popular image of the typical military bureaucrat, Guevara emphasized only the numerical strength of the Bolivian forces, which totaled about 20,000 men, of whom 16,000 were in the army, 2,500 in the air force, and 1,500 in the navy. In his judgment they would be totally incapable of "defending a country twice as large as France with borders touching five other nations." He ignored structural and political changes that had been effected by

General Alfredo Ovando Candia in the intervening years, increased combat capabilities, as well as the army's emphasis on civil actions and political training, and its growing awareness of what the communist goals in guerrilla actually entailed. (*Bolivian Diaries*, pp. 21-23).

10. See Gonzalez and Sánchez Salazar, *Great Rebel*, pp. 44-51.

11. Luis E. Aguilar, "Régis Debray: Where Logic Failed," *The Reporter*, (December 28, 1967), p. 31.

12. Politics of both wings, the Muscovites and the Maoists of the Partido Comunista Boliviana (PCB), as well as the Trotskyite Partido Obrero Revolucionario (POR), are discussed in detail in "The Communist Betrayer and Leftist Abandonment of Guerrilla," Harris, *Death of a Revolutionary*, pp. 145-67.

13. Gonzalez and Sánchez Salazar (*Great Rebel*, pp. 234-39) assert that of 60 Guevara partisans, 18 were Cubans, 36 Bolivians, 2 Argentinians, 2 Peruvians, and 2 of unknown nationality. Somewhat different figures are given in Harris, *Death of a Revolutionary* (p. 76): 17 Cubans, 22 Bolivians, 3 Peruvians, and 2 Argentinians, or 44 in all. Che's actual fighting force, at its height in March 1967, totaled, according to his *Bolivian Diaries* (pp. 323-27), only 41 guerrillas: 18 Cubans, 20 Bolivians, and 3 Peruvians.

14. He still firmly believed that "all our problems will be solved by our friends," the motto he had cherished for a long time preceding his arrival in Bolivia. See *Look* (April 9, 1953).

15. Harris, *Death of a Revolutionary*, p. 69.

16. In the message he sent to the Second Tricontinental Conference in 1967, Guevara said: "We can summarize our hopes for victory as follows: the destruction of imperialism through the elimination of its strongest bulwark: the imperial dominion of its subject peoples, either one by one or by groups, drawing the enemy into a difficult struggle outside of its territory; and cutting it off from its basis of subsistence, i.e., its dependent territories."

17. The center of guerrilla activities.

18. *Bolivian Diaries*, p. 59.

19. "The Absence of Popular Support," in Harris, *Death of a Revolutionary*, pp. 135-44.

20. In fact, he had instituted classes in Quechua, the leading Indian dialect of Bolivia, but the spoken language of the region he operated in was Guarini, which none of the guerrillas, including the Bolivians, could speak (*Bolivian Diaries*, pp. 60-61).

21. *Bolivian Diaries*, pp. 96, 108, 151, 164, 176, 190, 202, 219.

22. *Ibid.*, p. 60.

23. Gonzalez and Sánchez Salazar, *Great Rebel*, p. 51.

24. Pomeroy (*Guerrilla Warfare* p. 183) cites the view of leaders of the PCB as follows: "The guerrillas began (their action) without an adequate evaluation having been given to political and social factors indispensable for their development, and they came into existence prematurely."

25. Rojo, *My Friend Ché*, pp. 196-97. For comments on the meeting and Guevara's increasing dissatisfaction with Monje, see also *Bolivian Diaries*, pp. 97, 108.

26. Harris, *Death of a Revolutionary*, p. 159.

27. It is rumored that some members of the PCB were indirectly involved in the killing of Guevara. This theory, as yet unsubstantiated, seems to spring not so much from available evidence that Richard Harris can put his finger on, as from the almost inescapable conclusion that Bolivian communists, faced with Che's arbitrariness and high-handedness, simply had to react one way or another.

28. Rojo (*My Friend Ché*, p. 196) indicates that Monje and other Bolivian hard liners were bound by a pact with Moscow that greatly limited their maneuvering space in their relations with Castro and Guevara.

29. Commenting on the fact that no help was coming from Fidel, Daniel James (*Bolivian Diaries*, p. 66) raises a reasonable question as to whether Mario Monje Molina was the only culprit in the matter of Guevara's death.

30. See Harris (*Death of a Revolutionary*, pp. 169-78) and Rojo (*My Friend Ché*, pp. 213-14) for discussions of the changed character of the Bolivian army and the impact of U.S. advisers in defeating the guerrillas.

31. In the matter of reprisals, the emphasis on saving the population furnishes yet another example of the difference between the old school of Marxists and Guevara. The traditional line of communist guerrillas to provoke enemy brutality in order to force the population to join the partisans is probably best reflected in a 1941 slogan of Tito's partisans, "Sto bolje, to gore" (The worse it is the better it is!) At the time when the German occupation forces had carried out literally Keitel's order that a hundred civilian hostages should be executed on the spot for every German soldier killed or fifty for every wounded German, the partisans went to great lengths to select just such targets as were most likely to induce this German reaction.

32. "There were no political ties with the city," said Bustos. "I said something once to Che about the political liaison, and he said ironically, 'Yes, we have three people.' He did not even seem to want it. There was no support at all." (Geyer, "Interview with Debray," p. 16).

33. The texts of the diaries of Rolando, Pombo, and Braulio are given in *Bolivian Diaries*, pp. 225-322.

34. For an illuminating discussion of Che's military conduct in Bolivia, see *Bolivian Diaries*, pp. 67-69.

35. Debray, *Revolution in the Revolution?*, p. 67.

36. *Ibid.*, p. 19.

37. *Ibid.*, p. 20.

38. *Ibid.*

39. *Ibid.*, p. 21.

40. *Ibid.*
41. *Ibid.*, p. 68.
42. *Ibid.*, pp. 68-69.
43. *Ibid.*, p. 71.
44. *Ibid.*, p. 70.
45. *Ibid.*, p. 71.
46. *Ibid.*, p. 73.
47. *Ibid.*, p. 76-77.
48. *Ibid.*, p. 84.
49. *Ibid.*, p. 74.
50. *Ibid.*, p. 86.
51. *Ibid.*, p. 82.
52. *Ibid.*, pp. 82-83.
53. *Ibid.*, p. 83.
54. *Ibid.*
55. *Ibid.*, pp. 83-84.
56. *Ibid.*
57. *Ibid.*, p. 76.
58. Fidel's letter of Oct. 10, 1958.
59. Quoted from Debray, *Revolution in the Revolution?*, p. 75.
60. *Ibid.*, p. 88.
61. *Ibid.*
62. *Ibid.*, p. 98.
63. *Ibid.*, pp. 98-99. "By the name they bear and the ideology they proclaim, they (the communist parties) occupy *de jure* the place of the popular vanguard; if they do not occupy it *de facto*, they must not be permitted to keep the post vacant. There is no exclusive ownership of the revolution," comments Debray at the end of his work. (p. 125.)
64. *Ibid* p. 102.
65. Pomeroy, *Guerrilla Warfare*, p. 284.
66. See Publisher's Preface in *Régis Debray and the Latin American Revolution*, Leo Huberman and Paul M. Sweezy, eds. (New York: Monthly Review Press, 1968).
67. See Simón Torres and Julio Aronde, "Debray and the Cuban Experience," in Huberman and Sweezy, *Régis Debray*, pp. 44-63.
68. *Ibid.*, p. 47.
69. *Ibid.*, p. 46.
70. See Andre Gunder Frank and S. A. Shah, "Class, Politics and Debray," in Huberman and Sweezy, *Régis Debray*, pp. 12-17.
71. Full Text in *New Left Review* (Sept.-Oct. 1967).
72. Huberman and Sweezy, *Régis Debray*, p. 8.
73. *Ibid.*, p. 9.
74. In Huberman and Sweezy, *Régis Debray*, pp. 36-43.
75. *Ibid.*, p. 37.
76. *Ibid.*, pp. 38-39.
77. *Ibid.*, pp. 40-41.

78. See Huberman and Sweezy, *Régis Debray*, pp. 9-11.

79. See Robin Blackburn and Perry Anderson, "The Marxism of Régis Debray," in Huberman and Sweezy, *Régis Debray*, pp. 67-69.

80. See Clea Silva, "The Errors of the Foco Theory," in Huberman and Sweezy, *Régis Debray*, pp. 27-30.

81. *Ibid.*, p. 24.

82. For an illustration of Debray's semantic imprecision in employing Marxist jargon, see his essay "Latin America: The Long March," *New Left Review*, (Sept.-Oct. 1965).

# 3 The African School on Guerrilla

A number of contemporary African authors have made significant contributions to the existing literature on modern guerrilla warfare. While their total output, in terms of adding substantially to the body of knowledge on the subject, has been minimal, their work has been notable in two directions. In the first place, it undermines the theoretical monopoly of orthodox Marxism in the area of guerrilla as Debray and others have done. In the second place, because their findings are derived from the uniquely complex political setting of Africa, their conclusions lay open to doubt the belief in guerrilla as a "magic, irreplaceable weapon of political change." Whatever other characteristics may be ascribed to their works, it is perhaps this African political uniqueness that bears the most significance for the student of guerrilla warfare.

The attempt to discover common threads in the writings of Kwame Nkrumah, Ahmed Sékou Touré, Amilcar Cabral, Julius Nyerere, Frantz Fanon, and other African writers on guerrilla becomes a laborious task. We have here a group of authors from the same continent, all contemporaries, all discussing the same subject, all apparently trying to determine the most effective means of adapting guerrilla methods to furthering the struggle of African nations against colonialism and racial prejudice. All tend for the most part to follow many Eastern patterns up to a point, only to set off each in his own direction. A majority of them operate within the same premises. All advocate a united Africa, continent-wide liberation, the creation of an all-African army at some future time, a uniform code of conduct for the black rebel, African nationalism and neutralism one and indivisible—a collection of ideals as unpopular among the architects of bloc politics as they are confusing when an attempt is made to incorporate all of them into a conventional political spectrum. On some points these writers resemble full-fledged Marxists. Their semantics, their dialectical method of reasoning, for example, and their hostile attitude toward the West seem to place them unmistakably in the hard-liner camp. Yet at other times they sound more like the hard liner's distant relative.[1]

The student is thus faced with a confusing situation. In a class at the University of California at Berkeley, for example, students recently raised the following questions: Are the African authors Marxists or continental nationalists? If they are Marxists, why doesn't their internationalism embrace other continents as well? If they are nationalists, why do they so religiously pay lip service to the theses of the Eastern bloc?[2] Some of the students tended to view these Africans as "an extension of the Eastern school on guerrilla," some as a *sui generis* breed of theoreticians, while still others—the most numerous group—considered any attempt at classification irrelevant and unnecessary.

On the other hand, contemporary Eastern authors appear to maintain total silence on these points. In materials published in the East during the late forties and early fifties, it is not at all uncommon to find reference to such heretical matters as African vulgarizers of Marxist-Leninist teachings on guerrilla, bourgeois-radical Afro-militantism, Afro-chauvinism, African anarcho-leftism, African nihilism, or African heresy.[3] As a matter of fact, African authors as a rule insist on cooperation with the socialist camp, with the Latin American and Asian revolutionaries, with the militants of the

New Left. In the view of these writers Africa, poor and oppressed itself, is naturally receptive to all ideologies of protest. Besides, the fighting experience, particularly in the case of the Eastern bloc, is of tremendous advantage. This bloc is capable of dispatching politico-military help, advice, training, or diplomatic support at the state level or by proxy. It has in actual practice proposed and checked out a number of tactical formulas for the struggle against imperialists. In the eyes of the African writers, cooperation with such an ally, therefore, seems not only rational but even imperative.[4]

At the same time, however, within their concept of cooperation, these Africans stipulate that the entire continent must be considered a world unto itself. On the one hand, they envision socialism as the end-product of their grand designs for Africa. Nkrumah, for instance, who has drafted a plan for an All-African Union of Socialist Republics,[5] which is to be an integral part of the world socialist bloc, in effect leaves the impression that he has in mind the Eastern brand of socialism. Nkrumah lends weight to this interpretation by sharply criticizing all those who believe the so-called original version of African socialism.[6] Upon closer examination, however, it appears that this theoretical affinity is superficial for the most part because Nkrumah's concept of socialism contains only fragments of theories espoused in the East. But even if the reader is sufficiently astute to detect these fragments and is able to combine them, he may still be unable to assess their political significance.

Among the various African writers, the most persistent resemblance lies in their semantics and their methodology, for most of them rely heavily on black-white distinctions, on an either-or logic. They appear quite accomplished in fitting reality into prepared simplistic dogma. Terms such as imperialist conspiracy, export and accumulation of capital, monopoly masters and client states, people's party and people's war, and many others constantly turn up in their work in essentially the same context as in the works of Eastern authors.

In the case of the Africans, too, it was the Western European states that in the past were regarded as the culprits chiefly responsible for all tragedies in Africa. Today it is the United States. Americans, continues the popular line, destroyed the old-fashioned type of colonies that were enslaved by a single metropolitan power and replaced the "National imperialisms" with a more dangerous, collective imperialism, in which they play the commanding role. To the great dismay of the United States, the world balance of power has now shifted inexorably; and it is the turn of the capitalist-imperialist states to be confronted "with a real danger of encirclement." This gives them a taste of their own medicine. To salvage whatever remnants of colonialism can be saved in Africa, the West is accused of resorting to subterfuge, subversion, fraudulent propaganda, corruption of leaders, and exploitation of differences in religion, culture, race, and political ideologies.[7] Accordingly, the compulsive aggression of the Americans and the West in general forces the Africans to consider themselves engaged in a protracted war with the neo-imperialists and obligated to support at all international gatherings proposals of representatives of the Eastern states, primarily those of the U.S.S.R.

Such phraseology and such charges against the West, outwardly similar to those of the hard liners, often take on special meaning, however, when employed by Africans. For instance, when a hard liner specifies a target for guerrilla, he has in mind a capitalist, a kulak, a member of the hostile network or army, any anti-communist, or even a neutral for that matter. To an African author, an enemy is chiefly a foreigner, a white man or his trusted agent, quite apart from the class status of each in the Marxist sense of the term. In Eastern jargon the party can be the "guiding light" of guerrilla, its membership scarcely ever including the professional revolutionary discussed by Lenin. To an Easterner a neo-imperialist is always an American or a Westerner. To an African, the neo-imperialist bloc may under certain conditions include even the Russians or the Chinese. The East views itself as the camp of peace, of socialism, of progress. Though the African would not deny this in principle, he would go along with this position only to the extent that the interests of the Eastern bloc happened to coincide with those of Africa.

Such is definitely not always the case, however. As Julius Nyerere reminded his audience in Peking in February 1965, "When elephants fight it is the grass which gets crushed. We have therefore determined to adopt a policy of non-alignment in relation to international conflicts which do not concern us. Where there are hostile blocs facing each other on the world stage Tanzania will ignore the threats or blandishments from both sides, and pursue her own interests."[8]

These divergencies between the hard liners and the Africans also spill over into the area of guerrilla warfare. At the outset the Africans appear a little reluctant to add anything to what the Marxist classics have already said on that score. Their accent is put on the same priorities as in the East. It seems that at first the Africans adopt enthusiastically and almost in toto all the theoretical formulas of the hard liners. Then, when it has become all too obvious that these formulas are inapplicable to African conditions, they dismiss them as irrelevant.

Furthermore, the African authors, with the exception of Amilcar Cabral, the Guevara of black Africa,[9] are mainly civilian politicians who treat the phenomenon of guerrilla either incidentally or only when they can no longer avoid it. Jomo Kenyatta, Kwame Nkrumah, or Ferhat Abbas, for instance, treat the subject as statesmen with a flair for theory; Sékou Touré and Julius Nyerere as practical politicians; Patrice Lumumba as an armed poet; and Frantz Fanon as a politically enlightened psychiatrist. Most of these figures come from states that attained their national independence not by the violent means of guerrilla but in a much less painful manner, through traditional methods of political intercourse. They tend to consider guerrilla methods as not the all-important issue, therefore, in the struggle for progress, as did the hard liners or the Latin Americans.

This conclusion appears quite obvious if we may judge from the space they devote to the subject. In his *Handbook of Revolutionary Warfare*,[10] Nkrumah dedicates four-fifths of the text to analysis of the political milieu of Africa and only one-fifth to the techniques of guerrilla warfare, or 102 pages out of a total of 122. To the problems of military training he allocates only 17 lines; to the technical training of both regulars and guerrillas, 14 lines; to the medical training of women, 4 lines; to logistics and composition of armed forces, 25 lines; and to analysis of the structure and strategy of the All-African People's Revolutionary Army (AAPRA), 36 lines and one chart that poses more questions than it answers.[11]

Politically, the Africans direct the guerrilla to fight first of all for the liberation of his race and his continent, and only then for socialism, a concept on which many of them tend to place their own interpretation and which each pursues in his own way. Unlike his Eastern counterpart, a guerrilla in Africa is first a political and then a class soldier. He may be a peasant, a worker, or a student, rich or poor, pro-communist or not. Representing a variety of class and tribal origins, the African embarks on guerrilla activities with a different set of goals from those of the Eastern partisans. His tactics, his strategy, and his philosophy must therefore differ from theirs.

The degree of frequency and the general impact of these similarities-dissimilarities between the hard liners and the African authors, as well as some common traits that appear to characterize the Africans as a group or as an independent school of thought, are somewhat easier to trace in the works of Kwame Nkrumah than in the others because he is the most prolific. His *Handbook of Revolutionary Warfare*, the Holy Bible of many African militants, is often accepted as the foundation of African thinking on guerrilla. Nkrumah's aphorisms, though not always clear, are applicable to virtually any situation in the context of the anti-imperialist struggle. As such, they have become an integral part of the revolutionary credo of a large segment of the younger generation in Africa.

In his *Handbook* Nkrumah assumes two differing positions. On the one hand, he is a theoretician of continental unity who applauds guerrilla methods as "the main part of the armed revolutionary struggle" of the peoples of Africa. On the other hand, an ex-premier of Ghana, he is a cagey politician, who, aware of the dubious efficacy of guerrilla methods, assigns to them only a limited role. Between these two extremes Nkrumah seems to find difficulty in threading his way: and in the end he sometimes leaves the reader more confused than enlightened.[12]

## Nkrumah: The Concept of Continental Guerrilla

In Nkrumah's opinion an African guerrilla must reckon with three categories of enemies: the classical colonial master, such as England, France, Spain, or Portugal; indigenous quislings, whom he designates as "lackeys," "hirelings," and "stalwarts" of imperialists; and neo-colonialists. Under this last heading he puts the United States and what he calls bogus, puppet African governments, formally independent but subservient to Washington. These foes he should take on in three separate stages: first, before his own country has attained independence; next, after it has been liberated technically; and lastly, when the initially progressive government of his country has degenerated into a "neo-imperialist tool." But when one period ends and another begins, who is to instruct the guerrilla that the target has changed? Who is to pinpoint the exact moment when a progressive government transforms itself into its opposite? To these questions Nkrumah fails to supply the answer.

Besides, this already confused guerrilla, according to

Nkrumah, must now meet two further challenges. First of all, in addition to performing his patriotic duty to his own country, he must be prepared to aid rebels in neighboring states. Then, since his prime allegiance is not toward his fatherland but rather to Africa as a whole, he must put himself under the standard of a Union government and of an All-African People's Revolutionary Army, neither of which exists as yet but which, Nkrumah assures us, will become a reality in the near future.

This perplexing situation of the African guerrilla has resulted in some measure from the generally confused conditons that prevailed on the continent during the struggle for independence, when the whole atmosphere was charged with contradictions and inconsistencies and revolutionary ferment, and when few leaders with political sophistication had been developed. Nkrumah charges that the former colonial powers, led today by Washington, when they found themselves powerless to arrest the Zeitgeist and the burgeoning of liberation movements, were forced to recognize that formal independence of many African states could no longer be withheld. Under pressure from the socialist bloc and from progressive forces throughout the world, the Americans acquiesced in the formation of many new states—even to the point in some cases of giving the process a reluctant boost. The United States offered large-scale financial, medical, and technical assistance, and was quick to extend diplomatic recognition to the new states.

From the standpoint of advancing the interests of the neocolonial powers, this enlightened policy has not been without merit. Nkrumah grants repeatedly that it was elastic, subtle, and cunning.[13] In time the powers were forced to recognize that mass popular resistance against the status quo in Africa spelled the doom of African colonialism; and the Western European imperialist states, having been reduced in the post-World War II period to the status of second-rate military powers, were much too weak to put their own houses in order, let alone to reenslave an entire continent.

When in a few cases they resorted to the use of arms, as in Algeria and Kenya, their ineffectiveness caused the West to lose even those positions that might have been preserved with minimal skill. Besides, the international public outcries against the use of brute force in Africa became so strident that the Americans decided, though somewhat reluctantly, to swim with the current.

According to Nkrumah, this course of action was part of a uniform plan of neo-imperialists to restore the golden era of colonial exploitation, based this time on more realistic foundations. It was thought that by means of bribery the inexperienced and politically naïve leaders of the new African governments could be induced to resume their countries' former functions as exporters of raw materials and importers of foreign capital. A majority of these men were personally honest, well-intentioned patriots, but politically far too unsophisticated to be a match for the Western "artists of subterfuge and machinations." They took great pride in the fact that their home region had become free for the first time in history, and made enthusiastic plans for contributing to its growth. As time went on, however, these leaders became too preoccupied with local interests and oblivious to the needs of Africa as a whole. Nkrumah appears to believe that with their initial revolutionary ardor thus dampened, many of them became easy prey to well-seasoned neocolonialists, who forced them into "a brand of nationalism based on petty-minded and aggressive chauvinism."[14]

Neglect of the fact that a majority of contemporary African states were created artificially at the Berlin Congress of 1884, "where today's political map of Africa was drawn," constitutes the greatest weakness of these leaders. Many of them seem to have forgotten that various peoples of Africa were at that time "confined behind rigid frontiers" carved to suit the needs of Western European states. Today, as in the past, these arbitrary frontiers "neither originate from the ancient African civilization, nor do they fit in with our African way of life, or habits of exchange. They are not even, for the most part, economically viable."[15] Many African leaders possessed no resources for a critical appraisal of what Nkrumah called "a policy of 'Africanization,' devoid of any fundamental changes in political, economic and administrative structure of the territory." Finally, in spite of their feeling that an active political life would lead to progress and a better future, the more things changed the more they reverted to what they had formerly been.

The second weakness of these leaders, according to Nkrumah, lay in their inability to perceive that African peoples waged their wars of liberation "each one separately, in a pathetic and hopeless attempt to make progress, while the real obstacle to their development, imperialism . . . is operating on a pan-African scale." Many of them did little if anything to cure this age-old tragedy. Instead they continued to clash with neighbors and became the slaves of nationalist sentiment, thus, however unwittingly, playing into the hands of the enemy.

At this moment, according to Nkrumah, when the Americans and other imperialists had come to realize that they were facing an essentially disunited Africa, they initiated the policy of creating a split within a selected patriotic government. With the moderate wing they sought accommodation, at the same time trying to isolate and suppress the militant group. In most cases the entire scheme was carried out through "the ritual of so-called free elections, mostly organized through methods of intimidation." Once elected, these moderates would usually become imperialist stalwarts, reliable functionaries in a puppet government.

Although some of these governments, in spite of overwhelming odds, do remain in power (the struggle against them is discussed later), it happens more often that these "lackeys" misjudge the tolerance level of the people. They oppress them mercilessly. "The gap between the puppet administration and the neo-colonized workers widens every day." Despite whatever direct help officials may receive from their foreign masters, the internal situation becomes explosive. Under popular pressure the bogus regime is weakened and gives way to progressive, anti-colonial elements. A truly independent government now comes into being, "dedicated to national reconstruction in the liberated territories and determined to assist all those engaged in anti-imperialist struggle."[16]

Throughout his summary on the succession of governments Nkrumah is direct and clear. He appears well-informed, but only with respect to events that support or illustrate his theses. Meanwhile he carefully sidesteps facts that may challenge his views. Despite his reputation for criticizing foreign writers and observers who have failed to recognize the extraordinarily complex character of African conditions, he himself frequently refers to Africa as a homogeneous entity. In this context he avoids specifics. He treats one country pretty much like another and constantly discusses the model of an unspecified African country which is likely to be the prototype for all his findings. In Nkrumah's accounts, though the neo-imperialists clash, they pursue a uniform policy for the entire continent. But all the moderate elements are equally wishy-washy and susceptible to corruption at a later stage. Notable exceptions are the progressives. The more progressive are likely to prove untouchable, while the less progressive do have their price.[17]

The danger posed to imperialists if they permit progressive elements to attain power is in direct proportion to the number of militant revolutionary leaders, "the sole champions of national liberation," who are included in the government. With the militants one can never bargain. They enjoy wide popularity and have more political sophistication than the first generation of patriotic leaders who held the reins immediately after the attainment of independence. Because the militants are not too susceptible to petty intrigue and maneuvering, they compel the neocolonialists to employ two new weapons: first, the coup d'état, assassinations, tribal revolts, or palace revolutions; and second, exploitation of the "conglomerate nature of the ruling party." The first method is intended to eliminate as many physical obstacles as possible through subversion and violence, while the second is aimed at dislodging all militants from public life, leaving the stage clear to those politicians, more liberal than truly progressive or anti-imperialist, who may be induced to switch sides.

The imperialists know from experience that in most cases a progressive party in Africa is "made up of several groups, each with its distinct economic and political interests." They tend to group themselves into two principal factions, one radically anti-imperialist, the other officially anti-imperialist yet not unwilling to parley with the West if certain demands are met. In Nkrumah's opinion, the most effective way of bringing about a split between the two is to force "decentralization of political power within the ruling party, one group being strong in the state machinery, the other being strong in the party machine." If, for example, the radicals hold the government, neo-imperialists and their local agents sabotage all government measures, spread "rumors of economic run-down, maladministration and corruption." The party machine in the hands of nonradicals often influences heads of individual institutions or entire branches of the administration to ignore or refuse to carry out the orders of radical ministers. The whole scheme produces a power vacuum, or a condition bordering on anarchy.

By this time the people have been subjected to an unceasing barrage of propaganda to the effect that the radical ministers are incompetent administrators, troublemakers, and Eastern agents besides. It follows that since people do not like a vacuum, they accept with resignation the overthrow or even the liquidation of the radicals. The key posts are now given to nonradicals. Ostensibly the same party remains in power, but a qualitative change in the nature of that power has actually come about.[18]

The first problem of the new regime is to conceal its reactionary character. For the sake of avoiding friction, the regime tends at first to pursue the policies of the ousted radicals. It continues to insist upon cooperation with other African nations, and it may even go so far as to promote somewhat indirectly the concept of continental unity or the all-African anti-imperialist struggle.

To extend this unnatural honeymoon between the non-radical government and the people, the foreign sponsors of the new regime rush to support the government even before the first indication of trouble. They extend financial and economic aid, grant loans, dispatch capital or consumer goods—all designed to improve the standard of living and alleviate some of the more pressing needs the radicals have not managed to attend to. As the confidence of the foreigners in the new regime grows, without public knowl-edge secret military agreements are signed and special units for repression of popular insurrection are formed. Condi-tional loans and credit extended by the International Monetary Fund, the International Bank for Reconstruction and Development, or other imperialist banking institutions begin to flow in.[19]

The presence of this government, at first nonradical, then moderately proimperialist, and finally reactionary, serves, in Nkrumah's view, as the prerequisite for an armed struggle in which the African guerrilla will find his place. Nkrumah sees this guerrilla as a political activist totally committed to the cause of African unity. At one and the same time he must be a nationalist of his own country and a pan-African national, with the weight on the latter role. These roles are easy to combine, since most Africans clearly understand that their own state can develop only "within a continental frame-work."

It requires little effort to convince the average patriot that Africa, "young, strong and resilient," is not a continent of states, but rather a continental nation that must confront all its foes on a continental basis. The African must never allow the struggle against the West to be "confined within any of the absurd limits of the microstate," for this is precisely what the enemy wants. The patriot should not perpetuate the present practice wherein so few freedom-fighters do so much for so many. By bearing the brunt of a continental struggle against a colonial enemy while an overwhelming majority of patriots are artificially cut off from one another, the freedom-fighters waste energy in local actions.

The task of the African revolutionary becomes slightly more complex when he attempts to explain to other patriots that without socialism, "the principles of which are abiding and universal," Africans would fail to secure "a new social synthesis in which the advanced technical society is achieved without the appalling evils and deep cleavages of the capitalist industrialist society." It goes without saying that the road to socialism is to be chosen by each individual country. Each may differ from the others in details of its policy or in the number of adjustments necessary to fit circumstances, but the basic course must invariably imply: 1) common ownership of the means of production, distribution, and exchange; 2) state planning of industrial and agricultural development; 3) political power in the hands of the people and egalitarian spirit applied in the modern context; and 4) application of scientific methods in all spheres of thought and production.[20]

As for the administrative arm to implement these goals— and this is Nkrumah's pet project—such an instrument must be established within a Union government, which would serve: 1) as a basic framework to link up all aspects of the struggle against the neocolonialists; 2) as a blueprint for popular activity; and 3) as "a yardstick for the evaluation of political development and phases in the history of Africa."[21]

Nkrumah's revolutionary now has the requisite political indoctrination. From this point on, the daily struggle against imperialists helps him to understand which concrete aims are to be achieved in each phase. The principles of scientific socialism offer him ideological guidance, while the Union government serves as the political general staff of a continent-wide planning of the African future. The next task, that of determining which cadres should carry on the struggle,

Nkrumah approaches with obvious optimism. He maintains that for the platform he has laid down—pan-Africanism, anti-imperialism, scientific socialism, and a Union government—the contemporary cadre situation is most suitable.

African leaders, according to Nkrumah, are fighters above all. They have not been born with a silver spoon, but have attained prominence either as outstanding heroes of a liberation war or as leaders of states that have had to fight foreigners and backwardness every step of the way. With few exceptions, these "children of oppression and imperialist pressure" follow their class instincts and the historic example of other militants and group themselves into a united front, "one of the primary conditions for a successful liberation movement" on a broader scale. Once this ideal leadership becomes a reality, Africans are approaching the moment to strike. The time is ripe. They know the battlefield far better than their adversaries. They are acutely aware of the ultimate goals to be achieved. Only the actual battle plan remains to be settled.

As for the precise time and place and method of launching the revolution, this depends initially on the selected target. Currently there are three categories of battlefields: liberated zones; zones under enemy control; and contested zones, or in Nkrumah's words, "hot points." On every field of combat the methods must differ according to the revolutionary readiness of the people and the dynamism of popular organizations that lead them into battle.

Liberated areas—those that have secured their independence either through an armed struggle, or through political action of a radical party, or as a result of the overthrow of a puppet regime—require of a militant that he remove every vestige of the colonial presence. Furthermore, he must be able to transform theory into practice, which must, of course, follow along the ideological lines drawn by his party; and he must commit himself to raising the political maturity level of the rank-and-file membership.

As for inter-African relations, a revolutionary from a

liberated area must actively support struggles in other parts of Africa, must contribute to their organization, and must attempt to synchronize the politics of his own government with the current needs of other fighting zones. "A truly liberated territory," envisioned by Nkrumah as a sanctuary for the rebels fighting in neighboring areas, must therefore help these fighters to establish rear bases, hospitals, schools, factories, workshops. An "organic liaison" between the liberated Africans and those actively fighting the imperialists would thus be established, "so that a continuous exchange of experience, advice and ideas will link the progressive parties in power with the parties struggling in the contested zone."[22]

In a zone under enemy control the revolutionary is a politician in uniform. His home territory is administered by foreigners or their local agents, or by a settler, minority government. It is one of the nerve centers of imperialist power in Africa, and plays the host for military installations, administrative and propaganda establishments, foreign banks, insurance firms, and mining, industrial, and trading companies. It is ruled by reactionaries, alienated from the rest of the African nation. Here the combat technique depends on the type of violence exerted against the people's liberation movement and on the nature of the economic-strategic interests of the imperialists.

If the regime's military capacity is negligible and the direct foreign help either limited or severely constricted, the area becomes an ideal target zone for direct military action. But in cases where the reactionary regime is militarily strong, where the foreign power is able to dispatch help at a moment's notice, and where the liberation movement is yet to be fully organized, other methods are called for. In such instances, national boycotts, strikes, sabotage, and mass unrest are the most effective tools. In either case, "our most vital asset is the degree of revolutionary awareness attained by the workers and the masses in the zone under enemy control." It is the readiness of the indigenous population to sacrifice and not the conditon of the colonial administration that tips the scales.

In actual practice it is not always possible to draw a line separating liberated areas and zones under enemy control. Very frequently it happens that a zone nominally held by the enemy is seething with revolutionary ferment, and a small incident can suddenly transform the situation into a full-blown armed conflict. Or, as Nkrumah says, at any moment the enemy may be thrown off balance, and instead of being the master he becomes merely one of the contestants.

In some sections of the country the enemy may still retain a strong grip; in others he may be "only superficially in command." Meanwhile a third section, where no one may claim dominance, becomes the principal battlefield. Here the bulk of the enemy's force resides either in the police, in the civil service, or in the army—all elements that are traditionally heterogeneous in Africa and that are inclined to waver and to side with the winner. When they change allegiance, the entire area is gradually transformed into a "hotly contested zone," which becomes a no man's land, a land of revolutionary transition. Here the local progressive party, whether underground or semi-legal, tries to organize the overthrow of the puppet government, which in its turn does everything in its power to isolate and destroy the party. The winner is determined by the amount of help the party receives from liberated zones, by its ability to organize the people, to train cadres, and to adopt such insurrectionary methods as are best suited to lead, first, to "the total destruction of the puppet government," and second, to the establishment of a people's government.[23]

Armed confrontation with the enemy has now become a reality. In order to win, the African patriots must be led by a uniform military command that will unite all forces in the contested zone and will devise a complete and coordinated program of military action. At this juncture, instead of elaborating on the structure of that command, Nkrumah shifts abruptly from the individual contested zone to a lengthy discussion of the military liberation of all Africa. In his opinion the entire continent represents one enormous contested zone. Victory in a single small section of it, therefore, must be thought of solely as an isolated battle, a phase, not as the whole war. No region in Africa can be free unless all are free. One tentacle cut off from an octopus does not prevent it from using the other seven; and when the first grows out again, the polyp may return to the source of its injury and attack once more. Since the octopus is vulnerable only in the head, one hand of the attacker must direct the spear. In the case of all-African, all-out war against imperialism, this hand is to be "a unified continental high command here and now."

This continental general staff should have two arms: the All-African People's Revolutionary Party (AAPRP) and the All-African People's Revolutionary Army (AAPRA). The first should link all progressive parties in Africa under a common ideology, coordinate their policies, and by assisting the prosecution of the "All-African People's War," smooth the way for continental unity. The second arm, the AAPRA, by coordinating the armed struggle should make possible all the tasks of the AAPRP.

An All-African Committee for Political Coordination (AACPC), an executive body at the level of the central committees of the progressive parties, would act as a sort of pro tempore government, because under the present situation the contemplated AAPRP would at best be an amorphous and awkward body. The Coordination Committee must concern itself with all the tasks relating to building socialism in the liberated areas; to strengthening the Organization of Solidarity with the Peoples of Africa, Asia, and Latin America (OSPAAL); and to maintaining relations with the socialist states in other parts of the world and with the workers' movements in the capitalist countries. The AACPC would thus become a centralized organizational instrument of the united struggle in Africa, a disciplinary organ to exert decisive influence over scattered centers of revolutionary activity in the first phase, and, in the second, a prototype of a Union government.

Nkrumah's outline of the structure of the general staff of the AAPRA and of the makeup of its forces is surprisingly sketchy. Military leaders prominent in various revolutionary movements are to establish its headquarters, to be located in one of the liberated areas, from which its field representatives will be assigned throughout the continent. Its operational area will be divided into five zones, North, West, South, Central, and East, each with its own army corps. The zonal army should be composed of local troops allocated to the corps by the individual progressive parties, who are formed into divisions, and of volunteers who will organize guerrilla detachments. In addition, peasants, workers, students, employees, and others, both men and women, will be organized into local militia units under the zonal command and will receive the necessary military training. The militia units, whose membership will be selective, will serve as the basic arm of the self-defense units. They will not be professional soldiers, but rather politically enlightened volunteers who would eventually be expected to master military technique as well as any professionals.[24]

The continent-wide plan for action designed by Nkrumah, though incomplete, is strikingly original. He proposes new, all-continental bodies, assigning to them the conduct of political and military affairs for all the Africans, in addition to a number of functions usually the prerogative of a sovereign state. He conceives of the greater part of the African people as united by an equally strong will to fight and as motivated by identical political ideals and a common ideology. Everywhere he envisions ideal technical cooperation, a grand political-military brotherhood. Like many plans designed to galvanize an entire continent, Nkrumah's grand strategy places the accent more on what is to be done than on what is possible under given circumstances. In *Africa Must Unite* he summarizes the three basic tasks of the future Union government: to achieve economic unity, to formulate a united military and defense strategy, and to develop a common foreign policy and diplomatic organization.

Africa, he says, dare not "remain balkanized, regionally or territorially." All the untold agricultural, mineral, and water power resources must be used "to the best advantage and the maximum benefit to all." For this reason, a continental transportation network must be developed, and a central bank, common currency, and uniform monetary system be established. Accordingly, overall economic planning must be the keynote of any development. "We should, therefore, be thinking seriously now of ways and means of building up a Common Market of a United Africa and not allow ourselves to be lured by the dubious advantages of association with the so-called European Common Market."[25] All these thoughts Nkrumah has crammed into half a printed page. And the same brief treatment, as has already been mentioned, is accorded other subjects as well.

Nkrumah takes the position that there is not "much virtue or wisdom" in the attempts of African states to build or to maintain their own armed forces, for none of them today can successfully defend their sovereignty against imperialist attacks. Because of this Nkrumah implores all of Africa to pool its military resources. Two such attempts have already been made by the Casablanca Powers and the Afro-Malagasy Union, "but how much better and stronger it would be if, instead of two such ventures, there was one over-all (land, sea, and air) Defense Command for Africa."[26]

Some sixty-odd states in Africa, about thirty-two of which were already independent in 1963 when Nkrumah wrote *Africa Must Unite*, in his opinion waste tremendous resources maintaining diplomatic representations all over the world. They seem unmindful of the desirability of a common foreign policy. He views the advantages of such a project as "so obvious that comment is hardly necessary." Again he recommends the establishment of the "All-African Parliament," to consist of a lower and an upper house: one elected on the basis of population and the other composed of an equal number of representatives from each African state. Technically, the wisest approach to this would be through the formation of a nucleus of states that already believe in the lasting value of this project, leaving the door open for the entry of other African states.[27]

Nkrumah's ability to improvise is apparent throughout his writings on revolutionary guerrilla warfare. He charges a revolutionary with a multiplicity of tasks: ideological, political, economic, diplomatic, educational, and military. His prime weapon is politics; at the present stage of African liberation, his military prowess is not uppermost. Most of the countries of Africa were able to attain independence for the most part without recourse to guerrilla fighting. Nkrumah even goes so far as to imply that the larger the number of trained guerrillas, the greater their team effectiveness and the less they will be needed.

### Amilcar Cabral: A Guerrilla Versus "a National Imperialism"

As defined by Nkrumah, the ideal militant must comport himself in such a way that a Union government knowing of his actions would approve. However, he must also take a measure of pride in belonging to the all-African movement, as distinct from and not bound by the program of the local party. What it boils down to is that he still has an obligation to support the local actions, but only to the extent that these complement the all-continental projects. Little by little, the ties that bind the militant to his homeland are thus loosened; and if Nkrumah's argument has merit, this alone would prevent an African revolutionary from playing the role of the classical guerrilla.

By way of contrast, Amilcar Cabral simplifies the issue by pointing out that a militant owes his first allegiance to his homeland, with the all-Africa cause a close second. The maneuvering terrain of this militant is his nation, his tribe, or his region. The local people are the source of his strength, and he must hold fast to the cord that binds him to them. Cabral, who, like Nkrumah, is a proponent of continental unity, cannot be considered the "petty-minded African chauvinist" described by Nkrumah. He is at the same time more realistic than Nkrumah and on firmer ground when he examines the aspects of the armed struggle. As a theoretician on the strategy and tactics of revolution, he is much more thorough than Nkrumah and his order of priority is different.

According to Cabral, the first responsibility of the Guinean patriot is to secure his own safety and that of his family and his village; then to free the region, and ultimately the whole of Guinea and the Cape Verde Islands. This accomplished, his next effort is to expel the Portuguese from the areas remaining under their control—Angola and Mozambique. Only then is he free to join the fight to expel all colonialists from Africa. Like Nkrumah, Cabral considers his home ground a zone under enemy control. The real oppressors are the unenlightened Portuguese imperialists who resort to force in solving all problems arising in their possessions. Hence, when a patriot from West Africa begins to shoot at a Portuguese mercenary, he wishes to destroy his flesh-and-blood enemy once and for all, not to change his ideological-political outlook.

It is largely as a result of his political apprenticeship in Portugal and West Africa that Cabral arrived at these conclusions. Born in 1921 in the Cape Verde Islands, he attended high school in São Vicente, where from early childhood he witnessed the brutal excesses of Portuguese imperialism. A gifted student, he went to Lisbon, where he studied at the Instituto Superior de Agronomia. It was here he came to realize that Portugal was itself an underdeveloped country, incapable of cleaning its own house yet master of an enormous colonial empire.

In 1948, with the aid of a few friends, Cabral established in Lisbon the Centro de Estudos Africanos. Here he studied the turbulent past of the empire, the slave trade, the wars against African tribes, the shortcomings of territorial admini-

stration, the judiciary, the police, and the military system, as
well as the metropolitan political structure and the party
system. Embittered by his findings, he returned to Guinea,
where he worked for the colonial administration from 1950
to 1954. The last two years of this assignment, which were
devoted to the census of the agricultural population, took
him to every corner of Guinea and Cape Verde. He observed
at first hand the class structure and the grievances of the
population and the abuses and difficulties they faced, as well
as the backward methods of production and the strengths
and weaknesses of the colonial government. He did the same
in Angola, where he worked on a sugar plantation from 1954
to 1956. In 1956 he took an active part in founding the
Partido Africano da Independencia da Guiné e Cabo Verde
(PAIGC) and the Movimento Popular de Libertação de
Angola (MPLA).

In the case of both parties the underlying principle was
that since the people under Portuguese rule were offered no
choice, they had nothing to lose. It was Cabral's firm belief
that nothing could be accomplished through negotiations,
political bargaining, or compromise. Nor could the colonized
people count on help from foreign quarters because the
Portuguese had kept the outside world from becoming aware
of conditions in West Africa. Meanwhile the colonial administrators were persecuting the people, obliging them "to go on
living in the most extreme misery, ignorance, and fear." For
according to Cabral, when the colonial power has a Fascist
government, the ignorant masses are cruelly exploited; and
this is especially true in the case of a metropolitan country
that is itself underdeveloped and has a weak economy.[28]

Cabral mentions three principal devices used by the
Portuguese for governing their colonies: economic depriva-
tion of the population, police and military suppression of
opposition, and a judicial mechanism that treats the African
as a second-class citizen. Cabral further classifies these devices
as either open or concealed. For instance, direct terror
cannot be hidden because of its physical manifestations,

while economic exploitation can easily be disguised. Regardless of which aspects of these activities Cabral undertakes to analyze, he winds up with the same conclusion: conditions in Guinea and Cape Verde can be changed only through total and unconditional expulsion of the Portuguese.

In the Cape Verde Islands, says Cabral, between 30,000 and 40,000 people died of hunger during the 1942-47 period. Another 10,000 succumbed in 1958-59. On some of these islands, such as São Vicente, chronic unemployment has reached catastrophic heights; while on others, primarily the agricultural islands of São Tiago, Santo Antao, São Nicolao, and Fogo, peasants tilling the land in the most primitive manner are at the mercy of weather cycles. Cabral charges the colonial government with trying to solve the perennial "agricultural crisis" in these areas through economic planning, which is "nothing more than a mystification, a source of enrichment for the colonial authorities."[29]

The islanders as well as the Guineans have resorted to every means of struggle at their disposal, ranging from passive resistance to individual protest and refusal to pay taxes, and collective actions such as mass revolt, strikes, and demonstrations. Many decide to go to other Portuguese territories as contract labor or to abandon their homeland forever, emigrating to Senegal or to the Republic of Guinea. In his statement to the United Nations Special Committee on Territories under Portuguese Administration,[30] Cabral declared in June 1962 that during the past forty years nearly 50,000 people had left Guinea. To replace them the administration has been offering strong incentives to encourage immigration from Portugal, "drawing an urgent plan for sending thousands of families of Portuguese settlers to Guinea." This is done, Cabral believes, in order to fortify the position of the white settlers, as well as "in the belief that increasing the European population will slow down the development of our liberation struggle."

The whole structure of colonial administration Cabral sees as resting on the force of arms. For over half a century,

1870-1936, "hardly a year went by . . . without some kind of military operations." He estimates that thousands upon thousands have been lost in these wars of conquest and occupation. In this era, "few adult Africans—the so-called natives—have escaped the palmatoria" (a wooden paddle with holes in the striking surface) "or the chicote" (a hide whip).[31] From 1936 to 1959 the colonial administration changed its tactics and adopted what Cabral calls the system of silent repression, i.e., one "of secret recourse to violence, of unsung victims, of disorganized individual reaction, of assault and crimes of all sorts, taking place within the four walls of the administrative buildings." Since 1959, however, when the liberation forces surfaced, the administration turned to "open and undisguised repression by the army and police, in the towns as in the countryside," massacring indigenous populations and murdering nationalist prisoners.[32]

Cabral maintains that two profoundly irrational concepts motivated Lisbon to apply open terror in Africa. The first is that possessions in Africa are an integral part of the Portuguese empire and that their progress outside the framework of the organic unity with the metropolis is unthinkable. For this reason the question of independence of any of these possessions cannot be measured by conventional criteria, right or wrong, because the question is in itself unarguable. The second concept is a logical extension of the first: any African who dares to subject this apocalyptic view of the empire to scrutiny, let alone one who acts in the direction of secession, puts himself automatically outside the law. In fact, he is not a political rival or an oppositionist in the ordinary sense, according to Cabral's understanding of the Portuguese philosophy, but a mortal enemy who must be eliminated.[33]

According to Cabral's data of 1962,[34] the oppressive apparatus in Guinea at that time consisted of the following elements: armed forces (4,000 European soldiers, 2,500 African soldiers, 5 jet fighters, 2 bombers, 2 armed patrol boats, as well as modern equipment including tanks and napalm bombs); security forces (300 Africans commanded by European officers); the political police (PIDE); (10 European special agents, and about 1,000 European and African agents, commanded by an inspector); as well as a number of European civilians who worked "as unpaid intelligence agents for PIDE." From 1957 to 1962 these forces incarcerated more than 1,000 African nationalists. In June 1962, when Cabral was interviewed by U.N. officials in Conakry, over 300 of these people were purportedly still held in the prisons of the PIDE. In addition, hundreds of Africans were sent to a concentration camp on the island of Galinhas, while dozens of people had been killed in the bush by Portuguese soldiers. An airbase was located in the Cape Verde Islands, one at Bissão, and several air strips spread through the interior of Guinea. With new contingents of soldiers constantly arriving, these ever-ready, highly mobile troops were capable of reacting with force against the slightest manifestation of dissatisfaction. Cabral says, for instance, that on August 3, 1959, the soldiers killed fifty African workers who had gone on strike on the docks at Pijiguiti (Bissão).[35]

Cabral's analysis of the situation in Guinea and Cape Verde was echoed by members of the U.N. Special Committee on Territories under Portuguese Administration in their 1962 Report. They also found the basic causes of unrest in these possessions to be, first, "the insistence of Portugal that there can be no change in its relationship with the Territories, which it considers are integral parts of its national territory;" and second, "the complete disregard for the legitimate aspirations of the indigenous people." In the opinion of the committee, labor conditions in the territories under Portuguese administration were generally deplorable; and the evidence this committee received from the ILO Commission "fully bears out that forced labor has not only existed in Angola, Mozambique, and Portuguese Guinea, but that it has been supported by law." In more precise terms than Cabral's, the committee called attention to "the fact that the illiteracy rates in these Territories are among the highest in the world," as well as that despite some improvements, noticeable mainly in the field of primary eduction, the "over-all educational situation . . . remains wholly unsatisfactory." The committee recommended the establishment of minimum, basic health services—"one physician per 10,000 population, one nurse per 5,000 population, one sanatorium per 15,000 population, and one sanitary engineer per 250,000 population." This committee stated in its report that "this situation cannot be maintained for long," and that if the attitude of the Portuguese administration remains unchanged, the indigenous population would undoubtedly be driven to "take up arms," abandoning any hope for peaceful solutions.[36]

Before the publishing of these findings, the Portuguese administration in Guinea had in effect tried to institute some reforms. This followed shortly after the adoption at the Fifteenth Session of the United Nations General Assembly of a firm resolution on decolonization dated December 14, 1960.[37] This reform package was intended to affect administrative organizations, land occupation, colonization, and judicial and political status of indigenous populations.[38] These acts, however, failed to bring about any significant change in these areas; in some cases, according to Cabral, they made the situation worse.

The Salazar government even turned the U.N. pressure for reform to its advantage. It promulgated new acts that further fortified the Portuguese position in Guinea and the Cape Verde Islands, and dispensed with even those minimal rights the African population had been accorded by earlier statutes. Since the majority of Guineans and Islanders were illiterate and entirely without experience in the political process anyway, their symbolic presence in the local governing bodies served to mollify the international community, but was a far cry from granting the Africans the right to manage their own affairs.

According to Cabral, decrees were enacted regarding the land commissions and settlement boards for the sole purpose of encouraging immigration of Portuguese settlers to Guinea. In addition to being offered special rights and a variety of unspecified privileges, these settlers were enticed with such "opportunities for the occupation of land which either never existed before or were very limited." To this end, the 1961 reform package also envisioned the establishment of cantons in Guinea and the Cape Verde Islands—nothing more, in Cabral's words, than the perpetuation of "the old system of replacing traditional chiefs by persons appointed by the colonial authorities." The new laws conferred Portuguese citizenship on Guineans and the people of Cape Verde without their participation in the drafting of the laws and without their consent. They were still sub-citizens whose lives had *"changed not one iota"* (Cabral's italics).

Cabral points out that the whole reform was implemented in the spirit of medieval dictatorial practices that still determine and shape Portugal's colonial legislation and administration.[39] Though their wording was different, members of the U.N. Special Committee on Territories under Portuguese Administration who investigated and reported on conditions in Portuguese West Africa in 1962 agreed in principle with Cabral's assessment of the 1961 acts. But taking the view that the immediate attainment of independence by these subject peoples was essential for safeguarding the peace of West Africa, they recommended the initiation of a comprehensive program of economic and social reforms.[40]

How far could these Africans be pushed before they were pushed too far? This was a question that Cabral felt Salazar did not even bother to ask. The complacency of Antonio de Oliveira Salazar, a ruler who for decades had maintained his authoritarian control over continental Portugal, appeared quite natural to Cabral. From the time Salazar succeeded Antonio Carmona as premier in 1932, he had given little heed to the people in the metropolis, let alone to those in the colonies. His goal was to preserve the Portuguese empire—in itself almost a myth—by restoring a medieval form of government.

On March 19, 1933, Salazar promulgated a constitution inspired by the *Rerum Novarum* of Pope Leo XIII and the *Quadragesimo Anno* of Pius XI, aimed at organizing a unitary and corporative state, a peculiar mixture of the Fascist one people-one leader-one state concept and the antiquated principle of a state without parties rather than a one-party state. The document provided for a two-chamber parliament: the Assembly, not divided along partisan lines but supposed to represent a cohesive national union; and the Corporative Assembly, designed to reconcile differences between capital and labor, producer and consumer, the trades and the professions, urban and rural areas, physical and intellectual labor, the homeland and the colonies. In other words, the 1933 Constitution envisioned an ideal social harmony and provided for the exchange—without the clash—of ideas, a society bent on attaining the Portuguese millennium.

In actual practice, Salazar's regime—and here Cabral is employing arguments almost identical with those of Western critics[41]—was characterized by forcible suppression of opposition and protests in the metropolis and by continuous oppression and an illusory endeavor to arrest the tide of progress in the colonies. Cabral maintains that the status of the colonies was to remain forever as it had been envisioned in the beginning of the thirties. No outside influence—whether world opinion or U.N. intervention or the examples of other colonial empires that had been liquidated after World War II or the emergence of free states in Africa or even actual rebellions in Portuguese colonies themselves—could alter Salazar's determination.[42]

The absurdity of Salazar's rule in West Africa, berated even by Westerners, gradually led the Guineans and Cape Verdeans to believe that all avenues of communication between Salazar and Africans were definitely blocked. Cabral points out that the contemplated reforms—those proposed in the forties by the Movimento Democratica Unidade[43] or by the Africans themselves in the fifties, or by the U.N. representatives in the early sixties—amounted to more of the same. Each time the

Africans grouped themselves into a force that might help the colonial administration to solve burning problems by peaceful means, their efforts were repulsed. In November 1950, for instance, Guinean workers established the first and only labor union—Sindicato Nacional dos Empregados do Comércio e da Indústria—but they were prohibited from negotiating contracts, from making demonstrations, or from striking. In 1953, when the workers of São Tomé disregarded this ban and demanded a raise, the Portuguese police opened fire on the picket lines and massacred a number of pickets. The following year the colonial government revoked the license of the Sport and Recreation Association because its by-laws provided for open membership of both assimilated and indigenous Africans.[44]

Under such conditions the only recourse of the Africans seemed to be to go underground. The first clandestine political organization—Movimento para a Independência Nacional da Guiné Portuguese—was established in 1954 by Guinean commercial and civil service employees.[45] Having lost all illusions that progress might be made through assimilation or by cooperating with the Portuguese, these Guineans concluded reluctantly that direct confrontation with the ruling element was inevitable. But on what basis? This politically naïve, poorly organized group was completely at sea. However, its members did keep uppermost in mind three principal points: the importance of the party, which, in tune with the times, was monolithic; the party program; and the necessity for a detailed plan of armed action. No longer was the expulsion of the Portuguese to be left to improvisation or guesswork. But first the party leaders must engage in a long-term dialogue with the people; and only after a mass army of followers was assured could clearly outlined tactics and strategy be put into effect. The record of the Movimento obviously influenced Cabral when he founded the PAIGC in Bissão in 1956, and determined to a great extent the program and structure of his party as well as its insurrectionary techniques.[46]

The program of the PAIGC envisioned the following goals: 1) total and unconditional national independence of the Guineans and Cape Verdeans; 2) people's power; 3) revision or revocation of all agreements, treaties, alliances, and concessions made by the Portuguese rulers; 4) recognition of the national and international sovereignty of Guinea and the Cape Verde Islands; and 5) "permanent vigilance, based on the will of the people, to avoid or destroy all attempts of imperialsim and colonialism to reestablish themselves in new forms in Guinea and the Cape Verde Islands."[47]

According to the program, the Guineans and Cape Verdeans were also to struggle for the unity of the African peoples, but only after their own national independence was assured. A republican, democratic, anti-colonialist, and anti-imperialist government would guarantee to all citizens freedom and equality before the law; would prohibit religious, racial, and tribal prejudice; would guarantee free general elections; would protect all foreigners living and working in the area; and would deprive "all individuals or groups of individuals who by their action or behavior favor imperialism, colonialism, or the destruction of the unity of the people" of their fundamental freedoms. In the realm of economy, state planning organized on principles of democratic socialism, modernization of agriculture and industry, agrarian reform, stabilization of prices, a balanced budget, and elimination of speculation and unfair profits were to be the guidelines of the future harmonious development. Four types of property—state, cooperative, private, and personal—would be sanctioned, whereas the national resources and the principal means of production and the communications network would be nationally owned.

The program emphasized especially the "progressive elimination of exploitation of man by man, of all forms of subordination of the human individual to degrading interests, to the profit of individuals, groups or classes." Peaceful coexistence, nonaggression, and non-interference in internal affairs, respect for the principles of the U.N. Charter, non-adherence to military blocs, and the complete ban of foreign military bases on the national territory, would govern the foreign policy of PAIGC.

With this program a militant would be armed with a clear-cut political platform around which the future guerillas would rally. Cabral points out that for real success in national liberation the new social order, ready to take hold as soon as the fire is extinguished, must be carefully planned. Only then may a militant consider himself politically armed, fully motivated, free to meet the foe in combat, and to show the way to others.

Cabral looked to the longshoremen of Guinea and Cape Verde for the nucleus of his guerrilla forces. These workers had already acquired significant experience in the strikes and protests against the police. Constituting an absolute majority of the indigene elements ("individuals of the black race who do not possess the enlightenment and the personal and social habits . . . of Portuguese citizens," as defined by the 1954 statute, and stripped of the possibility of ever becoming *assimilados*), these workers were predestined to be rebels. The excesses of the Portuguese administration had hit this group first; and even without the PAIGC, they were already engaged in a protracted war with the colonial administration. Cabral's chief problem in connection with the longshoremen was its relatively small number, because Guinea and Cape Verde were areas virtually without a proletariat in the classical sense. The group's activities, therefore, had to be coordinated with those of city militants, students, and members of the petty bourgeoisie. Only in this manner could the militancy of the workers be given definite political goals; but by the same token the program of the PAIGC militants could acquire a fighting fist.

During this 1956-58 period this plan of Cabral produced expected thought somewhat limited results. Throughout these years workers continued to protest, to strike, to demonstrate, their activities culminating in the massacre in Pijiguiti, where nearly fifty dock workers were killed and a number of others arrested. Twenty-one of the participants were tried on charges of subversion and rebellion and were subsequently sentenced to terms of from one to five years.[48] According to Cabral and other leaders of the PAIGC, events were unfolding at a rate faster than anticipated in 1956. It was apparently becoming clear to them that the party was lacking the mass base of support, as well as the organizational ability, to use incidents such as Pijiguiti as "a revolutionary spark that would start a prairie fire." Therefore, at an illegal meeting in Bissão in September 1959 they adopted a new eight-point program that insisted on combining the struggle in the cities with that in the countryside, an action that would change the face of the liberation war. The battle-ground was now to be switched from the urban to the rural scene; open guerrilla in the countryside would supplant strikes and demonstrations.

To implement this shift, Amilcar Cabral, with Rafael Barbosa and other leaders of the party, set about establishing a basic network. During the three years 1956-59 they organized the party apparatus based on a system of cells of from three to five reliable and campaign-hardened members. Secrecy, contacts, and control of execution of orders had by 1959 reached a creditable level. City militants established several intersecting circles of collaborators and set up channels for secreting members fleeing from the city. Security was well in hand, and the possibility for infiltration of PIDE informers was reduced to tolerable limits. In addition, Cabral founded during this period the first clandestine trade union in Guinea, the União Nacional dos Trabalhadores da Guiné (UNTG), an organization calculated to assist political actions within the cities as well as to keep the unpredictable longshoremen under control.

The next step envisioned the strengthening of bonds between the PAIGC and the insurrectionary movements in other Portuguese colonies of Africa. This was formalized in January 1960 through the creation in Tunis of Frente Revolucionária Africana para a Independência Nacional das

Colônias Portuguesas (FRAIN), and was superseded in April 1961 in Casablanca by the Conferencia das Organizações Nacionalistas das Colônias Portuguesas (CONCP). From a technical standpoint this move was executed in the best Leninist tradition, because through these organizations the PAIGC was aiming at acquiring, first, international publicity; then, a headquarters for politico-military planning of operations throughout Portuguese West Africa; and finally, a means of improving its chances in the struggle against the rival organizations—the Movimento de Libertação da Guiné (MLG) and the Frente de Luta pela Independência Nacional da Guiné (FLING).[49] Since it was geographically distant from Guinea, however, the Moroccan super headquarters was to have a field office in Conakry, where Cabral established in 1960 the Movimento de Libertação da Guiné e Cabo Verde (MLGCV), to handle at close range issues of cooperation among the liberation movements in the colonies as well as to serve as a school for training of political cadres.

Having thus secured the three basic prerequisites—a well-defined political program, a party to lead the struggle, and international assistance—Cabral then focused his attention on future battles in Guinea. He divided the country into six regions, which in turn were subdivided into zones.[50] This division was elastic, allowing the leadership of the PAIGC to effect whatever reorganizations circumstances might require. The party activists had been dispatched to the countryside with specific directives for agitation and propaganda work among the *homem grande*[51] and members of individual tribes, to acquaint them with PAIGC plans and politics, and to prepare the ground for the first armed actions.

Cabral's initial plan was as simple strategically as it was imaginative. It counted heavily on the stubborn refusal of the Portuguese to learn anything from the city confrontations with the Guineans or from the experiences of other colonial powers in Africa. The first guerrilla actions were to take place in the zone most susceptible to subversion, preferably in the south. The predictable colonial administration would then send the regulars and the police units to that zone, fully expecting the guerrillas to accept frontal battles in which they would be quickly crushed. Cabral's partisan was then to follow two courses of action simultaneously. First of all, he would be obliged to adhere to the elementary rule of guerrilla action: hit and run. Secondly, in the case of obvious superiority of the enemy, the guerrillas would shift their activity from one zone to another. If heavily attacked at one point, the Guinean partisans were to disperse and to regroup in order to return fire at another, more vulnerable spot. In the first case, the guerrilla should disappear; in the second, attack and destroy isolated patrols, theoretically an easy prey.

If, however, the Portuguese concentrated overwhelming forces in one zone, the PAIGC guerrilla in that zone would simply lie low and wait for his compatriots in another area to stir up trouble there, causing the regulars to divert some of their forces to deal with the matter. By their simultaneous campaigns and pressuring of the enemy they could compel the Portuguese to keep shifting their regulars, their mercenaries, or the forces of the PIDE from one hot spot to another, constantly in pursuit of a phantom.

It is generally agreed that this plan of Cabral did work for the most part—not so much because of any outstanding military talent of Cabral as because of the failure of the Portuguese to defeat the guerrillas militarily, to detach the indigenous population from the PAIGC, and to restore governmental authority. Whether it was the Portuguese lack of understanding of the nature of guerrilla warfare or their failure to understand the PAIGC rebels themselves, both factors contribute to Cabral's success.

From the very beginning, 1962-63, there was considerable confusion in the minds of the Portuguese soldiers as to what this war was all about. The official line of Lisbon was that all guerrillas in Guinea were *bandoleiros*, ordinary criminals, who, by defying law and order, intended to profit from the resultant anarchy. Later on, during the early months of 1964, this line was modified. The guerrillas, instead of being labeled exclusively as chauvinistic rebels from the Cape Verde Islands who chose to fight in Guinea in order to spare their own islanders from the sufferings inherent in guerrilla warfare, were represented as fighting to liberate their archipelago, while the interests of Guinea were definitely not their concern.

In addition to being exposed to this fuzzy argument, the Portuguese regular was told with increasing frequency after 1965 that the PAIGC guerrillas were political bandits attempting to export unrest from Guinea to Angola and Mozambique. As such, they were purportedly a part of a West African conspiracy against Portugal, and the participants in a much broader international conspiracy against the West as a whole. But since neither of these conspiracies could successfully be carried out without the assistance of the Eastern bloc, Cabral's men, continued the official line, must invariably be pro-communist or full-fledged communists.[52] What kind of communists, Lisbon and Bissão failed to make clear.

Already confused as to the true nature of his enemy, the Portuguese regular in Guinea was even more in the dark as to how to fight him. If the guerrilla was an ordinary bandit, simultaneously pitted against the colonial administration and the population at large, then the population could naturally be considered as friendly, or at worst neutral. If the partisan was a rebel from the Cape Verde Islands, indifferent to the interests of the Guineans, then it would seem entirely logical for a regular to view all islanders as his foes and the Guineans as semi-allies. However, if the guerrilla was neither a bandit nor a Cape Verde rebel, but instead a communist who had succeeded in enlisting the sympathy and the cooperation of a wide segment of the population, than all Africans from both areas must be considered hostile.

In their statements to the PAIGC partisans, a handful of Portuguese deserters[53] said that the first seeds of confusion were sown in the minds of many regulars at the moment when they discovered that the PAIGC was involved in a political revolution, while the Portuguese troops were opposing them only with military hardware. A regular was told to shoot at an enemy to whom a political victory was apparently far more significant than temporary military success.

The soldiers, these deserters complained, had been shunted relentlessly from south to north to east and back to their garrisons. They charged that no planner of counterguerrilla operations seemed to know what he was doing. Because the enemy had never been where their officers had assured them he would be, they were constantly under fire from an invisible enemy. New casualties became commonplace. And the courage of Cabral's men, who were becoming fascinated with the love of fighting and the prospect of easy victories, rose in direct proportion to the frustration that plagued the Portuguese troops.

Apparently unaware that a definite political strategy was imperative, the commanders of the counterguerrilla forces took a course quite characteristic of the politically uniformed professional soldier. From 1962 to 1965, the Portuguese increased their force from 10,000 to 25,000 and stationed them in entrenched camps. Except for drilling, which seemed a futile exercise, a majority of them were left with little or nothing to do. After 1966, when their morale had dropped radically, the military leadership decided to put prime emphasis on air strikes. Rivalry between the ground troops, either left idle or dispatched to unskillfully led actions, and the air force, whose members were engaged mostly in bombarding villages in the countryside from a safe altitude, mounted. The officers, on the other hand, sensing the general decline of morale and fighting spirit of the ground troops, were inclined to spare their men by holding them in the garrisons or, against all logic of guerrilla, by sending them on massive search and destroy missions or relying exclusively on commando teams.[54]

Given such conditions, Amilcar Cabral faced if not a demoralized enemy, then at best one who was for all political purposes neutralized. He quite rightly guessed that a guerrilla in a clash with the Portuguese might win by default, for it is such an enemy who tightens the noose around his own neck.

Except for the cities, such as Bissão, Bafata, Bissora, Mansoa, and Bolama,[55] the main contacts between the colonial administration and the indigenous population consisted of such sporadic and inherently coercive activities as the collection of taxes and fines and the enforcement of court sentences. The principal link in the administrative system was the Bissão-appointed village chief, who was frequently torn between loyalty to his tribe and loyalty to the capital. This delicate balance was apparently never appreciated by the Lisbon government, particularly during the fifties, when the PAIGC cadres were most actively engaged in laying the groundwork for the revolution.

During this period it seemed that Lisbon constantly demanded of the administrators in Bissão that they institute uniform rigid policies for the entire territory of Guinea and Cape Verde, disregarding the extraordinarily complex religious and tribal diversity of these colonies.[56] The administrators in turn demanded the same rigid conformity of the village chiefs, quite oblivious that some measures might stir up resistance. The chiefs in their turn, according to the direction of their own loyalties, either openly refused to carry out government orders or accused the entire village of recalcitrance. In either case, when the Bissão orders were disregarded, the PIDE or the army regulars were sent in to restore order. The first casualty was naturally the chief himself; friend or foe of Bissão, he was their only link to the indigenous population.

When the PAIGC guerrillas began in 1962 to disrupt communications, in most cases they killed any chiefs remaining loyal to Bissão, and, as happened in the south, overnight turned entire regions into contested zones. Without the village chief to act as intermediary, Bissão was obliged to send regulars to restore communications or to appoint a new chief. No sooner had the troops departed than the guerrillas promptly came out of hiding, killed the new chiefs, and ruptured communications once again. From this moment, Cabral began to apply tactics called by Tito's partisans "guerrilla's teeter-totter." Bissão would again be forced to send new troop contingents, first to repair roads and bridges, then to protect them, and to appoint new chiefs once again. Numerous small isolated patrols were left to guard communication lines or to act as bodyguards of the new appointees, providing further tempting targets for the guerrillas. What then followed was more of the same, with Bissão having the added burden of sweeping through the surrounding area.

During these search and destroy operations, the only people the regulars usually found were the uninvolved villagers. Their houses were burned and their livestock were confiscated, while a few inhabitants chosen at random were imprisoned or killed outright. Their mission completed, the troops returned to their garrisons. This would be the signal for the guerrillas to come out of hiding and renew their attacks on patrols remaining on duty.

It was at this stage of the struggle, approximately the second half of 1962, that the Portuguese began to rely heavily on air strikes. The pilots proved even less able than the ground troops to determine which village was in fact hostile. They attacked, Cabral says, anything that moved, and bombarded those villages the ground troops had left intact. The villagers, unable to work in the fields or to return home, began a mass exodus. The refugees, men, women, and children, as well as livestock, crowding into the forest, provided the heaven-sent army of followers the handful of PAIGC activists so badly needed. The guerrillas first organized the feeding and lodging of the refugees, child care, and protection of livestock, then incorporated the populace into the PAIGC political program.

For these refugees there was no way out. Any time they wanted to leave the camp, a Portuguese pilot or an infantryman was waiting, ready to shoot them or burn their homes. Among these disoriented and idle villagers, a Cabral organizer readily enlisted new recruits. When the number was considered large enough, the party initiated a "sweep of revolutionary violence," i.e., the liquidation of those accused of cooperation with the Portuguese, of those who openly disregarded the PAIGC policy, and finally, of deserters from the forest camps. Thus even those who did not favor the PAIGC program gradually became willing supporters.[57]

Cabral's practice of turning large areas into liberated zones seems to carry both the Cuban theory of the *foco* and the Latin American concept of armed self-defense one step further. Whereas the *foco* presupposes a small nucleus of guerrillas located in an isolated area, virtually alone for long periods and gaining popular support only by degrees, Cabral's system, as formulated in Conakry at the Fourth Conference of the PAIGC cadres during August-September 1962, focused on the liberation and political reorganization of a vast region. In his view this system demanded from the onset of the struggle both the accelerated transformation of guerrilla units into a regular army capable of defending the south militarily, and the creation of a new network of local authorities that would organize the rear to carry on the struggle. Both of these concepts were adopted in embryonic form by the Castro brothers and Che Guevara toward the end of their campaign against Batista in the second half of 1958.

But the south of Guinea, as organized by the PAIGC, is not a classic example of a self-defense zone either. Unlike the case of Colombia in 1964 or of Bolivia in 1965, the liberation of the south of Guinea was not a goal in itself, but rather a first step in the activation of the north and the east. In other words, Cabral's zonal system, or inter-region system as it was renamed in 1966, is considerably broader in scope than the *foco*, less rigid in its dealings with the population, and less concerned with the defense of real estate per se than with self-defense. It seems that Cabral borrowed from the *foco* those features he considered applicable to Guinean conditons (a monolithic party, provision for dispatch of organizers to the countryside, and a strong accent on secrecy, infiltration of enemy ranks, intelligence, propaganda, and political work, and contacts with indigenous population and sympathizers abroad). From the self-defense system, he adopted the principle of exploiting any militancy of the local population. At the same time, he bypassed the unfavorable aspects of both arrangements, i.e., the narrow confines of the *foco* and the local exclusiveness of the self-defense zones. Cabral's interregional system, required less time for extending the battlefield to embrace the whole country and provided the smallest risk of the guerrilla's becoming engaged in frontal battles.

From the time of the PAIGC Conference of August-September 1962 until January 1963, Cabral was able to launch a guerrilla campaign on a broad scale in the southern section of Guinea. In the course of these several months, his guerrillas managed to win over a number of refugees from forest camps, to form the skeleton of the future local authorities, to initiate collective work projects, to organize distribution centers which were later to become "people's stores," and to found the first primary schools and health stations. Simultaneously, they engaged the Portuguese regulars in numerous skirmishes and battles. In fact, according to Portuguese Minister of Defense Gomes de Araujo, the PAIGC rebels by July 1963 already controlled 15 percent of Guinean territory.[58]

Since the south was only the first step toward liberation, the PAIGC organizers in the course of 1963 made numerous incursions into pockets of rebellion and "zones of insecurity" in the north, so that by "the end of that year the PAIGC estimated that it controlled nearly one-third of the national territory."[59]

At the next PAIGC Conference, February 13-17, 1964, Cabral and other leaders decided to combine the south and the north of Guinea into a uniform operational area. All armed actions were to be coordinated and under the direct command of the central party leadership. Drawing together hand-picked guerrillas and some guerrilla units, the leaders formed a regular army, the FARP (Revolutionary Armed Forces), while the local administration was ordered to function uniformly throughout the whole area, again under the direction of the central party leadership.

After a number of Portuguese counteroffensives in the course of 1965 and 1966, the PAIGC and FARP began gradually to activate an eastern front, following the same pattern established in the south and later applied in the north. Here again, once the enemy had bolstered its troop strength in the east, the guerrillas and FARP units in the south and the north interregions would intensify their activities, forcing the Portuguese commanders to divide their troops.

The tactic of constantly shifting activities from one region to another or the simultaneous activation of all three was particularly effective between 1966 and 1969. The Portuguese were kept busy redeploying their forces.[60] At best, they could leave behind them only isolated garrisons or entrenched strategic hamlets.[61] In either case the PAIGC found them easy prey.

At this juncture, late 1968 and early 1969, Cabral's fighters could have proceeded in either of two directions. They could have attacked some well-chosen Portuguese entrenched camps, for which they were technically prepared (as Cabral stated at the Khartoum Conference in January 1969);[62] or they could have continued to strengthen the positions they already held, waiting for international events to take a favorable turn and compel the Portuguese to negotiate or to abandon their holdings in Guinea altogether. In the first case, Cabral would have been forced to make a considerable "qualitative leap" toward transforming the tactically unenviable position of the Portuguese into a full military defeat; in the second, to count on others to terminate the struggle instead of the PAIGC. Cabral wisely postponed this thorny decision and adopted a third course. Keenly aware that his very presence constituted an ever-mounting threat to the Portuguese, he tried to channel international events in his favor. It appears he was hoping to enjoy the fruits of a new Geneva Conference without having to pay the high price of a Guinean Dienbienphy.[63]

Most unfortunately for his cause, Cabral was assassinated in January 1973. As of this writing (July 1973) no new leader has emerged to take his place. The party is carrying on, however, without a leader.

## The African Guerrilla and Factional Strife

Because Nkrumah is too much an African cosmopolitan and Cabral is primarily a designer-interpreter of what happened in Guinea,[64] between them they have left significant areas untouched. The African guerrilla is thus deprived of any real catechism of revolution. Through the years the success of this guerrilla has been impeded, first, by the absence of a uniquely African concept of insurrectionary warfare, and secondly, by the confusing array of manuals put on the market by various factions and oppositionist groups. Jomo Kenyatta, Frantz Fanon, Patrice Lumumba, and Julius Nyerere testify repeatedly that Africans have a long and admirable tradition of fighting the white colonizers.[65] But the lack of any common ideology, as much as any other single factor, has led inevitably to the formation of dozens of factions and splinter groups. It is one of Nkrumah's laments, in fact, that contemporary Africa, however else it may be defined, is an enormous breeding ground for factional strife. These factions have resulted from the coalescence of several long-term conditons, the most significant of which we propose to discuss briefly.

According to Nkrumah, the typical African rebel springs from a continent in which state frontiers have been established with a slide rule, and where the existence of countless tribes, nations, national minorities, races, religions, and sects is destined to remain a continuing cause for unrest. Such matters as religious and racial intolerance or clashes over land

and hunting rights have led time and again to new contro-
versies, and not infrequently to tribal wars. Not only has
suspicion between black and black become as much a part of
the political process in Africa as has rebellion against foreign
domination; but this very suspicion has given rise to the
conditions in which the principle "one tribe, one faction" for
the entire continent has inevitably gained momentum.

As for the economic structure, the typical African colony
has almost without exception been handicapped by the
imbalance between industry and agriculture resulting from
the dual economy of the colonial system—"the small, largely
Westernized 'modern sector' of sophisticated production and
consumption versus the huge hinterland of somewhat disturbed social life and ancient cultural tradition."[66] This
imbalance in itself has in the past led directly to internecine
clashes. The urban areas would antagonize the hinterland;
and educated minority and an illiterate majority were
constantly crossing swords. Tribes in the immediate vicinity
of the ·cities envied those located out in the bush. The
"natives" distrusted the assimilated segments of the population, who, quite like their foreign sponsors, tended to view
their less sophisticated brothers as subhuman. Frantz Fanon
points out that the colonizer was particularly methodical in
fomenting mutual distrust among Africans and in cutting off
at the roots any attempts at establishments or intertribal or
intergroup bonds. The foreigner tended to prepare a separate
cauldron for each African victim; and each victim, considering his lot the worst, gave no thought to a concerted plan for
extinguishing the fire.

A third source of factional turmoil, especially before the
middle fifties, was the lack of a cohesive social force or of
traditional political parties that might have been relied on in
some cases to end these rivalries or to provide a uniform
leadership for opposition to the white colonizers. Here again,
it was not in the interest of the white colonizer to encourage
the creation of strong nuclei from which an organized local
party might emerge. In the few instances when this was

permitted to occur, the resultant parties were likely to find themselves without a firm program or any clearly outlined strategy and tactics. What such parties really represented was a loose coalition of tribal, religious, political, or altogether undefinable factions whose interests happened to coincide momentarily. As it turned out, in each case, new, often bitter, intraparty and interparty disagreements were compounded with old grudges, resulting in a step backward on the road to liberation.[67]

If a stable middle class, a class-conscious proletariat, and the peasantry, in the traditional sense of the term, had surfaced in time on the political scene of some of the colonies, with viable political parties appearing as their spokesmen, the factionalism might have been averted in some degree. But lacking these instrumentalities, the colonial oppositionists could only rely on those small ad hoc or permanent enlightened groups that demonstrated some capacity for leadership. These groups could be organized either by charismatic figures, such as Kenyatta, Nkrumah, Sékou Touré, Nyerere, Lumumba, and others, by a wide range of leftists from hard liners to anarchists, by African students schooled abroad, or by outstanding local radicals, such as Ben Bella and Cabral. Common to all of these was the desire to put new heart into the struggle of their compatriots and to impose upon them their own special concepts of liberation.

The factions differed as to their ideology, as to the program to be followed once the colonizer had been defeated, and as to the boundaries to be established for each group, as well as in tactics and strategy. From the standpoint of ideology, the members of these factions ran the gamut from ultraconservative to ultraradical and represented every school of thought. Some of them defy classification. Accordingly their programs differed vastly. To varying degrees and in different versions the programs advocated self-determination of a given colony, or of a region, or of the whole of Africa. Some espoused a unitarian state, some a federation or a confederation, a one- or a multi-party system, a democratic form of government or a dictatorship of one party, class, national front or tribe, or of an alliance of tribes.

On the economic front these programs included every conceivable type of system from communal exploitation of land and the means of production to black capitalism and state capitalism, or the Soviet or Chinese version of "scientific" socialism. A majority of these factions were formed abroad because the colonial administrations, except to a very limited degree, rarely tolerated a militant revolutionary. The number of militants living abroad who have had a rough idea of the situation at home has ordinarily exceeded those who were in direct contact with the local population. Not until the beginning of the fifties, in fact, did this ratio begin to shift. Some of the headquarters were located in neighboring African countries, some in Europe and the United States, and a smaller number throughout the Eastern bloc. Each reflected the demands of the foreign sponsor. Some were given an opportunity to travel, others not.

To further complicate matters, a certain number of members of these factions were politically enlightened individuals, some professional refugees, some, in hard-liner parlance, "revolutionary tourists," and some professional revolutionaries. By the very logic of their situation, these factions constantly clashed; and in some cases, the tendency to bicker became their only common trait. When located in the same foreign country, they usually suspected one another, and all both respected and feared those groups who had never left the home country. Those who had remained at home on their part tended to assess the refugees as deserters, or simply as opportunists; those abroad criticized those they left behind for their lack of awareness of the world scene, of local exclusiveness, and often of chauvinism.

In some degree African students educated abroad and, to a greater degree, Marxist hard liners are the groups chiefly responsible for preventing the unification of African oppositionists and the development of broad-based guerrilla movements on both the national and the continental levels. The status of these two elitist groups, and especially the type of political training and education they received, forced them to become sowers of discord not only during the struggle for liberation but also afterward. The activities of these two groups seem destined to cast a shadow over the political process in Africa for a long time to come.

Though no reliable statistics are available in this area, a majority of the Africans who left their country for study abroad immediately following World War II were either gifted students, or came from well-to-do families of tribal or village chiefs, or from the local aristocracy that London or Paris, Moscow or Peking have always sought to attract. At the Cité Universitaire in Paris, for instance, or at the Patrice Lumumba Friendship University in Moscow or at Belgrade University, the typical African student is usually conceived of as a member of a privileged caste. Usually he is financially secure and enjoys a number of privileges denied to the average French or Russian or Serbian student. With many academic and administrative requirements waived outright, this young man, now an object-lesson of racial discrimination in reverse, tends to acquire a completely distorted picture of the host country and of his own position, as well as of his own compatriots back home. Many an African student has become *dépaysé*, and has found common bonds only among his colleagues schooled in foreign universities. With his horizons rather limited, his African compatriots enrolled at the same institution often have been the only partners with whom he could share his thoughts and discuss his future plans.

Since we have concerned ourselves here primarily with the period up to the middle fifties, when the selection of these youths depended mostly on the colonial administration, we should bear in mind that they often came from different tribes and spoke different dialects, and that only after having learned French, English, Russian, or another foreign language could they communicate with one another. The African students were thus forced to form various political and social groups, in the course of which many students acquired significant political experience. They developed contacts and attended international youth congresses. A number of them learned several foreign languages and became familiar with the differing structures of various host countries. Often they published a newspaper or wrote leaflets or memorandums. Above all, many of them developed skill in attacking their opponents and in acquiring the subtle techniques useful in factional struggles.

The longer the African remained abroad the more pronounced did the unnaturalness of his position become and the more painful his readjustment upon his return. Once at home his situation depended upon whether or not his country was free. For instance, returning to Nairobi at the end of the forties, a Kikuyu, an Oxford graduate, though he might have enjoyed some political rights, would find many doors closed to him. A majority of the positions for which he might consider himself qualified were either conditioned by political and other prerequisites or were reserved solely for whites. At that time, any Kikuyu represented a threat to a white settler, an educated Kikuyu an even greater menace. Similar experiences faced the African foreign student returning to French, Spanish, Portuguese, or other colonies; while a student returning from an Eastern-bloc university had a second cross to bear—the stigma of being labeled a communist agitator.

The only recourse for these young people was either to join one of the oppositionist groups, or, if such groups were disinclined to accept them, to choose from among the few remaining possibilities: to withdraw from the political arena, which they had never formally entered; to organize with other returnees a new faction to suit their thinking; to join hands with one or another leftist group sponsored by the Eastern bloc; or to emigrate.

As for the African student returning home to find his country liberated, his path was likely to be strewn with disappointments and frustrations. For instance, an Algerian student returning from Moscow after the French-Algerian war, instead of receiving a warm homecoming, could have found himself branded a shirker. Accustomed to privileges and pampering at the hands of his Soviet hosts, this returning student was in for a rude awakening. He was rarely placed in the position for which he felt qualified. The central institutions had already been staffed for the most part by veterans, while the returnee was assigned to construction projects primarily in the countryside. He was likely to consider such offers both a humiliation and a denial of his skill. To be regarded as any other run-of-the-mill Algerian represented a considerable letdown from his Moscow status. It is not too difficult to imagine his becoming what the French call an *opposant systématique*. Having learned his Moscow lessons well, he would, for instance, consider Ferhat Abbas a bourgeois politician, Ben Bella a Moslem fanatic, Houari Boumédienne no more than a soldier, a professional man of violence. Thoroughly grounded in the Soviet version of scientific socialism, he might also criticize Ben Bella's tentative efforts to introduce socialism to Algeria. All these circumstances served to alienate him from his fellows and to make him a dissatisfied human being always on the verge of rebellion.

Even today, when the general position of the foreign graduate has changed for the better, some of his problems of readjustment remain. Educated, attuned to the time, and often thoroughly trained in a special field, it is difficult for him to consider himself less than essential in the future development of his state. If his government is dominated by a strong central figure, the foreign graduate may either accept completely the philosophy of this founding father, or may side with one of the opposing factions. In the first case, he may be placed in the wrong spot and thus become disillusioned. In the second, he lays himself open to all sorts of troubles and inconveniences affecting his every-day life. If he finds no group at home that sponsors an ideology he may have formulated abroad, he must decide whether to join one of the existing groups and work from within to bring its program into line with his thinking or to organize an altogether new faction.

These disaffected young intellectuals are joined by the Marxist hard liners, an element ready to stir up factional strife and to initiate insurrection. The peculiarities of the African scene have traditionally baffled the Marxists. Even as far back as Marx and Engels, who found themselves confronted with a continent lacking proletariat, bourgeoisie, or nobility, Africa was given no serious consideration.[68] In the same way Lenin, though deeply interested in the problems of Asia and the Middle East, paid scant attention to the Dark Continent. He apparently believed that whatever held true for Asia and the Middle East was equally applicable to Africa.

The Second Congress of the Comintern, held in the summer of 1920, officially endorsed these general thoughts of Lenin. Lumping Asia, Africa, and the Middle East under one heading, "Colonies and Semi-Colonies," the Congress coined the term "Afro-Asian revolutionary." In the opinion of the delegates, this revolutionary, whether from Morocco or Manchuria, was the natural ally of the Third International. It was his duty to pry loose the colonial holdings from which the West drew its strength; and the International, in its turn, was to widen the geographic and political dimensions of every local conflict.

By the same token, the Second Congress judged Africa to be "sub-proletarian," and an African revolutionary to be at the same time progressive because of his struggle against white domination, and reactionary because of his chauvinism, his racial and religious prejudices, his independence of action, and his lack of cooperation in the larger struggle. Best described as a class maverick, the African rebel, in addition, refused to follow the party line or to live up to the Bolshevik image. Regarding him more as a Robin Hood and less as an organized instrument of the proletarian revolution, the delegates tacitly agreed to leave him to himself in his struggle. If he showed signs of winning in his fight for liberation, however, the International could always rush in to help and profit from his success; if again, his uprising proved temporarily abortive, he would have another chance to do better in the future.[69]

This "can win but cannot lose" policy of the International took on real substance at the Baku Congress held September 1-8, 1920. The leading speakers, Gregory Zinoviev, Karl Radek, and Bela Kun, demanded from the "Afro-Asians" that they create numberless "revolutionary pockets," and thus grant the young, struggling Soviet Union a breathing spell in which to extricate itself from the difficulties caused by the civil war.[71] "Savage Asians" and their colonial brothers were expected to achieve in this direction what "cultured Europeans" definitely had failed to accomplish.[72] The African delegates were led to believe that they had been invited to Baku to declare a Holy War against the West and to be assigned their overall roles in the struggle. However, the representatives of the Comintern exposed them instead to endless tirades on the needs of Moscow. The Africans, of course, gained the impression that the Soviets regarded them merely as auxiliary troops at the beck and call of Moscow. Inasmuch as the successful liberation of Africa depended in the last analysis upon the outcome of the global showdown between Marxist socialism and imperialism, the Africans, Radek hinted, were expected to invest every resource at their command in aiding the first land of socialism. Or, by inversion, they would be entitled to use for domestic aims only that surplus of revolutionary strength remaining to them after fulfilling their first obligation.[73]

The same insistence on the part of Moscow that the Africans should help the Soviet cause before they helped themselves prevailed in 1928 at the Sixth Congress of the Comintern.[74] Time and again the delegates appealed to the African militants to put their role in the global struggle between socialism and imperialism ahead of their individual struggles for freedom. Nikolai Bukharin, Otto Kuusinen, and others made it all too clear at this gathering that the Kremlin, the only conceivable leader of this struggle, was to direct it through special "transmission belts," i.e., controlled factions and those trained Africans who deserved to be called "black Bolsheviks."[75]

The Seventh Congress of the Comintern,[76] held in 1935, touched upon the Dark Continent in even more general terms than the previous ones. From the podium the chief speaker, Gheorghi Dimitrov, after deploring the absence of strong communist parties in tropical Africa, simply let the matter drop. He could not identify the struggle of the Africans with anti-Fascism and the concept of the National Front—the basic topics of his address—nor could he appeal to the Westerners at one moment to join Moscow's offensive against Nazi Fascism and in the next breath accuse these hoped-for allies of tyranny over Africa.

During the entire 1935-39 period, the Kremlin and the Comintern seem to have clamped the lid on their attacks on Western oppression of Africa, referring to it only obliquely and without invective, as though duty-bound to do so. To them the only safe target during these years was Italy's policy in Abyssinia and in the Italian possessions in North Africa. From 1939 to 1941, however, while the Nazi-Soviet Pact was in force, this situation was completely reversed. After the German attack on Russia the Kremlin turned full circle, renewing its attacks against Italy and suspending its criticism of the West. Once again Africa seems to have been relegated to the sidelines. When the Comintern was abolished in 1943, the subject was dropped for the duration.

After the defeat of the Axis powers and the onset of the Cold War era, Africa again found a place, if only a minor one, in Moscow's agenda. Because the U.S.S.R. was preoccupied with the more pressing issues of the Cold War, the Kremlin continued for a time to give very little direct attention to Africa. But in their speeches and articles Stalin and his key lieutenants, Andrei Zhdanov, Andrei Vyshinski, Andrei Gromyko, and Pavel Yudin, persisted in their attacks against the West, demanding the expulsion of the colonial powers from Africa and the recognition of the historical rights of Africans to independence. Their criticism dealt almost exclusively with Africa as an integral part of the world colonial system that they insisted would ultimately be destroyed once the Western bloc could be put in its proper place. They employed all the pat phrases and the abusive language of the second and sixth congresses.[77]

During the years between 1945 and 1949, however, the Kremlin leaders were gradually beginning to feel the results of the shortsighted African policy pursued from 1917 on. Entire areas on the continent were now on the move. England and France, weakened by World War II, had been forced to stand by while insurrection, nourished by unprecedented conditions, was mushrooming on all sides. Groups, parties, factions, tribes, and sometimes even whole populations turned to every conceivable form of struggle, from passive resistance to large-scale guerrilla warfare. The situation confronting the colonial powers now, quite unlike any disorganized pattern of unrest in the past, was a continent-wide movement that could not be arrested. In the words of Nasser, the record would be set straight with the West once and for all.

The Soviet leaders reacted with mixed feelings to this awakening Africa. As in the past, they dutifully applauded the militancy of the black slave and his quest for dignity and recognition. In the press and at international forums they played up the political and military accomplishments of the Africans. However, with Stalin still in power, the Soviet leaders had to uphold such time-worn formulas as Lenin's and Stalin's teachings on the national question and the concept of the communist party as the sole guiding spirit of liberation. Unfortunately, what was happening in Africa at the time had been completely unforeseen and uncharted by Soviet leaders. According to Professor Alexander Dallin, the events in Africa forced the Kremlin, if not to reassess all the clichés of its African policy, at least to push for organization of an African studies program in 1949.[78]

From the very outset this long overdue project was doomed. Whether to interpret ambiguous processes in Africa in the light of reality, thus trespassing upon doctrine, or to retain the old clichés—these were the two unhappy alternatives between which the Soviet experts found themselves trapped. In the end, they opted for the clichés, creating in the process considerable confusion among these experts every time an unexpected event occurred in the colonies. For instance, when India and Egypt, in attaining independence, bypassed the only accepted road to independence according to the clichés, in the opinion of these experts the sovereignty of both new states had to be fictitious and the proclaimed neutrality utterly false.[79] The long practice of neglect and generalization of African problems had now placed the Soviet experts in a most uncomfortable position. On the one hand, they certainly had to recognize that India and Egypt were no longer colonies; on the other, they could not admit to the fact of an independence attained without proletarians, without the conscious role of the party and under the direction of such "pro-bourgeois leaders" as Nehru or Naguib.

This difficult situation brought Soviet experts in the beginning of the fifties to another, even more perplexing one: whether a communist in the colonies should be advised to cooperate with politicians like Nehru and Naguib or to attack them as enemies. If the party recommended cooperation, they laid themselves open to being accused of violating Stalin's teaching on the national question; and if they advised resistance, of inconsistency in following through with Stalin's policy of weakening the West. The Soviet experts were forced to return to the old patterns, counseling African communists to cooperate only with those local patriots they could control.[80]

The first tentative efforts in the direction of broadening the criteria for dealing with Africa were noted in 1953 after the death of Stalin. The new leadership under Malenkov, realizing that with respect to Africa Stalin could not have been more wrong, tacitly ignored some of his crudest formulas but refrained from officially admitting that the entire Soviet doctrine had been compromised beyond salvation.[81] It was not in the interest of the new regime to continue Stalin's policy of alienating new states, as he had in the case of Egypt. Nor could they oppose anti-Western liberation movements, such as those in Kenya, Algeria, or the Gold Coast. At the same time, it would have been difficult at that moment to execute a new shift in outlook and strategy. This position of the Kremlin left its imprint on Soviet Africanology. The experts were supposed to assess realistically the forces at work in Africa and to cease attacking individual African leaders.[82] Lacking directives from the Kremlin, Soviet scholars did make a significant contribution by way of collecting and synthesizing new evidence, but left their interpretations for the most part inconclusive.[83] The new monographs on Africa that flooded the market were on the whole dry and monotonous. Those few that did touch upon problems of contemporary Africa gave the impression that the authors were commenting on events from a vantage point half inside and half outside the old doctrine.[84]

The Khrushchev era, particularly in the interim between the twentieth and the twenty-second congresses of the CPSU, 1956-61, was a landmark in Soviet African policy.[85] One after another the colonies attained their independence. To a down-to-earth Khrushchev, this could mean only one thing: the West was definitely on its way out of Africa, leaving a vacuum into which the Kremlin could move. In Khrushchev's opinion it mattered little whether the leader of a given insurrection or the chief of a new state was officially a Marxist; what was really important was the chief's actual contribution to undermining the Western position. Not wanting to quarrel with the victors, the Soviet premier felt besides that since a majority of the new African states would move to the left anyway, i.e., toward the U.S.S.R., the matter of doctrinal righteousness had best be left to another day.[86]

As a result of Khrushchev's influence the Kremlin gradually abandoned the doctrine of Stalin that in the liberation of Africa there were only two roads: his own and the wrong one. Khrushchev insisted that in the final analysis the question of who was ultimately to expel the Western intruder from a colony, a Marxist or a non-Marxist, was irrelevant, especially if there were no Marxists in the colony in question. In his words, the emancipation of any colony is historically a positive step. Its population becomes master of its own destiny, while the West irretrievably loses another link from the chain it has been using to choke Africa. The process snowballs. The newly emancipated colonly joins the bloc of other liberated countries in Africa, Asia, and South America, and together they exercise irresistible pressure upon the Western colonizer to relinquish his mortal grip on the rest of the colonial slaves.[87]

From whatever angle it is viewed, such a development in Africa, according to Khrushchev, actually strengthens the position of the U.S.S.R. Though it is all too clear that the colonial system is definitely marked for extinction, there would always be individual Western governments that would try to arrest this avalanche toward freedom. Since their shortsighted policies toward the ex-colonies force the population to look for an ally in the socialist bloc, the U.S.S.R. gathers up new friends all along the way.

Except for a few pockets such as the Union of South Africa and Rhodesia, the continent of Africa has ceased to be an enormous zone under enemy control. Depending on the degree of their militancy and their attitude toward socialism, the new states have either joined the "zones of peace," as in the case of Algeria, Tunisia, Egypt, and Guinea, or have become contested zones. While the first group, Khrushchev maintained, are already outside the West's embrace, the second may very easily be maneuvered into the socialist camp.[88]

This Soviet policy, which with minor variations has prevailed until the present time, has enabled the Kremlin leaders to interpret all processes in Africa in the light of their own state interests without appearing to deviate from Marxist doctrine. Khrushchev recognized that upheavals in Africa often ended in military dictatorship or that new governments, following the path of least resistance, tended to adhere to some of the outmoded formulas of their former colonial masters. The new governments might also be so overwhelmed with a multitude of unforeseen problems that they unwisely accepted financial aid from the West. Though such practices are frowned upon the Soviet concept of new democracies, Khrushchev believed that with some efforts in the direction of accommodation a viable body of socialism might yet be created in these countries. An erstwhile slave, Khrushchev insisted, will never knowingly endorse his oppressor's ideology or his policies.[89]

It is to this Soviet leader's credit that as a Marxist he dared to sanction a revolution in Africa despite the fact that it had developed spontaneously and without consultation with Moscow. In Africa, "the neglected corner of the globe," the Kremlin had failed to secure a sufficient number of faithful black Bolsheviks capable of accomplishing the "first phase" of the revolution, i.e., the expulsion of the Westerners. Be that as it may, this failure was not so serious in Khrushchev's eyes as to prevent the Kremlin from taking an active part during the "second phase," i.e., the attraction of the new African states into the Soviet camp.[90]

In practice, the new Soviet African policy placed the emphasis on two principal goals. The first entailed all-out cooperation with these governments because "there are no better forces, and particularly no reliable African communist parties toward which to turn."[91] The second, and equally important, goal was to stand by and reap the benefits of the broad programs of industrialization the new states would have to initiate. The process of industrialization itself would in its turn create not only a labor force, the natural ally of the Soviet bloc, but also a bourgeois class, the natural ally of the West. Between these two groups an antagonism would be generated that would inevitably push the African labor force to turn to the Kremlin for advice and practical assistance.

Such a general strategy would have the added advantage, as Khrushchev saw it, of enabling the Kremlin to retain unchanged its maximum objective of control of the entire African continent and its near-term objective of denying the West access to selected areas. Since the short-term strategy was to some extent dependent on the ultimate goal, Khrushchev's policy was to retain enough overall flexibility to adjust to the character of any new African government. According to Alexander Dallin, during the 1960-62 period a significant number of Soviet Africanologists, whose habits of definitive classification acquired during the Stalin era lingered on, divided all African states into the following groups: (1) "progressive," one-party states, such as Ghana, Guinea, and Mali, with socialist elements among the rulers generally sympathetic toward the Kremlin; (2) states pursuing an anti-Western policy or a policy of "positive neutralism," such as Morocco and the United Arab Republic; (3) states such as Ethiopia, the Sudan, Liberia, and the Somali Republic by and large maintaining "correct" and businesslike relations with the U.S.S.R., inclined to accept Soviet aid and technical assistance while rejecting Western aid; (4) Nigeria, Togo, Tanganyika, and Senegal, still in danger of following the capitalist path and of adopting bourgeois democratic models; and (5) "reactionary" and "fascist" states, such as French Africa, the Congo, the Ivory Coast, and Mauritania.[92]

These schematic attempts of the Soviet experts to project an African state through its current policy toward the U.S.S.R. simply disregarded all those areas of the continent in relation to which the Kremlin's attitude in the beginning of the sixties was not quite crystallized. Before Nasser's visits to Moscow, Egypt, for instance, was classified as a state which maintained "positive neutrality;" but after his parleys with Khrushchev, it was thought of also as a state with strong domestic socialist tendencies.[93] Currently, with the Soviet influence more pronounced, Egypt tends to be viewed by

Soviet experts as even more "progressive," more "positively neutral." Or, in the case of Algeria, from 1962 to 1965, during the Ben Bella government, this country was definitely labeled "progressive" and pro-socialist. Following June 1965, under Houari Boumédienne it has remained for the most part "progressive" and socialist, but sometimes more and sometimes less, depending upon the extent to which the politics of Boumédienne have paralleled the Soviet line.

In the opinion of a number of Soviet experts, while Patrice Lumumba was alive, socialism in the Congo was just around the corner. Following his death its advent was threatened by the "fascist" Moise Tshombe, and the Congo dropped lower on the approved list. After Tshombe's exile it was once again reclassified, to become sometimes a pro-bourgeois and sometimes a "positively neutral" state. On the other hand, Ghana was labeled progressive during Nkrumah's rule, then dictatorial after he was deposed. Rhodesia has now joined the company of "reactionary" and "fascist" states, while Ethiopia, Morocco, Kenya, Tanzania, and others have had to be moved up and down on the list several times, often to the discomfiture of the Soviets.[94]

These practices of Khrushchev were adopted by the Brezhnev government and implemented with what we may call the same inflexible flexibility. In general, Khrushchev's successors have attempted to assist "progressive" and "positively neutral" states. The current regime has done its utmost to expand "correct" and "businesslike" relations with friendly African states, has encouraged the "pro-bourgeois" regimes to seek more propitious socialist patterns, and finally, it has sternly opposed "fascist" and "reactionary" governments. The only departures from this general line occurred after Mao Tse-tung's China and Tito's Yugoslavia made their influence felt on the African scene.

Nowadays in order to be classified progressive by Soviet politicians and scholars, an African state, in addition to harboring strong anti-Western sentiments and pro-Soviet sympathies, must apparently display the approved political attitude vis-à-vis the "intrigues of the Chinese warmongers" and the "Yugoslav revisionists." The Chinese consider an African state progressive if it is able to combine its struggle against the West with "healthy proletarian suppression" of the Soviet and Yugoslav brands of revisionism;[95] the Yugoslavs, if the state pursues socialism in its internal and anti-Westernism and nonalignment in its foreign policy.[96] The only point upon which all three governments agree is the weakness of the communist parties in Africa. Early in the sixties Moscow, Peking, and Belgrade seem to have concluded independently that little could be accomplished in Africa through the African communists. Accordingly, each sought supporters elsewhere for its respective policies: Moscow in friendly governments, Peking in controlled factions, and the Yugoslavs through diplomatic channels.

Confronted with these three varieties of Marxism, the African Marxist is hard put to decide which to follow. As an African he is on safe ground only so long as he is fighting the white colonizer, as in Portuguese Guinea; the "pro-bourgeois" tendencies of his government, as in Nigeria; or the "fascists," as in South Africa or in Rhodesia. In these cases he is engaged in a struggle for freedom from Western domination or influence, against one, easily definable, enemy. Here, according to Nyerere, there is no room for differences.[97] As a true Marxist, however, our African must increase his list of enemies: a pro-Soviet hard liner must add to their number "Chinese sectarians" and the "pro-bourgeois Marxist Titoists;" a pro-Maoist, adherents of the Moscow and Belgrade concepts; and a Titoist, "Marxist foreign oppressors," the Russians and the Chinese. If he happens to be a Marxist with strong ties to his homeland, he may choose his own road, only to find himself against all of them. Hence he is bound to make enemies among communist factions and to end up fighting them as hard as he does the Westerners. Taken together, all the Marxists alienate other local patriots, who look upon them as a divisive force, or just another agent of a foreign power in a new disguise.

As an insurrectionary, such a Marxist is severely handicapped. Politically, he is expected to accomplish a great deal for his ideological alma mater, whether Moscow or Peking or Belgrade. However, he is often left without even the symbolic protection normally offered a self-sacrificing supporter by a communist state. For instance, when Nasser prosecuted and jailed pro-Soviet communists, the Kremlin not only did not lift a finger to help them but continued its cordial relations with Cairo. Already in head-on ideological confrontation with a majority of his compatriots, this African communist resembles a faithful servant whose master accords him only infrequent attention. The casual observer would have difficulty believing that he represents such a master. In addition, a majority of the citizens of any new African state are likely to be completely ignorant of the causes of the violent conflict between local Marxist factions.

The man on the street sees it all as a curious puzzle, with factions accusing one another of all sorts of evils. Since valid evidence is rarely offered, the majority of politically awakened but ideologically nonaligned local people tend to equate the battling of Marxists with a struggle for supremacy. Nevertheless, each faction in attracting followers will prevent others from gaining either much popular support or an absolute majority. This situation is aggravated by the fact that followers of a given faction are bound more firmly by their joint antagonism toward other Marxist factions than by a positive program for reform or revolutionary plans to overthrow a non-Marxist government.

The pro-Soviet hard liners in Egypt who were prosecuted and jailed by Nasser may illustrate this point. As prisoners they had to be against Nasser and to accuse him of "terror and torture of freedom fighters." They had to tread lightly however, because in Khrushchev's time a friendly Egypt was crucial for Soviet plans in the Middle East. In order to preserve his political identity, an Egyptian communist was expected as a matter of course to mount an offensive against the "reactionary Moslem officers' clique;" but as a pro-Soviet hard liner he had to praise the same clique for its anti-Western policies and correct relations with the Kremlin. All that he could safely do was to oppose the Egyptian Maoists and the few Trotskyites while bypassing the Titoists in view of the bonds of friendship between Nasser and Tito. At this moment in history the last thing this Egyptian communist could expect was Moscow's concurrence or tangible aid in the attempt he felt duty-bound to make at overthrowing Nasser's government. Without a program of his own, and forced to support the government that had let him down, this revolutionary who was discouraged from instigating revolution but encouraged to neutralize the Maoists and others, was forced to abandon completely his role of professional revolutionary.

The possibilities for an African Marxist, irrespective of his faction, to stir up revolutionary ferment in his homeland, though not identical to those of this Egyptian hard liner, are thus severely limited. The assumption of course, is that white rulers and native-born white "reactionaries" and "fascists" are not among his targets. Caught in the web of this inter-factional struggle, and deriving his strength and support primarily from foreign quarters, the African Marxist is best qualified to remain "the yeast of discord" on the African scene, the "maneuverer" and the "quarrelsome factionalist" attacked by Lenin.

All of these factions often employ some standard guerrilla tactics. However effective such methods may be against the white intruder, they tend to produce only limited results when directed at the black compatriot. They simply force him in his turn to take reprisals; or, what is worse, they create a climate in which the political struggle between two factions may lead to a blood feud resulting in the downfall of both. To repeat what we have already mentioned, therefore, the principal cause of the decline in the use of guerrilla to promote revolutionary change lies in the peculiar political realities of the African scene. With the possible exception of Algeria and a few other areas, the colonies have for the most part gained their independence without recourse to guerrilla and without paying the usual blood tribute. The only cases in Africa wherein full use has been made of guerrilla warfare have been those instances when the colonizer has stubbornly refused to revise his attitude toward his African possessions in the light of historical evolution. In these cases, the colonial subject has taken up arms only as a last resort. In all other cases, the subject of guerrilla has been treated either with academic detachment, as is true of Nkrumah and Fanon, or it is discussed in passing as a fashionable aspect of modern politics—this holds for Lumumba and Nyerere, Sekou Touré, Kenyatta, Ferhat Abbas, Kaunda, Tshombe—or it is considered as a tactic of factional strife and of dubious value.

The constant quarreling of these various factions, Marxist and non-Marxist alike, has tended to impede any significant contribution to the technique of guerrilla warfare. Few factions can claim a broad-based following or the unswerving loyalty of their membership. Most of them lack the basic requirements for waging this type of warfare; and without a long-term program, mass support, and assistance from friendly foreign countries, their cause is all but lost.

## Notes

1. André Malraux's description of Catayee, a politician from French Guiana. "Neither the International nor the proletariat formed part of his vocabulary. Whatever his label, he was a distant brother of the Communards." (*Anti-Memoirs*, trans. by Terence Kelmartin [New York: Holt, Rinehart and Winston, 1968], p. 117.)

2. Reference to the course in Political Science (198b) at the University of California, Berkeley, Spring Quarter 1971, conducted by Professor James A. Gregor.

3. Referring to the period from 1949 to the times when a number

of African states attained independence, Alexander Dallin, "The Soviet Union: Political Activity" published in *Africa and the Communist World*, Zbigniew Brzezinski, ed. (Stanford, Calif.: Stanford University Press, 1963), p. 10, points out that "Soviet journals at this period contain what must now seem an embarrassing number of vicious attacks on 'bourgeois' leaders," such as Dr. Nnamdi Azikiwe, who was called an African Gandhi, or Kwame Nkrumah, who was labeled a "representative of the 'big bourgeoisie' and his party a 'screen covering up the domination of English imperialism' in the Gold Coast." A careful scrutiny of leading Soviet journals of the times would unearth a much longer list of colorful attacks on African leaders, their policies and writings.

4. See Henry L. Bretton, *The Rise and Fall of Kwame Nkrumah: A Study of Personal Rule in Africa*, (New York: Praeger, 1966), p. 30.

5. *Ibid.*, p. 36.

6. For discussion of African socialism and African socialist thought, see Fenner Brockway, *African Socialism* (London: Bodley Head, 1963); William H. Friedland and Carl G. Rosberg, Jr., eds., *African Socialism* (Stanford, Calif., Stanford University Press, 1964); John F. K. Phillips, *Kwame Nkrumah and the Future of Africa* (New York: Praeger, 1960); Brzezinski, *Africa and the Communist World*; James S. Coleman and Carl G. Rosberg, Jr., *Political Parties and National Integration in Tropical Africa* (Berkeley: University of California Press, 1964); Charles F. Andrian, "Patterns of Socialist Thought," *African Forum*, Vol. 1, no. 3 (Winter 1966), pp. 48-49; and Samuel P. Huntington, "Political Development and Political Decay," *World Politics*, Vol. 17, no. 3 (April 1965), pp. 386-430.

7. See Frantz Fanon, *Toward the African Revolution: Political Essays*, trans. Haakon Chevalier (New York: Monthly Review Press, 1967), pp. 57-173; Frantz Fanon, *Studies in a Dying Colonialism*, trans. Haakon Chevalier (New York: Monthly Review Press, 1965); James Cameron, *The African Revolution* (New York: Random House, 1961); Patrice Lumumba, *Congo, My Country* (New York: Praeger, 1962); Kenneth Kaunda, *Zambia Shall Be Free: An Autobiography* (New York: Praeger, 1963); Gwendolen M. Carter, *Independence for Africa* (New York: Praeger, 1960); James Duffy, *Portuguese Africa* (Cambridge, Mass.: Harvard University Press, 1959); D. A. Ol'derogge and I. I. Potekhin, eds. *Narody Afriki* (Moscow: 1954).

8. Julius K. Nyerere, *Freedom and Unity: Uhuru na umoja: A Selection from Writings and Speeches, 1952-65* (London: Oxford University Press, 1967) p. 323.

9. David Caute, *Frantz Fanon* (New York: Viking Press, 1970), p. 3.

10. See Kwame Nkrumah, *Handbook of Revolutionary Warfare: A Guide to the Armed Phase of the African Revolution* (New York: International Publishers, 1969).

11. *Ibid.*, pp. 63-67.

12. The summary of Nkrumah's thoughts on revolutionary warfare

is based on a number of his works, including the following: *Africa Must Unite* (New York: Praeger, 1963); *Neo-Colonialism: The Last Stage of Imperialism* (New York: International Publishers, 1966); *Consciencism: Philosophy and Ideology for Decolonization and Development*, (London: Heinemann, 1964); *I Speak of Freedom: A statement of African Ideology* (New York: Praeger, 1961); *Dark Days in Ghana*, 1nd ed. (New York: International Publishers, 1968) ; *The Autobiograph of Kwame Nkrumah* (New York: University Place Bookshop, 1957); and *Class Struggle in Africa* (London: Panaf, 1970).

13. See Nkrumah, *Neo-Colonialism: The Last Stage of Imperialism*, p. 239; also Nkrumah, *Handbook of Revolutionary Warfare: A Guide to the Armed Phase of the African Revolution*, pp. 8-15.

14. Nkrumah, *Handbook of Revolutionary Warfare: A Guide to the Armed Phase of the African Revolution*, p. 9.

15. *Ibid.*, p. 25. For the general background of the history and politics of colonialism, see L. H. Gann and Peter Duignan, eds., *Colonialism in Africa 1870-1960*, Vol. I: *The History and Politics of Colonialism 1870-1914* (London: Cambridge University Press, 1969); J. D. Fage, *Ghana: A Historical Interpretation* (Madison: University of Wisconsin Press, 1959); Norman R. Bennet, *Studies in East African History* (Boston: Boston University Press, 1963); J. D. Fage, *An Introduction to the History of West Africa*, 3rd ed. (London: Cambridge University Press, 1962); Jan Vansina, Raymond Mauny, and L. V. Thomas, eds., *The Historian in Tropical Africa: Studies Presented and Discussed at the Fourth International African Seminar at the University of Dakar, Senegal, 1961* (London: Oxford University Press, 1964); and Robert W. July, *A History of the African People* (New York: Scribners, 1970).

16. Nkrumah, *Handbook of Revolutionary Warfare: A Guide to the Armed Phase of the African Revolution*, p. 11.

17. *Ibid.*

18. *Ibid.*, p. 11.

19. See Nkrumah, *Neo-Colonialism: The Last Stage of Imperialism*, pp. 220-27; 239-54; *Africa Must Unite*, pp. 173-93; *Handbook of Revolutionary Warfare: A Guide to the Armed Phase of the African Revolution*, pp. 6-7.

20. Nkrumah, *Handbook of Revolutionary Warfare: A Guide to the Armed Phase of the African Revolution*, p. 28.

21. *Ibid.*, p. 30.

22. For discussion on the role of liberated areas, see *Ibid.*, pp. 43-46.

23. *Ibid.*, pp. 48-50.

24. The preceding four paragraphs are a summary of Nkrumah's discussion on coordinated revolutionary action in Africa, *Ibid.*, pp. 51-67.

25. Nkrumah, *Africa Must Unite*, pp. 218-19.

26. *Ibid.*, pp. 219-20.

27. *Ibid.*, pp. 220-21.

28. Amilcar Cabral, "Guinea and Cabo Verde against Portuguese Colonialism," Speech delivered at the Third Conference of the African Peoples, held in Cairo, March 25-31, 1961, *Revolution in Guinea: Selected Texts*, trans. and ed. by Richard Handyside (New York: Monthly Review Press, 1970), pp. 11-12.

29. *Ibid.*, p. 21.

30. Cabral, "At the United Nations," *Revolution in Guinea*, p. 34.

31. *Ibid.*, p. 32.

32. *Ibid.*, p. 30.

33. For a better understanding of these thoughts of Cabral, see "Brief Analysis on the Social Structure in Guinea," a condensed text of a seminar held in the Frantz Fanon Centre in Treviglio, Milan, May 1-3, 1964; "The Nationalist Movements of the Portuguese Colonies," opening address at the CONCP Conference held in Dar Es Salaam, 1965; and "Message to the People of Portugal," Declaration to Voz de Liberdade radio (Khartoum, January 1969), in Cabral, *Revolution in Guinea*, pp. 56-75; 76-85; 152-55. See also Amilcar Cabral "The Struggle in Guinea," *International Socialist Journal* (Rome, August 1964); "The War the Portuguese are Losing," *The Economist* (April 27, 1968); "In 'Portuguese' Guinea," *West Africa* (September 5, 1964); "In 'Portuguese Guinea': Seeing for Oneself," *West Africa* (November 4, 1967); "Unknown War in Portuguese West Africa," *Times* (London) (November 10, 1967).

34. "At the United Nations," pp. 32-33.

35. *Ibid.*, p. 32.

36. See *Report of the Special Committee on Territories Under Portuguese Administration* (United Nations, New York, 1962, A/5160), pp. 132, 134-36, 139-40, 142-43.

37. For the U.S. attitude toward the Portuguese colonies in Africa, see Adlai Stevenson's speech to the U.N. Security Council on March 15, 1961 (*New York Times*, March 16, 1961).

38. Cabral singled out for attack the following acts: a) Decree no. 43,730, revising Articles 489,511 and 516 of the Overseas Administrative Reform Act; b) Decree no. 43,894, regulating land concessions; c) Decree no. 43,895, establishing provincial settlement boards in the colonies; d) Decree no. 43,896, organizing cantons in the colonies; e) Decree no. 43,897, regulating matters of private law; and f) Decree no. 43,893, repealing the Native Statute of May 1954. (Except for the first, all these decrees were promulgated on September 6, 1961.) For Cabral's discussion of legal aspects of these reforms, see "At the United Nations," pp. 24-29.

39. "At the United Nations," p. 29.

40. See T. Walter Wallbank, ed., *Documents on Modern Africa* (Princeton, N. J.: Van Nostrand, 1964), p. 168.

41. For Salazar's biography, analysis of his policies in the metropolis and in the colonies, and comments characteristic of Western authors,

see Antonio Ferro, *Salazar: Portugal and Her Leader*, trans. by H. de Barros Gomes and John Gibbons (London, 1939); Charles E. Nowell, *A History of Portugal* (New York: Van Nostrand), pp. 233-42; Harold V. Livermore, *A New History of Portugal* (London: Cambridge University Press, 1966), pp. 330-45; as well as Richard J. Hammond, *Portugal's African Problems: Some Economic Facets* (New York: Carnegie Endowment for International Peace, 1962); Richard Hammond, "Economic Imperialism: Sidelights on a Stereotype," *Journal of Economic History*, Vol. 21 (December, 1961); James S. Coleman, "Nationalism in Tropical Africa," *American Political Science Review*, Vol. 48 (June 1954); F. Clement C. Egerton, *Angola in Perspective: Endeavor and Achievement in Portuguese West Africa* (London: Routledge & Paul, 1957); C. F. Spence, *The Portuguese Colony of Moçambique: An Economic Survey* (Cape Town: A. A. Balkema, 1951); Ronald H. Chilcote, *Portuguese Africa* (Englewood Cliffs, N. J.: Prentice-Hall, 1967); Franco Nogueira, *The United Nations and Portugal: A Study of Anti-Colonialism* (London: Sidgwick and Jackson, 1963; Tandem Books, 1964); Adriano Moreira, *Portugal's Stand in Africa*, trans. William Davis and others (New York: University Publishers, 1962); *The United States in Africa*, The American Assembly Papers (New York: 1958); and Arnold Rivkin, "Lost Goals in Africa," *Foreign Affairs*, Vol. 40 (October 1965).

42. Not suprisingly, Cabral's analysis of Salazar's regime is sketchy, and of concern to him only insofar as Lisbon closes all opportunities of settling problems in Guinea by peaceful means. He says that his people are fighting only Portuguese colonialism, and that the struggle against Portuguese fascism must be waged by the Portuguese people. He argues that while the defeat of fascism in Portugal might not signal the end of Portuguese colonialism, the destruction of Portuguese colonialism would surely spell the doom of Portuguese fascism. ("Guinea and Cabo Verde against Portuguese Colonialism," *Revolution in Guinea*, p. 18.)

43. A movement composed of democratic, liberal, and left-wing groups, which tried to oppose Salazar in the 1945 elections in Portugal but which instructed its members to abstain from voting because of alleged repressive measures. In 1948 the Movimento was outlawed on the grounds that it was a communist front.

44. The assimilated elements (*assimilados*), about 8,000 in number at the time of the establishment of the PAIGC, whose presence constituted one of the notable differences between Portuguese colonialism and the colonialism of other European states, were Africans employed by the colonial administration or by some banks and businesses, middle class businessmen, and store clerks. They were regarded as integrated into the Portuguese colonial society: citizens "no longer thought to be natives."

45. See Chilcote, *Portuguese Africa*, p. 99.

46. For a somewhat glowing report of the structure and policies of

the PAIGC, see Gerard Chaliand, *Armed Struggle in Africa: With the Guerrillas in Portuguese Guinea*, trans. by David Rattray and Robert Leonhardt (New York: Monthly Review Press, 1969), pp. 21-27.

47. For the full text of the PAIGC program, see Cabral, *Revolution in Guinea*, pp. 169-174.

48. Chilcote, *Portuguese Africa*, p. 99.

49. Nkrumah (*Handbook of Revolutionary Warfare: A Guide to the Armed Phase of the African Revolution*, p. 10) views the FLING as an example of a group set up by imperialists and their local agents to serve both "as a worthy partner for negotiations and as an intelligence and/or repression agency against the genuine liberation movements supported by the oppressed masses." See also Chaliand, *Armed Struggle*, p. 80.

50. *Ibid.*, p. 22. For details on the steps outlined by Cabral in preparing the PAIGC for guerrilla, see Basil Davidson, *The Liberation of Guiné: Aspects of an African Revolution* (London: Harmondsworth, 1969; and Baltimore: Penguin, 1969).

51. Old men who enjoy special prestige and moral authority in village communities; not to be confounded with the village chiefs, in most cases appointed by the Portuguese to exercise administrative authority. The PAIGC activists view the chiefs predominantly as Portuguese agents.

52. Cabral's repeated insistence on the Bolshevik slogan, "A revolution is dead when it has no friends in the outside world!" particularly stimulated this changeover of the official line.

53. For illustration see a statement of the deserter Jose Augusto Texeira Mourao, in Chaliand, *Armed Struggle*, pp. 57-58; and also "Deux déserteurs portuguais parlent," *Révolution Africaine* (January 2, 1964).

54. For an illustration of the growing awareness of the Portuguese officers that the commandos are the only reliable and militarily competent units for combating the PAIGC, see "The Commando Doesn't Miss," in Chaliand, *Armed Struggle*, pp. 130-31. It should also be noted that the less officers knew what to do with their troops in Guinea, the more insistent they were upon the prolongation of their tours of duty in Africa. During the period 1962-66, the length of this tour was increased several times, until in December 1966 it was finally set at from two to four years.

55. These are small cities: Bissau, 25,000; Bafata, 10,000; and Bissora, Mansoa, and Bolama, approximately 5,000 people each according to the 1960 statistics. Due to an over-concentration in these centers of the Portuguese administration, the army, the PIDE, and the *assimilados*, they are still considered by many Guineans, particularly by the indigenous elements, as foreign bodies on Guinean territory.

56. For the complex structure of Guinea, its brief history, and its tribal division, see Chilcote, *Portuguese Africa*, pp. 83-98; Cabral,

*Revolution in Guinea*, pp. 56-57; and Chaliand, *Armed Struggle*, pp. 3-21.

57. For an enthusiastic description of changes that had taken place in the lives of these refugees, see Chaliand, *Armed Struggle*, pp. 38-42, 45-50, 62-65, 76-77, 91-94. All aspects of the life of these refugees seemed to be under the firm grip of PAIGC leaders. "In the liberated areas we have a real state," said Cabral in his speech in the Manchester Free Trade Hall, October 28, 1971. "We have all elements of a state; we even have prisons."

58. *Diario de Lisboa*, July 18, 1963.

59. Chaliand, *Armed Struggle*, p. 23.

60. See Cabral's December 1968 report, "The Development of the Struggle," *Revolution in Guinea*, pp. 112-26.

61. For brief references to the technique of strategic hamlets, see Cabral, *Revolution in Guinea*, p. 115; and Robert Thompson, *Revolutionary War in World Strateggy 1945-69* (New York: Taplinger, 1970). pp. 103-4.

62. "Towards Final Victory," Cabral, *Revolution in Guinea*, pp. 156-64.

63. See "Towards What Future?" and "With What Wider Meaning?" in Davidson, *Liberation of Guinê*, pp. 129-60.

64. See Amilcar Cabral, *On the Situation of the Struggle: January - August 1971* (Manchester: The PAIGC Publication, September 1971.

65. For summaries of Jomo Kenyatta's views, see Jomo Kenyatta, *Facing Mount Kenya* (London: Secker and Warburg, 1938); Jomo Kenyatta, *Kenya: The Land of Conflict* (Panaf: 1945); L. S. B. Leaky, *Mau Mau and the Kikuyu* (New York: Methuen, 1952); John C. Carothers, *The Psychology of the Mau Mau* (Nairobi: Government Printer, 1954); Ione Leigh, *In the Shadow of the Mau* (London: W. H. Allen 1955); Edward W. M. Grigg Altrincham, *Kenya's Opportunity: Memories, Hopes and Ideas* (London: Faber and Faber and Faber, 1955); and Carl Rosberg, Jr., and John Nottingham, *The Myth of Mau Mau: Nationalism in Kenya* (Stanford, Calif.: Stanford University Press, 1966).

For some of the key thoughts of Frantz Fanon, see Fanon, *A Dying Colonialism*; Fanon, *Toward the African Revolution*; Fanon, *Black Skin, White Masks* (New York: Grove Press, 1967); Fanon, *The Wretched of the Earth* (New York: Grove Press, 1963); and David Caute, *Frantz Fanon* (New York: Viking Press, 1970).

For the views of Lumumba see Patrice Lumumba, *Congo, My Country* (New York: Praeger, 1962); and Alan P. Merriam, *Congo: Background to Conflict* (Evanston, Ill.: Northwestern University Press, 1961).

For Nyerere's concepts, see Julius K. Nyerere, *Freedom and Unity*

(London: Oxford University Press, 1967); Julius K. Nyerere, *Freedom and Socialism* (London: Oxford University Press, 1968); Julius K. Nyerere, *Essays on Socialism* (London: Oxford University Press, 1968).

66. Guy Hunter in "New Africa," *Foreign Affairs*, (July 1970), p. 712.

67. For a broader understanding of these meanderings, see John Hatch, *Africa Today and Tomorrow* (New York: Praeger, 1960); Herbert J. Spiro, *Politics in Africa* (Englewood Cliffs, N. J.: Prentice-Hall, 1962); Immanuel Wallerstein, *Africa: The Politics of Independence* (New York: Vintage Books, 1961); Margery Perham, *The Colonial Reckoning* (London: Collins, 1961); Guy Hunter, *The New Societies of Tropical Africa* (London: Oxford University Press, 1962); Melville J. Herskovits, *The Human Factor in Changing Africa* (New York: Knopf, 1962); and Arnold Rivkin, "Lost Goals in Africa," *Foreign Affairs*, 40 (October 1965): 44.

68. Alexander Dallin, "The Soviet Union: Political Activity," in *Africa and the Communist World*, Zbigniew K. Brzezinski, ed. (Stanford, Calif.: Stanford University Press, 1963), pp. 7-48.

69. For summaries of some of the Marxist discussions on these points, see Dallin, "Soviet Union," pp. 7-9; Bela Kun, *Communist International in Documents 1919-1932* (Moscow: Partine Izdatel'stvo, 1933); V. I. Lenin, "The Conditions of Affiliation to the Communist International," *Selected Works* (New York: International Publishers, 1943); "Thesis on the National and Colonial Question," *The Communist International* (Russian ed., no. 13, September 28, 1920), pp. 2425-34; and *The National-Liberation Movement in the East* (Moscow: Foreign Languages Publishing House, 1957).

70. For the text of the addresses, see the Russian edition of the stenographic record of the Baku Congress: *Kommunisticheskiy Internatsional i Osvovozdenie Vostoka-Piervui Zyezd Narodov Vostoka 1920, Baku 1-8 September 1920* (Petrograd: Smolnyi 63, 1920), pp. 9-15, 30-48, 63-72, 173-83, 224-32. For discussion, see George Lenczowski, *Russia and the West in Iran 1918-1948* (Ithaca: Cornell University Press, 1949), pp. 6-9; Franz Borkenau, *The Communist International* (London: Faber and Faber, 1938), pp. 284-95; Karl Radek, *Five Years of the Comintern* (Moscow: Krasnaia Nov', Glavpolitprosvet, 1924), pp. 211-31; and Grigorii Z. Sorkin, *Piervyi Zyezd Narodov Vostoka* (Moscow: Eastern Literature Publications, 1961).

71. See William H. Chamberlin, *The Russian Revolution 1917-1921* (New York: Macmillan, 1960), II. 392-94.

72. The reference to Lenin's articles, "Cultured Europeans and Savage Asians," *Pravda*, May 18, 1913.

73. *Kommunisticheskiy Internatsional i Osvovozdenie Vostoka-Piervui Zyezd Narodov Vostoka 1920, Baku 1-8 September 1920* pp. 53-72.

74. For the full record of the Sixth Congress, see *International Press Correspondence*, Vol. 8 (1928).

75. These thoughts first emerge during the discussions among the members of the Colonial Commission of the Sixth Congress presided over by Otto Kuusinen. For the text of "Thesis on the Revolutionary Movement in the Colonies and Semi-Colonies," adopted at the Sixth Congress, see *International Press Correspondence*, Dec. 12, 1928, pp. 1659-76.

76. For the text of the proceedings, see *International Press Correspondence*, Vol. 15 (1935); and for Dimitrov's speech, Gheorghi Dimitrov, *United Front Against Fascism* (New York: New Century Publishers, 1935).

77. For illustrations of this line, see V. M. Molotov, *On Armed Forces of the United Nations on Foreign Territory* (Washington, D.C.: Embassy of the U.S.S.R., 1946), pp. 3-31; A. Y. Vyshinskii, *For the Peace and Friendship of Nations Against the Instigators of A New War* (Washington, D.C.: Embassy of the U.S.S.R., 1947) pp. 3-28; and L. P. Beria, *Thirty-Fourth Anniversary of the Great October Socialist Revolution* (Washington, D.C.: Embassy of the U.S.S.R., 1951), pp. 5-31. For an enlightening summary on Soviet postwar foreign policy, see J. M. Mackintosh, *Strategy and Tactics of Soviet Foreign Policy* (London: Oxford University Press, 1962), pp. 1-32.

78. Dallin, "Soviet Union," pp. 10-11.

79. *Ibid.*

80. See, for instance, "The National Liberation Movement of the Peoples Against Imperialism," in *Fundamentals of Marxism-Leninism*, pp. 394-430.

81. Dallin, "Soviet Union," pp. 10-11.

82. Professor Dallin points out that the work by I. I. Potekhin and D. D. Ol'derogge, eds., *Narody Afriki* (Moscow: 1954) remains in this respect a landmark in Soviet Africanology ("Soviet Union," p. 34).

83. For a discussion, see Walter Kolarz, *Communism and Colonialism* (New York: St. Martin's Press, 1964), pp. 114-24.

84. Many Soviet Africanists were thrown into a state of confusion when they found themselves dealing with a proletariat that exercised a leading role in the liberation process. This applied as well when the "rate of transition" and "democratic" and "socialist" transformation were determined by the rate of liberation of a colony, especially in treatises that dealt with areas that had no proletariat worth mentioning. For an example of a successful sophism in this area and an imaginative use of Marxist jargon, see I. I. Potekhin, *Formirovanije natsional'noy obshchanosti Yuzhno-Afrikanskikh Bantu* (Moscow: 1955).

85. Several good sources on Soviet Africanology during this period have appeared in the Western languages. Some of the most useful are Brzezinski, *Africa and the Communist World*; Manfred Halpern, *The Politics of Social Change in the Middle East and North Africa* (Princeton, J. J.: Princeton University Press, 1963); Sergius Yakobson, "Russia and Africa," *Russian Foreign Policy: Essays in Historical Perspective*, Ivo J. Lederer, ed. (New Haven, Conn.: Yale University

Press, 1962), pp. 453-87; Mary Holdsworth, *Soviet African Studies, 1918-1959: An Annotated Bibliography* (London: Oxford University Press, 1961); Thomas P. Thornton, "Communist Attitudes Toward Asia, Africa, and Latin America," in *Communism and Revolution*, Cyril E. Black and Thomas P. Thornton, eds. (Princeton, N. J.: Princeton University Press, 1964), pp. 245-69; and William H. Lewis, "Sub-Saharan Africa," in *Communism and Revolution*, pp. 367-90.

86. See Nikita S. Khrushchev, *Conquest Without War*, comp. and ed. by N. H. Mager and Jacques Katel (New York: Simon and Schuster, 1961), pp. 144-47.

87. *Ibid.*, pp. 11-30.

88. See Khrushchev's speech at the Kremlin luncheon for Gamal Abdel Nasser, *Pravda* (May 1, 1958), and the letter to Hassanayu Haykak of Al-Ahram, Egypt, *Pravda* (November 25, 1957).

89. See Khrushchev, *Conquest Without War*, pp. 116-18.

90. See Ernest Block, "Communism in the (Underdeveloped) Countries," *Problems of Communism*, July-August, 1958.

91. Dallin, "Soviet Union," p. 13.

92. *Ibid.*, p. 14.

93. See *Khrushchev Remembers* (Boston and Toronto: Little, Brown, 1970), pp. 430-51.

94. A tendency to classify an ex-colony in Africa in one or another category prematurely is particularly noticeable in the writings of I. I. Potekhin, I. Kuzminov, G. Mirsky, A. M. Sivolobov, S. I. Tyulpanov, and several other prominent Soviet Africanists.

95. For the Chinese views, see Richard Lowenthal, "China" in *Africa and the Communist World*, pp. 142-203; and Bruce D. Larkin, *China and Africa 1949-1970* (Berkeley: University of California Press, 1971).

96. See Ales Bebler, "Africa Rediscovered," *Review of International Affairs* (Belgrade), February 16, 1960, and his "Problems of Social and Political Change of Black Africa," in *Socijalizam* (Belgrade), no. 6 (1959). A comprehensive account of Yugoslav attitudes toward Africa is given by William E. Griffith, "Yugoslavia," in Brzezinski, ed., *Africa and the Communist World*, pp. 116-41.

97. Nyerere, *Freedom and Unity*, p. 106.

# 4     The International Radical Left

The representative writers of the New Left whose work I propose to examine display an amazing diversity of views. These authors differ substantially not only with their predecessors but with one another as well. Within the short span of time since the middle of the 1960s, they have put forth a number of novel and intriguing thoughts on insurrection that challenge the postulates of all other schools. The one area in which we find some agreement is in the desire on the part of all these writers to overturn the status quo. Their campaigns promoting unrest have elicited strong reactions not only from political scientists and from public figures in every walk of life, but even from the communist hard liners and other official enemies of the establishment.

This lack of a uniform school of thought with easily distinguishable traits makes it especially difficult to assess the contribution of this New Left to the body of knowledge on guerrilla and to understand the reasons for its clash with classical concepts on revolutionary violence. We are dealing here with a loose confederation of ideologues and activists from different countries, from different groups within the same country, and from East and West as well as from the Third World. The late Senator Thomas J. Dodd describes the movement—if it may be so termed—as one that defies classification. It fits into no conventional category. While it does embrace a number of tightly knit groups, some agreeing, some violently at odds with others, it is a phenomenon of far greater significance than the combined weight of its many parts.[1] In the beginning of the sixties it was considered as a purely American phenomenon, by the middle of the decade as a Western movement, and after events in some Eastern European and African universities toward the end of the sixties, as a force to be reckoned with on a world wide basis. Whether the New Left is simply a national movement of protest, a new type of student International, an alliance of contemporary youth of every complexion, a fraternity of the discontented, or an unclassifiable "mixture of theory, sociological action, and bitter protest" remains to be determined.

A majority of the special characteristics of the New Left are in the process of crystallization. This very absence of a cohesive organization makes it possible for analysts to trace irreconcilable portraits of the movement, often on the basis of identical factography. Some defend it without reserve and applaud its every aspect. Others see it only as an anti-intellectual, disruptive, or subversive force. A third group, still the most numerous, write of the New Left as an embryo which is yet to find "its true soul."

It is characteristic of the first group that they label the New Left as "the avant-garde that knows the story in advance;" as the enlightened youth who, convinced of the regressive character of the establishment, both in the West and in the East, stubbornly refuse to follow its dictates. In the opinion of these analysts the movement is composed of those segments of youth who are the most keenly aware that the older generations have left them without a cause to believe in, without a flag to fight under. If "God is dead," as many dissident priests proclaim, if Marxism as an ideology has definitely lost its battle with reality, and if democracy, as many of them insist, is desperately in need of a thorough overhaul, what is a young man to believe in? What hope can he hold out for the future? Thus, in the opinion of Kingman

Brewster, president of Yale University, the New Left will henceforth be the official representative of today's "cool" or "with it" generation, having its own sense of right and wrong; or as Clark Kerr, former president of the University of California, views it, the movement is made up of "activists" who challenge society to produce answers that have meaning.

On the other hand, the late director of the F.B.I., J. Edgar Hoover, regarded the New Left simply as "a serious threat to both the academic community and a lawful and orderly society." Leslie Fiedler, an opponent of the New Left, calls it "the mindless unity of an impassioned crowd whose immediate cause is felt rather than thought out, whose ultimate cause is itself." George Kateb, a political analyst, assesses the movement as "crude in mind and simple in feeling, marked sometimes by posturing, sometimes by mindless activism, sometimes by irrational hatred." After the events of June 1968, the Yugoslav press labeled the rebellious students of Belgrade University bourgeois radicals, nationalists, "an unruly mob that forgot history;" and the Czechoslovakian press after the Soviet invasion of that year accused the students of the University of Prague of Trotskyism and of pro-capitalist or of pro-liberal sentiments.

Milovan Djilas, author of *The New Class*, describes the students in the West as "revolutionaries without revolution" and those in Prague as "unarmed guerrillas." And one of the active participants in the shaping of the movement in the United States, Carl Oglesby, though predicting a great future for it, believes that the movement has yet "to discover or create its historic identity."

What is the philosophical outlook of the New Left? Can it reach out to all young dissidents irrespective of country or bloc? What are its positive contributions, if any, to the progress of a contemporary society faced with outmoded ideologies? How can a definite borderline be established between the New Left and the great body of youth in general? All these are questions that still await satisfactory answers.

It is not surprising that in dealing with such a complex, multi-faceted movement, most authors examine first its external manifestations. The typical new left militant is likely to be described as under the influence of young Marx or old Marx or Lenin; of Mao Tse-tung or Trotsky or Djilas; of Castro, Albert Camus, or Jean-Paul Sartre; of Herbert Marcuse, Erich Fromm, George Mandel, or C. Wright Mills. Often he is said to style himself a pupil of Mihail Bakunin, Mohandas Gandhi, or Che Guevara; of individual leaders of the Third World, of Malcolm X, or of founders of different religions. Not infrequently he is said to take pride in being a political *auto-didacta*, a self-taught follower of no one, who is seeking to write his own Ten Commandments. Whether he is motivated by a definite school or a cohesive body of thought is a question that must be examined in each individual case with no guarantee of a satisfactory answer.

According to Oglesby, a New Leftist enters the political arena holding to one of four basic postures.[2] First is the belief widely held by the left-wing liberals that the system itself is inherently capable of producing "worthwhile self-reform." No matter how much out of balance the present system may be, it still contains elements sufficiently strong and viable to be awakened and forced into activity by the New Left. To what extent these liberals are truly a part of the movement and to what extent only its satellites is difficult to determine and will remain so until all ferments of the New Left surface.

The second of Oglesby's basic four, "the most familiarly radical position," is held by Marxist hard liners. They maintain that "the industrial workers remain the essential driving force of an inevitable socialist revolution," a process that the New Left may accelerate by radicalizing intellectuals and members of minority groups and bringing them closer to the proletarians in the factory. In this context, the hard liners appear sometimes more sometimes less assertive, i.e., they officially grant the New Left the right to achieve its stated aims, but under the guidance and following the unalterable teachings of the communist party. For instance, in its letter to the *Harvard Crimson*, the Boston Youth Club of the Communist Party U.S.A. (CPUSA) makes clear that its purpose is not to turn organizations into junior communist parties, but rather to further the goals of these organizations by offering relevant activities.[3] And Gus Hall, the party's leader, makes the point somewhat clearer. He argues that the choice lies between reforming capitalism as an end in itself or in replacing it with socialism through a revolutionary process.[4] This concept of "controlled freedom" for the New Left, as sponsored by the hard liners, does not essentially differ from classical Stalinist formulas on "transmission belts"—the mass organizations (trade unions, youth, women, professional and other front organizations) encouraged to carry on their individual, independent type of activities but geared in the final analysis to mesh with the party's overall tactics and strategy. In terms of numbers, how much influence do the hard liners actually wield? Can they divert or subvert the activities of the movement to serve party needs? These are questions that cannot be completely answered on the basis of available information. But it is a foregone conclusion that the communist parties in the West, continuously on the lookout for "new blood and new cadres," will always be found waiting in the wings whenever the atmosphere becomes highly charged over a new move-ment or a fresh cause.

The third, exclusively New Leftist posture, in Oglesby's opinion, is best expressed through the concept that great technological developments in industry have significantly affected the character of the work force. The workers are now students and students are the new working class.[5] This position is best summarized in the first thesis of "The Appeals from the Sorbonne" of June 13-14, 1968. In this document, the students regard themselves as privileged persons because only they have the time and the opportunity to acquire an understanding of the state and of society. They recommend that the privilege be spread around so that all may enjoy it.[6]

The last, and the least elaborated, principle espoused by certain of the New Leftists holds that "students constitute the beginning of a new historical class, produced by a workers' revolution which (within the West) is not still to come but has already taken place." This concept implies several serious departures from classical Marxism, placing this "unnamed, and no doubt at this point unnamable," new class at loggerheads with the Marxist hard liners, as we shall see. Though the present study examines in detail only the area of this movement directly concerned with insurrection and guerrilla warfare, brief mention of a few peripheral issues will help to explain some of the precepts that distinguish the New Left from all other schools.

Disagreeing with the Marxist postulate that "the bourgeois society (or any other) is the last of the contradictory social systems," the New Left emphasizes that its cause represents only one movement among many in a historical sequence. The bourgeoisie, after destroying the regressive, contradictory feudal class, made sure, first, that the remnants of the nobility were prevented from returning to power. This accomplished, it went about securing its newly won positions. The chief danger lay in the growing proletariat, whose historical mission, according to the New Left, is not the replacement of capitalism by socialism; rather it is the industrialization of society. This the bourgeoisie has proved itself capable of achieving, if only to a limited degree. The latent capabilities of the proletariat to carry on the project are undeniably greater, and its contribution has therefore been noteworthy. Where the struggle for industrialization is still in progress, the role of the proletariat continues to grow. However, in all those societies where the goal has already been achieved, as in the West, its role is substantially reduced, and to all intents and purposes has practically been eliminated. The burden of the struggle must now be shouldered by new forces, and it is exactly at this point that the New Left enters the stage.

In those countries in the Eastern bloc where the Marxists acceded to power in the name of the proletariat, the proletarian government destroyed the bourgeoisie and then sought to secure itself against the threat of any opposition, often employing harsher means than had its bourgeois antecedents. The once progressive proletariat and its official representatives thus became regressive and contradictory. To continue worshipping the proletariat under any and all conditions despite its changed role, as the hard liners demand, does not seem reasonable to some of the New Leftists; nor would such a course, in their opinion, contribute to the awakening of new progressive elements in a society destined to take up the banner of progress from the hands of a tired proletariat.[7]

The question as to whether and to what extent a militant of the New Left should consider himself tied to the official, Marxist-designed ideology and slogans of the proletariat remains unsettled among the movement's ideologues. On this point there is very little consistency in their advice to the militant. Some of them, as in the case of Daniel Cohn-Bendit,[8] one of the leaders of the 1968 Paris revolution, imply that the entire theoretical heritage of Marxism and its practical manifestations, such as Bolshevism, Maoism, and the institution of the party, are definitely obsolete. They may even go so far, in fact, as to recommend the erection of a completely new structure, starting with the first brick. Others, such as leading New Leftists Rudi Dutschke or Leszek Kolakowski, espouse some elements of Marxist philosophy, reject others, and completely ignore a third segment. If he were to rely solely on suggestions of these authors as to whether Marxist teachings should be treated as a conditional guideline, as an impediment, or as a hostile ideology, our New Leftist militant would surely find himself at sea. His confusion would be increased by exposure to what "practical politicians of the Movement," such as Mario Savio,

Tom Hayden, Jerry Rubin, or Huey Newton, have to say about the subject. Though these leaders may on occasion recommend cooperation with organized labor or with the Marxists, at other times they completely disregard this issue.

Finally, the militant may settle on a compromise by following the advice of authors such as Oglesby, who on the one hand directs the leftist militant to repudiate, and on the other to carry forward, the classical proletarian ideology, "in much the same way that the proletariat both absorbed and transcended the bourgeois culture."[9] In other words, a New Leftist should seek to ally himself with the proletariat in view of its past progressive role, its present numerical strength, and its organization, but must by no means allow himself to be dominated by it.

The New Left, according to Oglesby, who is still the most ardent defender of the movement, has arrived only step by step at these ideological positions.[10] The first stimuli in this direction were provided by the communist hard liners and other older generations of radical oppositionists—the Old Left, as he names it, whose philosophy was by and large "liquidated in the fifties because it was defenseless."

Adhering to Stalin's formulas, the Old Left demanded above all economic security for "the masses" despite the fact that the better portion of the "masses in question" believed themselves already secure. It further sought to overthrow the system, insisting that capitalism could not "deliver the goods." When it became undeniable that "the goods (were) being delivered," the whole practical argument for socialism advanced by the Old Left collapsed. Having stubbornly maintained that the postwar American prosperity was a bluff—and they pointed out such problem areas as the South, the ghettos, and race relations—Old Leftists insisted that even where relative opulence existed, it came primarily as a result of the irrational system of subsidizing the Cold War economy through the Pentagon and military spending. The first argument, that capitalism could not deliver the goods, was specious on the face of it because "things were better here than any place else and (were) getting better," while the second argument, the Cold War theory, could not be rightfully detached from Stalin's and Khrushchev's contributions to the very existence of this state of affairs. From the standpoint of tactics, therefore, this argument was ill-advised.

During the Eisenhower fifties, "when a flagging growth rate and occasional recessions gave some substance to the conventional left-wing critic, the intellectual initiative lay with those whose chief point was that within the West, there were no more fundamental economic problems to be solved." Some critics, like Daniel Bell, argued that the Americans were entering an era of "the end of ideology," meaning in Oglesby's words that "an achieved welfare-state capitalism, equipped with Keynesian control devices, had met all the objections of the nineteenth century and the thirties, and there being apparently no new objections, the matter was closed." Finally, according to Oglesby, the Hoover concept of a coalition of management, labor, and government not only dealt a severe blow to ideological thought but was itself sidetracked by the technological advance.[11]

As a result of this state of domestic tranquility and political inertia, young Americans of the fifties appear to have become what the French called "depoliticized, docile and serene bumpkins." Being "almost purposefully quiet," this Silent Generation appears to have played a passive role, to have melted into the population, either in a grey flannel suit or wearing a beard and a khaki jacket.[12] What these apparently silent young men and their not so silent offshoot, the beatniks, actually had been—a subcult, a nuisance, or an insult to American history—Oglesby leaves to speculation.

Deep in the minds of the young of that era, unspecified misgivings were churning about. The status seekers seem to have been seeking other objectives, too. The hidden persuaders were neither always hidden nor always capable of persuading; the waste makers were successful in more ways than one. The loneliness of the American crowd emerged as an issue, and "by the end of the decade, these themes were so commonplace as to become the property of all points of view—Left, Right, and Center."[13]

Paradoxically, the more secure the American intellectual became in a material sense, the more threatened he felt psychologically. For him, living as he did in an era of "post-scarcity" or the "post-industrial state," reality seemed to be sugar-coated. An ever-increasing number of those employed seemed to the New Leftist to be overpaid, and many of their followers were looking forward to the same happy fate. Class grudges from the past were gradually diminishing, and all the problems of the remaining economically underprivileged were to be settled once and for all by an advanced technocracy that would magically light the way to growth and prosperity. For this reason, a significant segment of American society seemed obsessed during the fifties by the desire to harness technology. It seemed that "there was no more need for ideology."[14] If the answers were not to be found in politics anyway, of what use was ideology?

To many, the making of revolution was in itself a holy cause in which workers were supposed to become involved in order that they never again would be wiped out by economic depression. (Oglesby makes it clear that he means only economic, not spiritual, depression). The term radical signified "either a Dostoevskian fanatic, or someone who believed that capitalism would fail to rationalize the industrial society—either a freak or a bore." At the same time, socialism or communism, because of the unfavorable examples provided by the Eastern empires, the U.S.S.R., and China, represented neither more nor less than "an extravagant horror produced by killer utopians."[15]

However, symptoms of the malady were to be seen on all sides. "Everybody knew it; something was wrong." The vertical line of technological breakthrough, to paraphrase Arthur Koestler, was accompanied by a slowly declining horizontal line of spiritual and intellectual progress. Despite promises that in the near future not only he himself but his neighbor as well would have five chickens in the pot, the politically elevated American felt insecure. There was a "big gap between what the world looked like and what it felt like," and "a soft, deft pessimism" became the main philosophical attitude of many a leading novelist or poet.

Oglesby credits the contributions of such widely read modern authors as J. D. Salinger, Philip Roth, John Updike, Saul Bellow, Robert Lowell and Theodore Roethke with developing a remarkably cogent point of view, "a set of implicit judgments amounting to an informal canon of the modern sensibility." He says that the inner experience is all-important, and that neurosis which is a very common condition, can be elevated "to a certain eerie grace."[16] The panacea society could offer to this disturbed intellectual, a going economy and a modernized version of *panem et circenses* in the political arena, was far from sufficient to redirect his inner misgivings or arrest the malady whose deepening seemed for the time being "beyond all known therapies."

From the communist hard liners, who were already anesthetized by their ideology, the weary American intellectual of the fifties could expect very little. Naturally, the hard liners insisted that solutions for all personal crises be sought in the examples of Russia and China. Since all such solutions, however, led essentially to the mass production of depersonalized, emasculated human beings, the hard liner's advice was likely to fall on deaf ears. After all, the tired, disillusioned American had already lived through this experience in his own country, and was likely to regard the hard liner as an antiquated, senile ideologue, desperately trying to turn the calendar back to the thirties.

For Oglesby's dissatisfied intellectual, the problem of where to turn would not have appeared so formidable had he not already become an involuntary slave of another national pastime—excessive introspection. Oglesby regarded this exercise as the undefined pleasure that could be drawn from a painstaking analysis of the concealed ins and outs of one's dissatisfaction, a tendency especially strong in a man free from want. What this individual was lacking, in particular, was that specific ability required for a "wild leap of the imagination to see that it was precisely politics that was being put into question," that the first steps toward settlement of the disaffection of the intellectual could be implemented only in and through politics.[17]

It was at this time that S. Wright Mills came into prominence by initiating the process of "[putting] political pieces together in a political way." in his book *The Causes of World War III*, he first attempted to systematize the causes that separate the oppositionists, and then to examine the reasons that prevent these forces from appearing on the political scene as a significant persuasive power.[18] Mills summarizes his own arguments in one sentence: "Drop the liberal rhetoric and the conservative default; they are now parts of one and the same official line; transcend that line.[19] The conservative, in Mills's opinion, accepts the status quo, all the efforts that have been necessary to build it, and views it as something desirable. "In brief, and in the consistent extreme, the conservative is the man who abdicates the willful making of history."[20] The radical—and to some extent the liberal, too—does not abdicate; in principle he sees that "more and more events in our epoch are not matters of fate; they are the results of decisions made and not made by identifiable men who command the new means of decision and power."[21]

Time is on the side of the radicals, Mills believes, because all around us in one form or another, either expressed or implied, there is a general outcry for reform and for overhaul of the status quo. We live in an era of highly organized irresponsibility, prevalent in the East as in the West. In both the East and the West the current concept of responsibility has come to a sorry pass, either drowned in rhetoric or crushed in purges explained away by trumped-up charges.[22]

Many critical remarks on some aspects of modern life put forward by a number of authors, such as Erich Fromm, Herbert Marcuse, Jean-Paul Sartre, and James Baldwin, are as enlightening as they are long overdue. However, the overall political influence of these figures has hardly created a ripple. Cautious and individualistic in outlook as many of them are, they appear to lose sight of the fact that an idea has a chance of succeeding only when followed up by a concrete action.

Of course, their need to air their grievances and unnamed fears is perfectly understandable. Like many others, these authors see on every side, in both the East and the West, a frightening convergence of what Mills calls "the cheerful robot," the technological idiot," the "crackpot realist." All of these types are said to embody a common ethos: "rationality without reason." To this group of writers the lost souls may turn for help in understanding the nature of their own insecurity and their own complaints. Then if this whole collection of gripes and grumblings can be laid open to broad inquiry, a cogent political issue may be formulated.

The driving force capable of transforming the dissatisfaction of millions into a uniform structure, according to Mills, must be sought in new agencies of change. Such force does not reside in the poor, whom he considers "chronically hard to organize" and an easy bite for the mass-consumer society that has, in Oglesby's view, already emasculated everyone else. Nor does Mills, on his part, see much help from the black population. "The odds again seemed to be with the system: over and over it had shown its skills at legalistic maneuver and cooptation; and what could the blacks demand except inclusion, access to the general behive?"[23] Finally, labor, "bureaucratized and politically docile," seems content to forget its prewar militancy; "socialism could find no more indifferent and the Cold War no more ardent a partisan."[24]

The only hope remaining, then, lies in the academic intellectuals, whose ability to solve the impasse Mills alternately believes in and doubts. The postwar record of this political subclass, actually a career group, has been undistinguished at best. Mills accuses them of following the establishment line of equating revolution with Stalinism. And their chief contribution to the radical cause, according to Mills, was an active interest in preserving welfare-state capitalism.[25]

However, this academic trade union has in its favor a number of pluses, too. Its members are trained and to some extent deprovincialized. They are self-assured. Because they enjoy job security, tenure, and seniority, they can allow themselves the luxury of indulging in the constructive use of their leisure time. "Considering themselves to be responsible to the humane criteria of classical liberalism, maybe they could be made to think some second and third thoughts. And then perhaps to make a few small waves,"[26] especially if it can be done with impunity.

For the most part Mills leaves us to wonder what is expected of these intellectuals. Should they challenge a seemingly rational culture? Must they formulate the new *Weltanschauung* or create the new radical forces that will crush the Leviathan wherever it rears its head? Even if we assume that the new agency of change, the academic intellectual, succeeds in helping the man in the street to understand the causes of his misgivings, Mills fails to spell out what should be this intellectual's next step: should he write a letter, sign a petition, join a committee, organize an insurrection, or merely continue to protest and "die happily ever after?"

This same elaborate uncertainty as to the driving force for bringing about social change characterizes the writings of Herbert Marcuse,[27] "a major source of the New Left's conceptualization, of its world and its tasks."[28] Marcuse insists upon a critical look at the technological society and its development. He uses such descriptive terms as "the increasing irrationality of the whole," "waste and restriction of productivity," "the need for aggressive expansion," "dehumanization." We seem to be conquered by the System, which assimilates minds and facts, thoughts with required behavior, and natural aspiration of an individual with automaton-like reality. The maneuvering space of this individual, his private realm, is shrinking at an alarming rate; and even the smallest action seems to be regulated and subjected to the depersonalized power and efficiency of the System. Who is the real master of this modern slave, the technocracy or technology? The many types of propaganda and manipulation he is exposed to? His own inability to know facts and evaluate alternatives? Or some combination of all these factors? The answer is less significant to him than is the way out. As seen by Marcuse, the exit is "the planned utilization of resources for the satisfaction of vital needs with a minimum of toil; the transformation of leisure into free time; the pacification of the struggle for existence."[29]

In this "world of mute objects without a subject," the question of who is to assume the burden of seeing this historical alternative through remains unsolved. Dialectic theory, even though not disputed, is surely not the answer. "It cannot be positive," argues Marcuse, because "it defines the historical possibilities, even necessities; but their realization can only be in the practice which responds to theory, and, at present, the practice gives no such response." What is certain is that the struggle for the solution to the contemporary dead end has outgrown the traditional forms of rendering known means of protest ineffective. What we are asked to call "the people" may contribute little toward this end, for they have "moved up" and have become the ferment of social cohesion.

In Marcuse's opinion, the greatest hope rests with the substratum of "the outcasts and outsiders, the exploited and persecuted of other races and other colors, the unemployed, and the unemployable.[30] Outside the democratic process they do not need to fabricate or import a cause, since they already have one. Bitter and mobile, they constitute an elementary force which the System either cannot absorb or relates itself to by using conventional means of maneuver and cooptation. Deprived of the most elementary civil rights, they are harassed and persecuted in all their goings and comings. And when finally they are no longer willing to play the game, the beginning of the end has approached.[31]

However, "nothing indicates that it will be a good end."

The still viable establishment may find sufficient strength to adjust or to make concessions to the underdogs. Its law enforcement arm is well trained and equipped to take care of emergency situations. But the specter remains, inside and beyond the frontier of the advanced societies. "The facile historical parallel with the barbarians threatening the empire of civilization prejudges the issue; the second period of barbarianism may well be the continued empire of civilization itself." At this yet distant point, "the critical theory of society possesses no concept which could bridge the gap between the present and its future; holding no promise and showing no success, it remains negative."[32]

What sort of revolutionary ferment could be brewed by these outcasts and outsiders? Are they a specter haunting society in order to devour it or to join it? These questions both Marcuse and Mills leave to the future. The exploited and the persecuted, the unemployed and the unemployable, may continue endlessly to harass and undermine the system, especially if it remains deaf to their demands. A sub-stratum, who may transform themselves from revolutionaries into a conventional political opposition, may be less militant and slower to act under pressure. These elements bicker, protest, and become participants in criticizing the system, a pastime that has already become fashionable.

The ranks are still further swelled by segments of the student body, with their extravagant hopes and bitter disappointments, who "want more and want it now;" by individualists who reject the process of surrender to mediocrity that is prevalent in all spheres of life; by apostles of various causes sternly disapproving of almost everything and everybody; by disillusioned radicals, by left-leaning liberals, and by others tired of their role as "the court opposition;" and finally, by a large segment of youth with boundless energy it does not know how to invest and welcoming any movement that promises relief from monotony. Taken together, all these actors—the underfed and the sated, the dreamers and the pragmatists, zealous students and disappointed veteran radicals from the old guard, the restless, the rootless, and the apathetic individualists and the conscience-stricken mediocre—constitute that orchestra of dissonances that is expected to make of society a harmonious ensemble.

## Cadres and Issues

More specifically we find among the adherents of the New Left dedicated militants ready for sacrifice; mature, deliberate agitators; and those who on the Berkeley campus are called "thrill seekers," "queer apostles," "fair-weather revolutionaries," or "Little League guerrillas." To these we may add, in the jargon of the Sorbonne, confirmed againsters, revolutionaries on a diet, or mama's little class fighters. Some consider a showdown with the regime a serious business, a calling or profession. To others it is a part-time occupation, a youthful hobby, or simply an integral part of campus activities.

In the United States many New Left activists view the system's manager, the federal government, as the prime target. Others take aim at the academic establishment, the military, big business, local and regional political machines, and trade union hierarchies, as well as at establishments based upon race, age group, sex, or profession. Many also try to neutralize adversaries from the old guard of radicals, those "clerks and paid apostles of revolution," who have wasted decades without a significant achievement.[33] The list of the New Leftist's actions increases with the number of his targets.

A "pure peace protester" from Columbia University or from Berkeley may have shied away from all actions not directly connected with the war in Vietnam. If he is only "a petty bourgeois pacifist," he normally refrains from any act of violence, and limits his activities to marches, demonstrations, petitions, and meetings. His politically more enlightened colleague, however, will incorporate the upheaval in

Southeast Asia into the broader struggle against Western imperialism, using it as a pretext to import violence into his home country. If he happens to be a true "forerunner"—a real cadre of the New Left—and, as such, intends to preside over revolutionary changes, he is likely to find one cause as attractive as the next. He may thus fight for such unrelated causes as equal rights of minorities or new laws on drugs and abortion; and against travel restrictions to communist countries, education fees and tuition, or the system of police records that refuses to distinguish a criminal from a political offender.

The list of activities may be expanded almost indefinitely. The dedicated cadre of the New Left may latch onto issues as they present themselves, or may place old issues in a fresh perspective; or he may dream up altogether new ones. He may even uphold a double standard of political morality. He could conceivably ignore such an action as the take-over of Prague by Soviet troops in 1968, or attack the Soviet invasion as another threat to world peace.

In Tokyo, a New Leftist or his ideological brother rises up against "a sterile feudal tradition," against "post-war industrial sharks," for expulsion of the Americans from Okinawa, for freedom of Southeast Asia, and for or against a new policy vis-à-vis China and Russia. In Seoul, students have protested against "the corrupt puppet regime of Syngman Rhee," but they also oppose Russian and Chinese ambitions to colonize South Korea. Turkish students demonstrated against the "Ankara military junta" and against Moscow's efforts to sovietize Turkey. In Paris, during the May Revolution of 1968, New Leftists demanded the overthrow of President de Gaulle. They were lined up against the "medieval century school curriculum" and absenteeism of professors; against the United States and NATO; against Moscow's imperialism and the opportunists and reactionaries assembled around the Communist Party of France; for student power, for student-worker power, and for the "alliance des misérables."

A month later, in June 1968, their colleagues from Belgrade struck out against the "red bourgeoisie," against Tito's oligarchy and his "red Cossacks," against the Croats, and against "Serbian communist quislings;" for better living conditions and for "a little more freedom to bark." The Yugoslav press, which only a few years before had applauded the tactics of Mario Savio at Berkeley, now failed to take note of any resemblance between Savio and his Belgrade counterparts, and attacked "the irresponsible youth that forgot history and the contributions of the elder generations." Students from the University of Prague, in opposing the 1968 Soviet invasion of their country, attacked the "toothlessness of the Dubcek government," the enemies of the Dubcek government, and the "handcuffs of the Warsaw Pact." In opposing a flesh-and-blood foreign intruder, Prague students adopted very much the same policy as had the Africans when confronted with the white colonizer. That is, they suppressed their factional strife to meet the new, more serious threat. The Czech students introduced the technique of "guerrilla without arms," a term used by Milovan Djilas to signify a peculiar blend of passive resistance, not-so-passive resistance, and traditonal communist devious techniques turned to serve anti-Soviet purposes.

In December 1971, nearly 700 students from the University of Zagreb were arrested, processed through summary procedural courts, and fined or sentenced to one or two months in jail for a variety of charges ranging from disturbing the peace, unlawful assembly, and incitement to riot, to "conspiracy to break up the Yugoslav Federal System."[34] Accused by the Yugoslav press as Croat separatists, Trotskyites, revisionists, anti-communists, or "rotten spoiled children of opulent parents," these Croatian students were rebelling against the "hegemeny of Belgrade," against the Croatian communist traitors, against "spiritually senile older generations," for "relevant, meaningful, and purposeful Croatian patriotism."

It may seem puzzling, or perhaps not so puzzling after all,

that the fighting techniques and the recurring slogans of all these diverse and geographically separated groups should somehow have formed a common meeting ground. All of the groups used demonstrations both peaceful and violent; all engaged in open confrontation with the police, mass meetings, and strikes of all sorts; teach-ins, sit-ins, and be-ins; letter campaigns, music, film and cultural festivals; arson, sabotage, and diversionary tactics; assassination of policemen, bombing and take-over of buildings; public heckling of opponents and physical attacks against them. What specific measures were to be adopted in any given instance, whether legal, illegal, or not yet covered by any law, depended on the revolutionary skill of the group's leaders, on the type of stand taken against them by the authorities, on geography, or on happenstance.

Currently the large number of actual or imaginary, ad hoc or permanent, elected or self-appointed leaders of the New Left groups also complicates the picture. Some of them exercise the prerogatives of leadership because their followers consider them natural helmsmen. Others are chosen as team captains by the news and television media. To what extent any of these leaders truly influences activities of the movement or a segment of it, and for how long, it is difficult to determine. Certain militants like Huey Newton and Bobby Seale have come to prominence as a result of their talent for organization and their ability to keep a firm grip on their followers; others, such as Mario Savio or Stokeley Carmichael, because of their charisma and their flair for muckraking; whereas Eldridge Cleaver, Daniel Cohn-Bendit, and Rudi Dutschke are considered natural captains of the movement because of their crusading, populist writings. Then again, some of them, Angela Davis and Tom Hayden to name two, have become known because they are constantly in the news; Jerry Rubin and others like him because of picturesque behavior and an unorthodox vocabulary. Bettina Aptheker reached center stage mainly because of her surname. A majority of the New Left factions, however, are still without recognized leaders, though some among the membership may be considered more equal than others. This last condition holds true particularly at universities in Eastern European countries where notoriety per se, especially in the foreign press, often results in persecution. In these cases we face what Belgrade students label *stado bes ovcara* (sheep without a shepherd), but with a direction nevertheless.

On the theory that strength lies in numbers, many New Leftist groups such as the Young Socialist League, the Students for a Democratic Society, various peace march organizations, or anti-draft movements in the United States can exist only with mass membership. The impact of others, the Yippies for one, is limited. And in some instances a faction "could be put in its entirety under one umbrella." In the case of the Black Panthers, it is *the* member and not *a* member that counts; whereas the Weathermen make a point of closing their doors to the "uninitiated." The New Left anarchists may or may not have a following; to them it matters little. Factions that do count on regular members or forerunners are outnumbered by those whose memberships swell with "trenchant activists" during campaigns organized for a specific objective. The New Left recruiter, when there is one, is constantly faced with a thousand problems. Who supports what leader or what cause? Why are some self-styled activists absent precisely at the moment when they are most needed, and why do they offer their services when the campaign is over? Why is the militancy of some New Leftists so pronounced during some periods, only to fade suddenly for no apparent reason? Who among them is most inclined to "retire politically" and why? What degree of responsibility should the leadership assume for a group's dissolution? These are only a few of the challenges he must deal with every day.

In some cases the recruiter imposes an age requirement for a novice. In other cases, the candidate's past may be taken into consideration, as well as his race, sex, social origin, behavior patterns, friends, professed political sympathies, and not infrequently his personal appearance. There are New

Leftist brotherhoods consisting only of students, while others count on workers, on social outcasts, or on the disaffected. To be recruited in Zagreb the novice must be a Croat, but if a young Croat tries to join the Belgrade militants, he is ordinarily considered an infiltrator. Similarly, the Canadian New Leftist-separatist tends to view his Anglo-Saxon contemporary as an enemy. In additon, in the early stage of the movement anyone over thirty years of age was suspect as a matter of course. Many New Leftists currently believe in this principle but do not apply it rigidly. A majority, particularly in Western European universities, attack in their elders only those traits that make them appear older than their chronological age.

Can we trace a true ideological-political profile of all these groups? Do they, indeed, represent a movement, and are its dimensions regional, national, or international? And if international, what are the specific characteristics or situations that laid the groundwork for the appearance of an international of oppositionists whose leadership for the first time in history is in the hands of youth? Are they reformers, crusaders, new Messiahs, or nothing more than a manifestation of the rebelliousness of youth that the media have glamorized and blown up out of all proportion? To which group should we look for new thoughts on insurrection? Will the New Left turn into something other than it started out to be? If so, for what reasons? Neither the New Leftist authors nor their critics have thus far produced any really satisfactory answers to these questions, nor do the answers appear on the horizon.

Unlike the younger generations of the fifties, who were considered apathetic, inward-looking, lacking in political and social awareness, and motivated toward conventionally defined success in life, the New Leftist is anything but restrained, reflective, or cautious. He is constantly on the move. He is either protesting, demonstrating, rioting, organizing, or participating in a campaign; and his activity may be accidental, incidental, well-thought out, or a cause in itself.

On the other hand, he may "actively withdraw," becoming a "mutant," as we shall see, and attempting to "create his own mankind in miniature."[35] Lacking such an issue as the war in Vietnam, he is prone to spread himself thin. Lurking somewhere within him is a compulsive need for action; and it is this trait that the older generation finds it most difficult to comprehend.

Our New Leftist may seek to cure or to reform society, or he may desire redress for his own grievances first and think of society later. In other words, he may be a "mutant" or a "forerunner;" that is, he may reject "the standardized games people play," in the words of Max Lerner, or he may aim to change or throw out the rule-book. Normally, if his goal is reform, he does not try to overthrow the system—which he doubts he could accomplish in any case. He simply displays his opposition to society by withdrawing. But if he belongs in the second category, he opposes the system actively and attempts to change it either with or without violence.

Some critics define the mutant as "a new irrationalist," a nonparticipant in the past of a nation, a drop-out from history. Leslie Fiedler characterizes this group as completely rejecting any notion of cultural continuity. Not only do they reject the past, but they disavow it, refusing to have any part of it.[36]

Many critics of the New Left tend to identify this mutant with the entire movement. He seems to be not only the safest but the favorite target. Generally they view him as belonging to those egotistical, anti-intellectual, arrogant, and anarchistic forces that reject all apostles of reason from Socrates on;[37] that sabotage all rational processes of government, whether intentionally or not; and that contribute to the creation of a society ungovernable except by force.[38] To their way of thinking the mutants in the West can afford this luxury because they spring from those strata of the population who have only a vague notion of the problems of daily life. They are indulged in their idealistic, anti-establishment whims by parents who want to free their children from material worries, or by an excessively tender welfare state that affords them an endless stream of grants, stipends, and scholarships; food coupons, unemployment checks, and free clinics. Since parents and society make a point of freeing these young people from all constraints or deprivations, they have no reason not to let their individualism run rampant. Moreover, they find it even less attractive to subscribe to the old-fashioned virtues of hard work, thrift, and respectable language, when the opposite course pays such handsome dividends.[39]

These disciples of Jean-Paul Sartre, believing that each man lives in his own world, soon become obsessed with the goal of acting as their own free, independent agents, each a world unto himself. They subscribe also to Erich Fromm's dictum that unless born "a mental or moral idiot," an individual must be forced by society to strive for mental health, for happiness, harmony, love, and productiveness, and for what is fashionably termed self-actualization;[40] and they readily turn this dictum about to read "everyone has the potentials for developing into a mature productive human being." The failure to do so may be laid at the door of society. Since ample proof exists for the expediency of this logic, right and wrong become in the mutant's way of thinking whatever each person feels them to be.

David Greenfield, one of the critics, says that nothing but the self matters, and anything that interferes must go by the wayside. Only to the extent that the outside world affects their own feelings does it have any meaning. They feel entirely free of any obligation toward persons or institutions.[41]

At this point the mutant is accused of acquiring a completely distorted conception of society. In his opinion society is theoretically an unnecessary evil that should be dispensed with, but one that should at the same time be preserved because it serves to guarantee his own life style. These "new irrationalists," Leslie Fiedler points out, can permit themselves to extend adolescence almost indefinitely. No longer do they need school as an excuse for leisure. The work-ethic has become obsolete, as has reason. Thus their attitude negates all regard for what society considers maturity.[42]

The mutant's lack of responsibility toward society is usually correlated by his critics with his oblivious attitude toward himself. Running away from reality in order to free himself from the concerns that have dominated the lives of his elders, this outcast often leaves school, thus, according to his critics, frequently preventing himself from ever becoming socially useful. Such a course is both a crime and an error, they believe, because these are the times of trips to the moon and of heart transplants, "the most scientific of all epochs."

The United States, for instance, is rapidly approaching what Daniel Bell calls the post-industrial society, where professional and technical work is bound to be revered.[43] In this society innovation will increasingly depend "on comprehension of theoretical knowledge." Thus the mutant who abandons the university—the main repository of codified knowledge—places himself irretrievably outside the mainstream of progress. Much less would there be room for him in "the technitronic society" that Zbigniew Brzezinski discusses, in which those with the greatest gifts, the best social talents and training are to govern. In this society the job market will be dominated by services. Here he will encounter, according to Daniel Seligman, "the new prominence of intellectuals, the central role of universities, and the likely extension of scientific modes of decision making."[44] Boundlessly affluent, this future society will afford every member an opportunity "to relax and enjoy it," and nobody will be under any pressure to do anything he does not choose to do.

Though it is quite impossible at this stage to know what the morrow may demand of its youth in the way of school qualifications and general skills, it is all too evident that the future cannot tolerate a withdrawal from today's world. Leaving school, joining a commune, wandering about aimlessly, or indulging in drugs or free love, will lead inexorably, according to the critics, to premature aging and to mental and spiritual senility. Therefore, no matter how strong his urge to be different, to once and forever break the vicious chain of sameness, he cannot help but resemble all other mutants. He reads the same poetry and literature, listens to the same music, cultivates identical jargon, and believes in the same principles. If this life style is allowed to persist, he slowly but surely loses all his individuality, becoming in the end just another automaton in the mass of depersonalized human beings in the name of whose liberation his rebellion began. Moreover, the young self-exile stubbornly refuses to note that he is in the minority.

The authors of a collection of essays on the New Left, *Youth in Turmoil*, maintain that something like 60 percent of about eight million Americans who in 1968 were enrolled at universities are already on good terms with their elders.[45] They are said to pursue "fairly conventional career objectives; i.e., they are mainly interested in college for the boost it will give to their earning potential and social status." The remaining 40 percent—something over three million young people under twenty-four years of age—take the earning and the status for granted, but nevertheless "hold attitudes about national performance and purpose, business, and many other matters that are quite at variance with those held by the college majority and by most adults." Not unexpectedly, the mutant is in the minority even in this last-mentioned group.

However, in these gloomy and oversimplified generalizations, many critics of the New Left intimate that the outcry of the mutants may be authentic and valid in its central message. In this respect, their comments follow the same line of reasoning as those of defenders of the New Left. These critics recognize that this rebellious young person protests against reality in the wrong manner; he calls for a showdown at the wrong time and place or for the wrong reason, and his methods are even worse. He is impatient, arrogant, calloused, and unruly—all characteristics not uncommon in the young. His demands for reform, rarely intelligent or intelligible, are burdened with exaggerations and naïveté, with the conviction that highly complex problems may be solved by simple means if the right people are in the right place. But the crux of the tragedy lies not so much in the fact that many of his demands may be impractical or irrational, but rather in the fact that there is no one to answer them. Even if he tries to change the order of things or to be heard, he is often ignored or shown the door. Thus his only recourse is discourteous behavior or violation of the law or complete withdrawal.

The sudden flexibility on the part of the mutant's critics appears for the most part when they come to analyze the list of his grievances. Only then do they find themselves forced to notice that some of the causes of the mutant's rebelliousness reflect the tiredness and disillusionment of society at large. Young and militant, he is only expressing openly what everyone else is thinking but keeping silent about. These gnawing suspicions that some dissidents may be speaking not only in their own names but in the name of society has moved some Western politicians and sociologists to examine the complaints with a more open mind. Toward the end of the sixties such efforts led toward a better understanding of the causes of the frustrations and disillusionment, and to a correspondingly clearer picture of the conditions under which the dissident felt impelled to use violence as a weapon.

At this time it has become fashionable to take the position that young dissidents are the product of a given society, reared in an environment for whose qualities and shortcomings they bear no responsibility. Their general behavior reflects to a considerable extent all the influences to which they have been exposed since birth: the family, religion, community, education, and the social system. In one capacity or another, for good or for evil they will leave their mark on the social fabric. Whatever their future holds, we can surely not write them off today nor limit our criticism of them exclusively to their unorthodox life style. Agreed, their sense of tactics leaves something to be desired; and their strategy is not credible because it often fails to articulate the desired goals and the methods for achieving them.

Such shortcomings, however, are by no means the exclusive sins of the young. In fact, many of the older generation, too, seem disaffected with the isolation and with what they consider the privation of their own lives, and with the apparent disregard on the part of many political leaders of traditional values. In the East, many oppose the mechanization of life, the denial of rights, and a future that promises more of the same. Since the young person tends to express this general anxiety in a more demonstrative manner, today's dissident should perhaps be considered only the most militant and the most outspoken representative of what is "eating at all of us." In fact, in the view of a growing number of analysts of the New Left, a young dissident is peculiarly fitted for this role because of his age and the special status he enjoys in the world of today.[46]

In support of this position, the University of California, Berkeley, may be taken as one listening post. The familiar complaint of students there—and we include in this number many who may be termed politically inactive—relates to their strong feeling of alienation. "We seem to be members of an unneeded generation;" "already it seems there are far too many of us;" "nobody knows what to do with us, and in the future there will be more of us;" "if it would be possible to dump in the ocean half of the world's youth of today, except for parents, friends, and girl friends, society would hardly miss us." Unfortunately, some of the same thoughts might be voiced by the older generation; many of them are not so indispensable either. "When I graduate," insisted one student, "I will resemble a part from the Ford assembly line, interchangeable, and almost identical to millions."

Many a student sees the university system as the prime culprit in delaying the recognition of his adult status. This is a normal reaction because college represents his first concrete experience with the establishment as a young adult. Here, under the influence of older students, he often begins to equate the educational system with an enormous baby-sitting service that society has devised to corral those between the ages of eighteen and the middle twenties, too old to be treated as children and too young to compete in the labor market. As evidence shows,[47] a number of students accept this exaggeration as a fact, and on the strength of it level their antagonism against universities as a whole. Their animosity, divided initially between administration and faculty, is finally directed against society at large and its official spokesman, the government.

In the essay we have mentioned, "A Special Kind of Rebellion," Seligman says that during the 1968-69 academic year there were nearly 6,7000,000 full-time college students in this country, twice as many as a decade before.[48] At Brandeis University in Massachussetts, for instance, the total number swelled from 1,300 to 2,800, and at the Milwaukee campus of the University of Wisconsin it increased from 5,000 to 12,000. A similar process was registered in other American universities. Because this unprecedented influx exceeded the capacities of the U.S. schools, many school administrations were forced to reorder their priorities almost overnight. Among the first problems that had to be solved were raising new funds for the construction of buildings and for expanded laboratory and other facilities and finding personnel. At that time local revenue sources and donations and endowments proved inadequate to cover the increasing needs, and in many cases they threatened to dry up because of student riots and adverse publicity. It became clear, then, that without the help of the federal or state governments or of foundations, the mass university could not carry on. At this juncture, when both the nature of American institutions of higher education and the relationship between students and school authorities changed, many New Leftist speakers and writers rose to prominence by criticizing the changes.

School authorities now plunged into a quest for finances, a process with which the average college student is completely unfamiliar and in which he usually has little interest. This scramble for funds brought school administrators into the limelight, and in time conferred on them a degree of power

far beyond that of their previous status. Distributing resources and controlling expenditures, they unavoidably com-
menced to exercise an effective control over the educational
process. They determined the number of students to be
admitted, the openings for teaching positions, the amounts to
be spent for books and laboratories, and for buildings,
stadiums, and restaurants. Since a majority of them were not
educators by profession, many of them were charged by
students with understanding only the value of real estate and
concrete. The whole process had in fact begun much earlier,
sometime in the middle fifties. But because students at that
time were fewer in number and less vocal on the whole,
critics have said that administrators were subjected to few
restraints. They are accused of tending to become self-
serving and of losing sight of the primary function of the
university: to serve the students. Students at Berkeley have
been heard to say in jest, "If it were not for the students, our
campus would be a very happy place for all the employees."

On the campus, a student is constantly exposed to new
and impressive construction projects: buildings of every
description, restaurants and dormitories and stores, magnificent fountains and beautiful landscaping. At the same time,
he hears the constant complaint about a lack of money. He
may be sitting in his $150 chair in the spacious new library,
built by the foremost architectural firms and incorporating
the most sophisticated electronic gadgetry; but all too often
he is told at the desk that the books and publications he
needs have not been ordered because of a financial crisis. In
the classroom, he may have access to movie projectors,
television sets, and padded chairs, but not enough instructors
to give him the individual attention he longs for. From these
glaring inconsistencies springs his antagonism toward real
estate, and it is easy to guess the origin of the sentiment
commonly expressed on American campuses that concrete is
more important than the student. In the same way that the
fifteenth-century English worker discussed by Marx, who,
having lost his job to a machine tried to demolish the

machines, many an American student, when sufficiently inflamed by an eloquent agitator, may give vent to his frustration by lashing out blindly at the concrete he believes comes between him and the education to which he feels entitled.

To make matters worse, school administrations have been forced to capitulate to our "world of paper" by increasing reliance on computers. The entire personality of a student, his profile, his school performance, his dreams and ambitions have been reduced to holes in the punch card; and in spite of the extent to which the computer may have simplified administrative operations and eliminated the unnecessary, the contemporary student has begun to feel that he is merely a "student unit" (a dubious term that entered administrative jargon in the early sixties). This has created a peculiar type of tension among the students that remains unrelieved to the present day. "If I am only a dead statistical unit that any machine may shuffle at the press of a button anyway, it does not make any difference what I do," became the complaint at Berkeley during the Free Speech Movement in 1964. Some of the students raised these other questions, too: Since the bureaucracy generates its own logic, one which does not reflect the sum of the individual logics involved, if I rebel against its excesses, who am I erring against? All school activities are based on committee work, a system geared to relieve any particular person from responsibility. Is it not then natural for students to organize their own opposing committee system? Or, no boat caught by a typhoon can be steered by a committee. Is it any wonder that the school administration is so toothless when we make a hurricane on the campus?

On a few American campuses open confrontation with professors is often added to clashes with the administration. This tendency is most prevalent among the students from middle class families where the children have been sheltered. A product of the television generation, the student from such a background approaches a book only when he is forced to.

He is said to be industrious and conscientious mainly when unimportant projects are involved.

Many critics insist that the typical American college student is the product of a grammer school system that puts the main emphasis on the question of how he gets along with other children, and that he has coasted through high school with a minimum of effort. Excessive permissiveness at home and the two institutions of their formative years are held responsible for the intellectual damage that handicaps many college freshmen. Once they have been programmed to learn a little about everything, they are naturally not anxious to disturb the harmony of their conclusions with facts. For instance, they can discuss for hours on end the peculiarities of the status of Eldridge Cleaver's life in Algeria without having the faintest notion of where Algeria is. Or, they may come up with a number of highly intriguing thoughts about the war in Southeast Asia while believing that Vietnam and Indochina are two separate states. Exposed early to no-holds-barred discussions about family life, career, and the "rat race," drugs, sex, and the pressure-ridden society, many of these young people soon become accomplished debaters, intolerant and discourteous toward opponents or impatient with evidence that they cannot refute. It often seems that the more limited their knowledge the more they are inclined to seek solutions for all problems in the counterculture, the new consciousness, the new utopia, the alternate society, or the green revolution. In any event, faced suddenly by extensive requirements that professors put before him, our young expert at making excuses and dilly-dallying is provided with a heaven-sent opportunity to declare war on the college educator.

The law of social conformity, usually strong in the American culture, apparently has no effect in his case, for our student is not impelled to follow the example of his serious-minded colleague. Rather he tends to classify him as the "young-old man," the "pitiful square," the "decent joker," that society mocks. In a sense, he derives a measure of support from society itself, which is so preoccupied with vocal dissenters that it manages to reserve only minimal attention for the silent one. Then, too, the news and television media thrive on the unusual or extraordinary.[49] The broken window of a squad car or the injured skull of a policeman is far more likely to give our student front-page coverage than academic distinction or high grades.

Finally, and to a much greater extent than is usually thought, the bright, pragmatic American student is aware of the many uncertainties about the direction of social life and shares with the greater portion of modern-day society the fears of the unknown. He is forced in one way or another to witness parents afraid of their children, officers distrustful of their men, congressmen and senators suspicious of the electorate, the majority afraid of the minority, the minority afraid of the majority, professors alienated from students. If he lodges a protest against the professor-student relationship, he believes he is only doing what society expects of him. If, in addition, an instructor supplies him with a ready excuse for protest on the grounds of absenteeism, of unintelligible jargon, political unawareness, obsolete teaching technique, or what the French students call *l'idiotisme doctoral*, our student has all the ammunition he needs for a knock-down-drag-out clash.

The American student's French counterpart meets a completely different set of problems, at least as regards pre-university education. In order to matriculate after high school and to become a candidate for a baccalaureate, the French high school student is expected to display a degree of seriousness that French society, according to the critics whose work we are discussing, rarely requires of an adult. At an early age, the French student begins the study of foreign languages. He must perform acceptably in a number of subjects "from gymnastics to philosophy," or as has been said in jest, he must "study chemistry and philosophy as though intending to become either Madmae Curie or the Cardinal."

It is fair to say that the entire high school system in the United States permits the young person to do a certain amount of coasting, his French counterpart may and often does view this period as one of endless mental torture. When he finally does graduate from high school and enters such an institution as the Sorbonne, the curriculum he finds there corresponds more or less to programs of all other big universities, and he has a sense of being liberated. The freshman in Paris finds the atomosphere stimulating. If he becomes politically active, he is only following tradition and fulfilling his own need. The French student, more politically minded in general than the average American, joins one or more of the existing student groups as a matter of course, and immediately sets about seeking the reforms in the school system and in society that he has dreamed about as a high school student.

Whereas some students in the United States, as we have indicated, clash with the school over grievances that a rapidly changing society has not caught up with, the clash in France results from long-overdue reforms. The story in Eastern universities is somewhat different. Here the student is likely to attack first the political system as such, and then the school, which he regards as a product of that system. From the point of view of the system, it is this student who constitutes a real danger. Unlike his American and French counterparts, he has much less to lose. He is impatient. It is not only that he does not want to wait for reform but that in view of economic, administrative, and political pressure exerted upon him he cannot wait. As the Proclamation of the University Council of the Alliance of Students of Belgrade of 1971 points out, "Waiting is not our alternative. No one should grant us the future. What we went is to change the present, and now."[50] Moreover, as the hard liners assure us, the majority of Eastern students seem to possess all the requisite traits for becoming the "outstanding yeast of insurrection." Their grievances are real, not imagined. For years they have been hearing from their Marxist professors

about the imperative of the organization in initiating upheaval, about the specific program, about the tactics and
strategy of rebels. Above all, they are not dealing with a
pluralistic society that leans toward accommodation and
concessions; rather they face an uncompromising, well-oiled
system bent on crushing any opposition.

If the foregoing generalized summary of the political
attitudes and life style of certain segments of the student
body appears expansive, it is only because of our purpose to
depict the capacity of the modern-day student to generate an
atmosphere of dissent. At a mass university, the young man
or woman is given the opportunity to evaluate and compare
his own grievances with those of his peers. He soon discovers
that the frustration and misgivings he feels are not his
monopoly because many of his contemporaries are similarly
disturbed. In the West the cause may lie in the emptiness of
the family life-style and in uncertainty as to the future; and
in the East, in the regimentation of thought and all aspects of
life. In the company of students who share the same
problems, his own private anxieties, joined with the concerns
of others, become transformed into a broader antagonism
toward society. This built-up, highly charged antagonism is
fortified during sporadic protests against unpopular decisions
of school administrations. And since these administrative
bodies cannot forever be separated from society as a whole,
the protests are ultimately directed against the status quo
itself. At this point, the formerly isolated disaffected youth
becomes a political oppositionist to the system, usually with
no precise goal.

The real politicization of the young dissident occurs
ordinarily under the tutelage of experienced hard liner and
other leftist militants who provide him with both the issues
and the means of struggle. In most cases the whole process is
conducted with such subtlety as to be almost imperceptible.
For instance, a student enrolled at Berkeley in 1964 who
attended the first rallies of the Free Speech Movement[51]

might readily have been in complete sympathy with the arguments of the speakers. Employing familiar jargon and time-worn arguments, they seemed to be attacking the very weaknesses in the social and political fabric that were disturbing him. Up to this point he could say they were speaking in his name.

However, as the leaders of the movement proceeded to introduce new issues, the activity of our novice protester took on a new dimension. He was told that the present stage of development of American society, the University of California, like all other institutions of higher learning, functioned only as a link in the chain with which the Johnson administration choked a young person and made a "soap opera out of his school experience." He was also given to understand that his prime target should not be the school administration per se, but the Federal government, because, as many speakers insisted, the university was only the field representative of the central authority.

This switch from one culprit to another the leaders of the movement executed with deftness and imagination. Toward the end of 1964, an endless supply of leaflets, pamphlets, and monographs became available. All aimed at convincing the student that he must gradually expand the base of his protest and pointed a finger at the real culprit, the political system of the land. Most of these publications pointed out that the importance of the lesser culprits—family, school administration, professors—should not be overestimated. If, for example, the school administrators seemed impervious to their demands, this was only a reflection of a much broader heartlessness on the part of the Washington rulers, as well as of the apathy of a general public that allowed itself to be manipulated at will. Again, if the computer at Berkeley shuffled a student about as an impersonal statistical unit, this too was merely a repetition of the accepted practices of the rulers to view the individual as a lifeless political marionette.

All along, in the same vein, he was told to devote but a minor portion of his energies to confrontation with the school establishment; the remainder was to be reserved for striking against the central establishment, Washington. Later on, sometime during the first quarter of 1965, another set of guidelines for protest began to circulate. The pamphlets and the speakers now insisted that years of endless labor on behalf of the general electorate would be required to alter a majority of the laws we live under; youth would therefore be better off to forget them altogether and try to pull down the whole structure. This could only mean open confrontation with society.

Meanwhile, the war in Vietnam emerged as a leading issue. If our dissident harbored any previous misgivings as to the rationale of open confrontation with the system, opposition toward the escalation of the war in Vietnam helped him to dispel any doubts he might have entertained about the Free Speech Movement. In cirticizing the policy of Washington in southeast Asia, the speakers were, in his opinion, giving expression to the general hatred of war and violence and to the traditional fairness of American youth, who have always been prone to side with David against Goliath.

He had solid backing for his position from many quarters: from politicians, congressmen and senators, men of the cloth, businessmen and professors who disagreed with Johnson's Asia policy. These public figures, adult and often highly respected, argued that the war in Vietnam was being waged at the wrong place, at the wrong time, and without long-term goals; further, that it indicated either political incompetence on the part of the administration or the arrogance of a superpower oblivious to the immense sufferings of the Vietnamese civilian population. To the aroused student it appeared that the dissident segment of American public opinion expressed the same objections toward Washington as did the hard-core militant from Berkeley.

In addition, the media were giving full-scale coverage to this growing body of criticism from members of the establishment, a process that was most welcome to the young protesters and made their position even stronger. Almost daily, every aspect of anti-war demonstrations claimed a significant amount of time on the air. The press gave detailed accounts of similar anti-war activities on other campuses and of the solid support of students from foreign universities for the position of their Berkeley colleagues. Besides, the Berkeley dissident could not help but observe that statements of leading protesters rated headlines and front-page coverage that elicited comments and reactions from government officials. Not burdened with very much knowledge of the ideological background of the war in southeast Asia, this young man could easily conclude, first, that the anti-war demonstrations were perhaps more important than the war itself, and second, that in spite of what could be objected to in the tactical excesses of protesters, they were forcing the Johnson administration to listen to the voice of the people in foreign policy matters. According to Jean-François Revel,[52] this participation of the college activist made a significant improvement in the democratic process, for it clearly raised the question of whether war was too important an affair to be left to Congress or the president alone.

Still another consideration seems to have entered the mind of the college activist. The more serious his chances of being drafted, the more urgency he felt to join first the anti-war movement and then the anti-draft movement. Though an outside speaker might have approached the subject from an academic standpoint, that is, opposing the war as a matter of youthful idealism and rejection of violence in any form, to the young dissident the possibility of being drafted and sent to Vietnam was a matter of his own skin. And since, in the final analysis, all draft notices were coming from Washington, the last barrier that prevented him from participating actively in the movement was removed.

About this time, however, early in 1966, the Free Speech Movement began to lose its appeal. To continue in full swing it needed new issues. Some leaders of the movement felt that the highly charged atmosphere existing over the Vietnam issue and the draft could be counted on to attract new followers. Sincere anti-war feelings of new members could readily be transformed into political opposition to the system responsible for the war. At the same time, those who could feel the draft-board breathing down their necks were good candidates to become full-fledged activists. Thus, the movement could expand and continue to flourish, even if under a different name. As it turned out, however, this was wishful thinking, partly because opposition to the war ceased to be the exclusive domain of the leftists and partly because the youthful war protesters themselves proved to be too diversified in interest and background to be welded into a homogeneous organization.

During the second half of the decade an increasing body of American public opinion was being directed against the Vietnam war. People in every walk of life were challenging the administration's conduct of a war we did not want to win and dared not lose. One segment of opinion criticized Washington for having involved us in the first place, another for carrying on the action in a half-hearted manner. The public search for a key issue led to an ever more critical study of such matters as problems of minorities other than the blacks, the decline of the U.S. image abroad, the unbalanced budget, and the situation in the military forces and in the State Department. Besides, it was pointed out, the Johnson administration had itself attempted on several occasions to extricate us from Vietnam; and all manner of organizations, as well as many congressmen and senators, were insisting on ending the war as quickly as possible. Though the young protesters had undoubtedly been responsible for awakening the American public to the situation in Vietnam, they were no longer the only advocates of withdrawal from Asia. Now their voices would be heard above the din only when the bombing of Hanoi was resumed or when the action spread to Laos and Cambodia.

Deprived of his monopoly over the war issue, the young militant was hard pressed for a new exclusive issue. His need became all the more immediate inasmuch as he had found by this time that the system was far more malleable than he had been led to believe. In many instances, for example, school administrators were beginning to think seriously about abandoning some antiquated rules and educators were taking a hard look at curricula. Various loans and grants, medical aid, and other forms of assistance were made available. Anti-discrimination sentiments became so fashionable on campuses from one end of the country to the other that it was not long before they were reflected in official university policy. Though many former student grievances still remained unresolved, the student did consider himself for the first time a political force to be reckoned with.

This new awareness was particularly evident when the voting-age was reduced to eighteen. The prime enemy of youth, the Establishment, had unexpectedly armed its adversary! This sudden flexibility of the system caught the New Left cadres by surprise. Was it not contrary to all their teachings for a foe to arm its rivals? Many of these militant cadres, geared not to build but to destroy, were completely at sea as to how to use this new political weapon. Their advice to the young remained virtually unchanged: tear down the structure and build anew. But they supplied no blueprint. The young were to rely on the old time-tested weapons: riots, protests, and outright refusal to believe that the evils of society could be cured by any means other than violence. Since the college activist could profit very little from such advice, and since the cadres persisted in following this course, the principal adherents of the movement found themselves paying tribute to the *Zeitgeist* they had formerly ignored, a sin with which they had charged the Establishment only a short time before.

In their contacts with students who enrolled at the university in the beginning of the seventies, many New Left cadres in the United States were guilty of two other tactical errors. Accustomed to being the spokesmen of youth, they often overlooked some facts of life. Whereas in 1964 the typical cadre was in his middle twenties, the same man was now entering his thirties. To a contemporary freshman, he was just another middle-aged man whose jargon and arguments were not always "with it." The same reasons that caused a middle-aged hard liner to lose status in the eyes of the 1964 participant in the Free Speech Movement made the middle-aged revolutionary from the early sixties sound like a rebel of bygone days. Many of these old-young activists failed to realize that by advising the young not to trust anyone over thirty they were cutting themselves out of the action.

A majority of these militants failed also to give sufficient consideration to problems of leadership and of organization. On the Berkeley and Columbia campuses, for instance, a typical faction was usually composed of one or more spokesmen and of an indeterminate number of followers. Rarely was there a long-term program. More often than not a spontaneous protest on a specific issue furnished the excuse for the members to assemble. To determine the actual strength of such a faction was difficult, since its ranks swelled in times of open confrontation, only to dwindle once the heat of the movement had passed. As a rule, discipline among the members was lax. As part of a broader movement that had itself arisen against the senselessness of the hierarchy, hard-core cadres made it a point to exert a minimum degree of pressure upon their less inspired followers. Fully aware of the precariousness of the times, the cadres apparently feared that if they demanded too much of the young activist, his loyalty to the cause might prove as tenuous as had his devotion to the Establishment.

That small number of cadres who rose to prominence owed their success primarily to the media. In the United States, with its penchant for glamorizing stars and celebrities, the first duty of a newsman covering the New Leftists was to single out the leader. Thus was the eager reporter provided with names, personalities, statements, and pictures, and thus was he spared the pains of delving into the intricacies of the movement and burdening himself with too many facts. Sometimes the leader was picked from among the most vocal of the militants; or sometimes he just happened to be the person closest to the microphone or the camera. On the other hand, he may have chanced to appear on the rostrum on several succeeding days; or he may have read petitions and the final announcements of the meeting. A few, such as Savio in Berkeley or Dutschke in Paris, were singled out because of a demonstrated ability to convey to their audience that they were a step ahead of events.

Regardless of how they attained their leadership roles, they were at best helmsmen of factions or of spontaneous campaigns, and could hardly be considered leaders of the movement as a whole. Once the campaign was over, they usually faded into obscurity, in much the same manner as did Mario Savio after the end of the Free Speech campaign or Rudi Dutschke after the May Revolution of 1968. Whenever new issues appeared, leadership was assumed by fresh leaders or by a group of them. The supply of leaders seemed inexhaustible. So fragmented did the New Left movement become that it left many a prospective follower dizzy on the merry-go-round of leaders, factions, and sub-factions. Once proclaimed as a movement that would be all things to all people, those factions that remained toward the end of the sixties became the last refuge for hard-core militants who had earlier chosen the movement as a substitute for a career. As matters stand today, they have passed through all the wanderings, fermentation, and factional strife that character-ized the movement during the previous decade and remain the final product of all the sifting of cadres.[53]

### Tactics of Confrontation

We arrive finally at the consideration of a small remnant of the New Left movement who were capable of formulating a theory bearing some semblance of insurrectionary technique and specific methods of struggle applicable to the revolution-ary clash with the system. After the first clashes with the police on the Berkeley campus in 1964, activists of the Free Speech Movement observed two puzzling aspects of law enforcement practices. The first concerned the fact that the police, even when forewarned of the possibility of a violation of the law, were powerless to act until after the fact; and the second, that the police were notably lacking in experience in dealing with a mass political violation. The first condition, of course, appears essential in a society based on law, and seems not unreasonable in the case of a conventionally defined crime. It affords protection from punishment to a possible violator for a misdeed he may have contemplated but has not committed. However, when a political violation of the law or an illegal demonstration or protest does occur, the police reaction is even more delayed.

It was precisely upon this delayed reaction that the activist counted. The police usually arrived on the scene after the demonstrators had already assembled, had distributed leaflets, and had made speeches; i.e., after the purpose of the meeting had for the most part been accomplished. The police would ask the demonstrators to disperse quietly, promising not to interfere, a request that might or might not be complied with. Even if they did disperse, the demonstrators had by this time proved their point that in today's society one might violate the law with impunity even in the presence of the police. If the crowd refused to disperse, it might gain other advantages, as we shall demonstrate.

On the Berkeley campus the early participants in the Free Speech Movement counted on uncertainty and deep confusion in the mind of a law-enforcement officer dispatched to the scene to restore order. This policeman would find himself suddenly confronted with a mass of hundreds or thousands of shouting, protesting young people, each of whom in his eyes could be charged with unlawful assembly and disturbance of the peace. If the man in the street had been in question, the officer would have known what to do with him; he would have warned the violator or taken him into custody. In the same manner, he would have handled a small group that was unlawfully assembled or disturbing the peace. He would have requested help from headquarters, and would have asked the crowd to disperse or have taken them to the station.

On the campus, however, the police officer was confronted with much too large a number of violators to be handled through ordinary procedures. Besides, these were political demonstrators who were exercising their right to express their opinions or beliefs freely and without reserve. A segment of society that is traditionally indulgent toward the student, many a police officer felt it wiser to act with more care in this situation. As he saw it, they were all young–too young, probably, to be familiar with the complicated procedure for securing permits for assemblies. Why should he discriminate against the protester of 1964 and have him charged with an offense when students of earlier years had carried on with impunity? This was a reasonable question and one that many demonstrators counted on a law enforcer to ask himself.

Whether this profile of the policeman invited by the school administration in 1964 to restore law and order was accurate seems less important than the fact the police in their first attempt to suppress the Free Speech Movement were characteristically uncertain of how to act. Unless the officer were possessed of an extraordinary degree of political acumen, he could hardly have seen any reason for suddenly treating these protesters any differently from those of past years.

Whatever the case, two opposing forces, the police and the students found themselves face to face during the demonstrations on the Berkeley campus. Not unexpectedly, the very presence of the police added fuel to the fire. Many students joined the demonstrations even without knowing or caring what they were all about. The number of police remained fairly constant, with replacements coming in shifts, while the ranks of the demonstrators steadily swelled. The law enforcers had the advantage in arms, the students in number. As experience has shown, only a spark is needed in such a highly charged atmosphere to ignite a mighty conflagration. Sometimes an inappropirate word, an insult or curse, the wrongly interpreted move of a student, or a rock or pop bottle flying in the direction of the police line was all it took. The more loosely the meeting was organized, the more likely were such incidents to occur.

To make matters worse, between the milling students and the police, as well as within either group, there were many newsmen and cameramen, each wanting to be where he thought the action was. All were running from place to place following the commotion, and sometimes by their very presence creating the feeling that an outburst was imminent. Hence many a protester with a flair for the dramatic, feeling himself the predestined hero of the story, made his move.

Philip Luce, a former member of the Progressive Labor Party, describes such a confrontation at Columbia University. He says that to set the stage for violence, people must be manipulated into a situation where they are in open conflict with a recognized authority. The first step is to enlist supporters by the raising of false issues. This is followed by a list of demands that cannot or will not be met. And finally, it is charged that the student has been disregarded, and the only recourse is peaceful, though extralegal, steps.[54]

As for the falseness of issues, Luce may be overstating the case. Many of the students' demands may clearly be said to have had merit. However, he is eminently correct in judging that the presence of the police on the campus is exactly what the New Leftist militant most desires, especially if the demonstration in which he is participating has not been organized. "Suddenly, from somewhere, a policeman is hit, and he, in turn, retaliates, and hits a demonstrator. This has a chain reaction and soon there is a near riot."

When a demonstration turns into a riot, its duration depends as much on the speed with which the police move in as on the ability of the rioters to withstand the first confrontation. As they watched the police advance, speakers and activists at Berkeley responsible for distribution of leaflets and propaganda material usually fled. In order not to furnish a target, others followed suit, though sometimes it was the other way around, the audience dispersing and leaving the speakers behind. Since most of them had no experience in matters of open clashes with police, few had thought about avenues of retreat. For this reason bottlenecks were created around the exits from the principal scene of the riot. The stronger pushed the weaker aside; the male students trampled the coeds. In the resulting stampede, those who fell could not get up and were injured. In some cases, the rioters tried to extricate from the crowd a friend they had left behind. In addition there were the curious who turned back to look at what was happening, as well as those who could not resist the urge to throw one last stone or bottle or whatever at the police. As the chaos mounted and the exits became more clogged, the police often seized the opportunity to surround and apprehend many protesters.

Against the demonstrators the police marched in a line. Because the straight line rarely corresponded to both the terrain and the position of the protesters, sooner or later the police themselves broke ranks and took off in pursuit of the more experienced agitators who were trying to restore order among the rioters. Or participants who did not notice that their comrades had left them, as well as groups who came back after running into a dead end in their retreat, were often taken into custody. Because many resisted arrest, several policemen were required to join in subduing them and escorting them to the paddy wagon. At this stage, the more seasoned rioters would notice that the ranks of the police were divided and would take advantage of the vacuum to move in. Thus they were often responsible for a second and a third clash of forces and renewed violence.

Lacking better organization, some of the rioters tried individually to correct the mistakes of the previous days. Many still counted on the belated arrival of the police on the scene. In most cases, however, the police and the authorities, aware of the potential danger and the physical damage that could be caused, would arrive at the scene long before the students.

The situation was at once reversed. Waiting in the arena now was only one contestant, the police, accompanied by large numbers of the press. The other adversary usually slept somewhat later in the morning and had not yet appeared. Arriving on the campus either individually or in small groups, the students would find the newsmen and the police already on the spot and irritable from their long wait. Assuming the police were waiting for them, the students would begin to assemble in anticipation of a demonstration even though nothing had been announced. This time, however, both sides, with some experience behind them, needed less time to clash.

Lest this over-simplified account of a riot lead us to think we are dealing with child's play, this was unfortunately far from the case on the Berkeley campus. True, a certain element of wait-and-see is likely to be present in a confrontation involving rivals who do not know one another and have yet to establish the rules of the game. It became clear in conversations with a number of Berkeley students who had participated in or had observed the riots that the basic problem of the rioter was one of securing his retreat. As a rule, he was less concerned about the Free Speech Movement than about the possibility of his being injured or being hauled off to jail. At the same time, it was observed by many bystanders that retreating rioters who sought shelter in campus buildings were in a much better position than those who tried to flee to the streets. Those who took refuge in the buildings found themselves facing only clerks or empty classrooms, while those on the streets had the police to contend with. Though quaking inwardly, the rioters inside the buildings found that university personnel were terrified of them and offered little resistance. Hence they felt safe to wait it out until the police had reestablished peace.

The knowledge gained from this experience may very logically have led to the next step in their tactics: if the university buildings afforded a reliable sanctuary in case of retreat, why not transfer the staging area of the riot from the campus terraces to the buildings in the first place? Whether or not the origin of this shift can be so exactly pinpointed, many students did in fact believe this to be the case. Nevertheless, the occupation of key buildings that immobilized university personnel and brought activities to a standstill soon became standard practice on many an American campus. From the point of view of a protester, this tactic had its pluses and its minuses. The number of such buildings on a modern university campus is large, and there is no way for school authorities to police them all properly. Most of them, therefore, offered inviting targets that could be taken over with ease.

Some of them, however, such as the administration building and the office of the president, were more important than others. According to the spokesmen for the Free Speech Movement, the officials within these nerve centers of the university who had been deaf for many years to the demands of the students were determining their academic fate and their whole future. The students charged further that the university operated on the basis of numberless outmoded and inflexible laws, statutes, and regulations. The institution was said to employ its own jargon, its tacit understandings, its evasiveness, and its delaying tactics. In order to see an administrative chief the student usually had to queue up in long lines or to have his name added to a lengthy waiting list. There were secretaries, deputies, assistants, and assistants to the assistants, each of whom could say no but very few of whom were empowered to say yes. To make matters worse, a student often went through the same painful process when he wished to confer with a faculty member.

It seems that by the early sixties enough students had come up against this stone wall to convince even those without a particular problem that the difficulties of dealing with the administration were insurmountable. A majority of them gradually came to look upon the administration as an enormous powerhouse that could manipulate their lives and careers at will. Since in their opinion the administration was responsible to no one, it was virtually beyond control.

At the same time, the spokesmen for the Free Speech Movement kept belaboring the point that the administration and other centers of power at the university were but paper tigers, exercising unprecedented strength because there was nobody to face up to them. In cases where demonstrators occupied administration buildings, many students were forced to acknowledge that these speakers knew what they were talking about, because in this "enemy headquarters," to use the term of Columbia University demonstrators, the activist found machines silenced, computers halted, the contents of yesterday's locked filing cabinets now open to all, and wide-eyed clerks whose arrogance of yesterday had given way to frightened compliance. Could this be that all-powerful bureacratic conductor that has for so long been shuffling our lives about like so many papers? some of these students were said to have asked. To many it looked more like a soap bubble, "a big zero, that had, in their terms, behaved like a halo."

The ease with which an administration building could be occupied and the publicity thus engendered encouraged the demonstrators to expand the list of targets to other nerve centers, such as the office of the president, of the chancellor, and of the deans, or of individual departments. In most cases, they found more or less the same mild resistance followed by complete capituation. In isolated instances, university personnel offered token arguments and anemic appeals to students to vacate the building. Very few stood firm. Interestingly enough, in 1968 following the May events in Paris, many students came to believe that under duress a professor or official of the Sorbonne would behave like a "turtle with a broken shell," "a hermit crab," or "a handcuffed rabbit." They became the butt of innumerable jokes, and were described as "mice-moonwalkers who in quivering voice, [using] impeccable language generously sprinkled with quotations from Descartes, tried to advise the cat to change its diet." Despite a few outstanding exceptions to this pattern of behavior, by the time the occasion for meaningful dialogue between the two sides arrived, the students had formed such a low opinion of university officials and faculty that they refused to take them seriously.

Particularly in the United States, as success followed upon success, demonstrators, widely believed to have been egged on by outside agitators, expanded their goals, singling out institutes, research centers, and military recruiting offices as added targets on the campus. At a mass university, according to the leading cadres of the New Left movement, institutes and centers generally have the weakest bonds with the students. They work either for the government or for big business, and are but field offices of the Establishment on the campus. The R.O.T.C. is an even more flagrant example of the Establishment's presence, the cadre argument continued. Open attacks against the personnel or attempts to occupy their offices, therefore, presented the activist with an opportunity to raise his militancy to a truly revolutionary level and to deliver the first blows against the principal enemy of the New Left—the status quo. In the program of some small groups of militants such as the Weathermen, the institutes became prime "ideological targets" for bombing or destruction.

In this type of confrontation a rioter placed himself at a disadvantage on several counts. Sealed inside the building he was occupying, he found his maneuvering space severely limited. The police could easily surround the premises while the occupier, as a rule young and full of energy, relinquished his prime weapon, his legs. Running from one scene of action to another was out of the question. Unarmed and untrained, he was hardly a match for the police or the National Guards assigned to clear the building. Since he could not run away, he was forced to fall back on his next basic tactic, passive resistance. Now, if standing, he could be handcuffed and marched out by any one of the police or guards. However, if he sat down or lay down, at least two men were required to pick him up and carry him out. The sit-in therefore became the tactic of the hour.

Clearing the building became a long, drawn-out process, requiring many hours and lots of manpower, a fact duly noted by the early Berkeley activists. Meanwhile, the press and photographers outside the building had plenty of time to set up all their equipment and take pictures of every rioter being removed from the scene. Since at this point the cameramen rarely had access to the inside, they were in no position to judge what might have caused the police to take such measures. What the public saw was two or three husky policemen manhandling a limp student or coed who showed few signs of struggle. This could not help but generate adverse publicity for the law enforcement agents.

Toward the end of the sixties, when one might have expected that the successful take-over of campus buildings, the prominence given to every aspect of its activities by press and television, and the experience acquired would close the ranks of the New Left, exactly the opposite began to happen. Whatever action was involved, numerous factions of the movement quarreled vigorously. The spokesmen for each group would insist on the revolutionary purity of their own platforms and methods.[55] While refusing others the right to speak in the name of the movement, they dissipated a good share of their energies in mutual recriminations or in attempts at reconciliation, with the result that little energy remained for actual confrontation with school authorities.

From the very beginning of the offensives against buildings, leaders clashed on such questions as duration of occupation, type of violence to be used, hostages to be taken, materials and documents to be destroyed, allies to be trusted, content of ultimatums to the authorities, and above all, over what should be done once the immediate objective had been attained. In other words even before they had fully secured their position in the "enemy's headquarters," they seem to have been in total disagreement.

The events at Columbia University in the spring of 1968 furnish a fine example of the utter chaos existing within the movement. In the last week of April and the first week of May some two hundred student militants with little difficulty seized five major buildings on the campus. They also entered the offices of President Grayson Kirk, held a dean of one of the colleges hostage for twenty-four hours, and brought the university to a standstill. The first target, Hamilton Hall, was occupied by joint forces of black and white militants. No sooner was the building captured, however, than the two groups began to clash. Blacks threw out their white class-mates, most of whom were members of Students for a Democratic Society, and invited non-student militants from neighboring Harlem to join them on the campus. The white rioters, enraged and feeling betrayed, then turned on Low Library, seized it, and established their own headquarters there.

A third group of students that included the remaining segments of militants occupied Avery and Fairweather Halls a little later and set up their headquarters. The militants from Hamilton Hall refused to have any dealings with those in Low Library. They "barricaded the building with its own furniture and began what amounted to a siege of the outside."[56] Making a point of repelling all white rioters from the vicinity, their leaders, Roy Innis and Charles Kenyatta, apparently looked upon their headquarters in Hamilton Hall as the general staff of the Black Revolution. Mark Rudd and his co-leaders in Low Library kept their distance from the Hamilton force and at the same time entertained vague misgivings about the group in Avery and Fairweather.

In the very beginning, the three groups had been held together by the two issues over which the riots had presumably started: first, objection to the construction of a gymnasium in Morningside Park (it was alleged that the gymnasium had been so designed as to provide separate facilites and entrances for community users and for univer-sity personnel, and that such planning was a symbol of segregation); and second, a demand for termination of contracts with the Institute of Defense Analysis (charged by the SDS with "works on military projects aimed at the oppression of the people in Vietnam" and with developing "riot equipment to commit mass genocide against the black people in the United States").

The combination of these two issues, which had been strong enough to attract the students initially, now proved quite insufficient to hold the various factions together once the riots were under way. In fact, as soon as the first buildings were occupied, all the groups seem to have lost sight of what had brought them together and each went off in its own direction: the Hamilton Hall group, as has been mentioned, in pursuit of the Black Revolution; the Low Library group, seeking "a total revolution;" and still another, a spin-off from the Low group led by Tom Hayden, controlled the Mathematics building and even proclaimed its own "Soviet." The members of this last-named group, in fact, spared no effort in making its headquarters a miniature replica of the Kremlin. The Red flag flew atop the building, while inside Tom Hayden was reportedly "chairing meetings and directing the coming overthrow of the state. With their big poster of Karl Marx in the window and their sentinels of bearded young men carrying staves and table-legs, the Soviets [were] the most colorful, if the least plausible."[57] As for the Avery-Fairweather group, after their initial ardor had cooled, they contributed little to advancing their cause.

In fact, two forms of anarchy coexisted on the campus: one caused by the occupation of buildings and the interruption of all functions of the University; and the other resulting from factional strife among the groups of rioters, each wanting to be the great leader of the insurrection. Both types of anarchy could exist side by side only so long as the university authorities, determined to postpone confrontation at any cost, held the police at bay at the campus gates. Left to themselves and free from direct police pressure, each group continued to enlarge the scope of its plans, to hold closed meetings, and to compose an endless stream of petitions and documents and appeals.

Since in this kind of disorganized attempt "to tailor history" only a few leading militants could be involved, the remainder turned to the traditional pastime of the part-time insurrectionist—destruction of property and senseless vandalism. They raided the office of the president, broke into his stock of liquor and cigars, and riffled through his personal correspondence. Here, as elsewhere, rioters took or destroyed records, documents, files and books.[58] They burned papers and notes of one of the professors of modern history that represented ten years of research. If the furniture in the buildings was in the way, it was thrown out of windows and broken parts used for barricades or demolished. Some groups worked slowly and methodically, moving from room to room; others struck out wildly, destroying everything within reach. Charles Kenyatta, one of the few who tried afterward to rationalize this behavior, was quoted as saying, "I don't care what some people may say about private property. This building [Hamilton Hall] is in the Eighteenth Congressional District, and belongs to the people."[59] Rap Brown was said to have threatened campus authorities that if the police moved against the black students, the university would be burned to the ground.[60]

However, this vandalism could not continue indefinitely. In the buildings, first of all, few pieces of furniture remained intact; and in the second place, the destruction itself entailed so many hours of arduous physical labor that the demonstrators eventually began to suffer from pangs of hunger and aching backs. The people in Low Library seem to have been hungrier than others. Left without breakfast on April 29, for instance, they dispatched supply teams to the city in quest of food. Though the police allowed the messengers to leave the campus, they barred their re-entry. At this, groups of bystanders who had meanwhile gathered expressed high indignation. Though ignorant of both the original cause of the riot and of the demands of the protesters, the observers looked upon the police as using brute force to prevent the heroes of the day from receiving needed sustenance. The innocent bystanders, especially the older ones, pointed out that the students were hungry and demanded that they be fed forthwith. Thus shortly after ten o'clock that morning, according to the Memorandum of the Senate Committee on the Judiciary,[61] a group of clergymen and one nun pushed their way through the mob of about three thousand students, teachers, administrators, and police only to be turned back "among shouting and fist fights and an atmosphere of growing anger."

The leaders at Columbia were apparently less successful in holding onto their initial followers and attracting new ones than were the Berkeley militants who organized the Free Speech Movement in 1964. At Berkeley, according to the Report of the President's Commission on Campus Unrest,[62] the protests began over "a sudden change in enforcement of campus rules governing political organizing, and the activists' objections had been couched in civil-libertarian terms." What they demanded at the outset amounted to a request for "the removal of restrictions on speech and political activity imposed by administrators and university regents." The Berkeley militants used few outside contacts, restricting their activities mainly to the campus. Fred M. Hechinger, Education Editor of the *New York Times*, who followed the disturbances at Columbia closely, concurs in this general assessment of the Berkeley situation. He says that the complaints of the Berkeley students centered around the dehumanizing influence brought about by mushroom growth. They wanted educational reform, which included closer contact with senior faculty. While the Berkeley unrest was stirred up by activists, it had strong student support and even the sympathy of many faculty members.

In contrast, the mass of students at Columbia seemed to resent the troublemakers.[63] This resentment appeared first among the nonparticipants and was directed at the rioters. What seems to have disturbed the students most, according to

Hechinger's analysis, was the demonstrators' apparent obsession with violence and burning. Actually, many Columbia students who had been complaining before the riots that the process of redressing grievances was moving much too slowly had subscribed wholeheartedly to the use of demonstrations. But they felt now that the rioters were substituting the means (demonstrations) for the goal (redress of grievances), and had permitted the protest to degenerate into senseless, counterproductive violence. Many thus dissociated themselves from the violent demonstrators, refusing to allow them to speak in the name of the student-body as a whole. Then many of the rioters themselves began to question the actions of their leaders. Even some of the civil rights activists from Harlem were having second thoughts about the tactical wisdom of the contingent in Hamilton Hall. Though they did not officially disown Rap Brown and his co-leaders, they stood off to one side to watch and wait.[64]

What the rioters objected to in their spokesmen, though the reasons for their disaffection were not spelled out, was essentially the same program of lawlessness as that criticized by the nonparticipating student body. In the opinion of many of those who had joined in the demonstrations at the very outset, the real issues at stake were the construction of the gymnasium and the relationship between the university and the Institute of Defense Analysis. With these issues in mind—and only these issues—they had occupied five buildings, believing as many did that by accomplishing this they were fortifying their bargaining position with school authorities. However, at this point the leaders had fanned out in all directions to involve their followers in full-blown revolution.

To illustrate the point, when Provost David Truman announced that "at the request of Mayor Lindsay, the university is suspending construction of the gymnasium," many demonstrators considered their battle half-won. Their spokesmen, however, all but ignored this announcement and disagreed among themselves as to how to react in the face of this major concession. Each of the leaders now came forward with his own program. Mark Rudd proclaimed that the original issues were of secondary importance anyhow, and directed the rioters to use the university as a revolutionary political weapon with which to attack the whole system.[65] Tom Hayden, securely entrenched in the Mathematics building, which he apparently considered the political-tactical headquarters of the general revolution, asked support for his Soviet. Rap Brown, on his part, threatened to burn to the ground Rudd's revolutionary weapon, the entire university.

Meanwhile, as Hechinger reported, the black militants from Hamilton Hall proposed to "carry on their own thing." Though few understood precisely what this might entail, the predominantly white occupiers of Low Library expressed the same sentiment, as did those from Avery and Fairweather Halls. Where was the individual rioter to turn for guidance— to a particular leader or to a group? Was he to fortify the campus as the headquarters of a revolution or to burn it down? Once they had observed how the leaders had disregarded the provost's announcement, many of the activists raised even more "defeatist" questions. What does the top echelon actually want—victory or publicity? How long is this to go on? The policy of a sudden shift from destruction of furniture in occupied buildings to destruction of an entire society appeared far too drastic. Furthermore they were troubled by many more prosaic problems, such as lack of food, fear of punishment or suspension from the university, a threatening clash with the police, and the challenge of carrying on negotiations with President Kirk. On these matters they waited in vain for a directive from their leaders. At this juncture many a participant began to weary of the endless and seemingly futile meetings and to seek a way out on his own.

When confrontation with the police finally did occur, the rioters closed ranks to meet a common enemy. The harmony, however, was of short duration. The police first cleared Hamilton Hall without serious incident, and then, with slightly greater effort, the remainder of the campus. According to the Report of the President's Commission, the Berkeley scenario was reenacted at Columbia with few variations: "occupation, faculty and administration confusion, police intervention and student injuries, indignation of moderate students and faculty, a major strike, and, finally, endless consideration of reforms in administration, governance, and disciplinary procedures."[66] There was considerable property damage, and added to it charges of police brutality. A few faculty members, some representatives of the press, and many students accused the principal school authorities of being unprepared to cope with the riots. They charged that when the crisis arose, "some administrators believed that their only options were to do nothing or to call in the police. If they did nothing, they would allow the extremists to take over the campus; if they called in the police, they could not be sure the police would act properly."[67]

The insurrectionary tactics of the riot leaders apparently backfired. To repeat, they instigated the riots on the basis of specified grievances and encouraged an ever-escalating violence. Then, in the midst of the crisis, they switched their line by insisting, as Mark Rudd did, that the grievances were simply a pretext for protest and had they not existed others would have been substituted. Incapable of improvising new issues on the spot, however, the leaders lost the majority of moderate students and then alienated even some of their hard-core followers.

Nevertheless, these leaders obviously profited from the disproportionate amount of publicity they drew. Their harangues and slogans, usually taken out of context, were quoted for months afterward. Some commentators advised student organizations to weed out from their ranks these "politically enlightened thugs." With others it became almost a game to speculate on which campus Hayden, Rudd, Brown, Kenyatta, and their followers would select as their next staging ground. In any event, the fame or notoriety of these activists spread throughout the country and far beyond its borders.

**Urban Guerrilla**

On the broader scene, the events at Columbia provided New Leftist extremists with a precedent and a sound base for the use of open threats against university officials and of widespread terrorist tactics. The impotence of Columbia administrators when confronted with riots has been equated by some extremists of the New Left with the inability of American society as a whole to take effective action in suppressing the growing unrest of young people. Each time the demonstrators resorted to violence, college administrators and faculty, as well as government officials, politicians, and newsmen, seemed to be caught completely off guard and struck dumb. They wavered from one extreme to another—school authorities from reluctant concessions to harsh disciplinary actions; the police from mollycoddling to brutality; public opinion from an outpouring of understanding and sympathy to outright condemnation of the students.

Some faculty members even defended the cause of the protesters better than the protesters themselves. Faculty members were able to put the students' demands more forcefully and to present them in the form of a highly plausible package. However, their assistance to the protesters, as a rule, was less than that rendered by those members of the faculty who not only disagreed with the methods and politics of the rioters, but also disagreed with the countermeasures of the administration. Some of these critics charged leading university officials with pusillanimity, while others criticized them for over-reacting. Since this faculty group often included many outstanding scientists and public figures, their comments and criticisms received wide press coverage. In defending themselves against these charges, college administrators found themselves in an anomalous situation, that is, of having to justify first their tolerance and then their harshness.

In addition to observing this division among educators, the extremist could note the ripples produced among the politicians by his threat of violence. Each riot, it seems, afforded the politician a controversial issue on which to comment and reams of free publicity. A California Democrat, for instance, in analyzing the disturbances at Berkeley, might use the demonstrations as a pretext for attacks against Republican Governor Reagan or the Board of Regents of the University. Or if he chose to lash out against the system of financing the university network, he could skillfully work in his own ideas on education or on the status of youth. A Republican could accuse the Democrats of hamstringing the administration in its courageous efforts to solve the student problems. Both sides could then enlarge upon these mutual recriminations to include the Federal government, the courts, the U.S. Congress, or the professors.

During the 1964-68 period the militant was likely to find a similar type of reaction on the national level. Many a congressman and senator in Washington, according to the New Left, was using the campus disruptions across the country as an opportunity to steal the limelight, to hold press conferences, to make speeches or to propose new legislation. Endless discussions of the riots and their causes, proposals and counterproposals, had become an integral part of the activities of the U.S. Congress and Senate. One after another new committees, commissions, and fact-finding groups sprang up and were funded without question. The problems of the dissident young not only came to assume a more prominent place at the president's press conferences but became a significant issue in the 1968 presidential campaign.

This tendency of the Establishment to overreact to every violent incident perpetrated by the militants only seemed to strengthen the position of those extremists who justified violence as a means to an end. Columbia rioters have been quoted as saying: "A ransacked office or a broken window is more descriptive than a thousand petitions;" or, "If you'd like to be heard, keep your mouth shut and pick up a brick." Some forerunners insist that black militants, Chicanos, and Indians have achieved more in the course of a few years through the use of violent means than they have during an entire century of political maneuvering or "sheep-like submission to the system."

As regards the gains made through the normal political process, these were considered merely symbolic. The minorities might succeed in one campaign only to be defeated in another. And of this "political teeter-totter," the line goes on, the Establishment made masterful use for decades, wearing down and anesthetizing the disaffected. Theoretically, the man in the street is guaranteed the right to determine his destiny by the ballot, since he may vote for congressmen and senators. But these public figures seem to him to be self-serving and beyond his reach; and it avails him little to complain, to write letters, to sign petitions, or to seek redress in the courts.

Robert Lawrence, in *Guerrilla Warfare in the United States*, a treatise on New Left terrorism, points out that during the sixties all these ineffectual and in a sense tragicomic measures to promote peaceful change disappointed and angered even the most patient and the most persistent among the disaffected.[68] In this period, Lawrence says, the alienated and the dissatisfied began en masse to apply what we are asked to call surgical methods of cure or last-ditch efforts, i.e., attempts at destruction of the underpinnings of American society. According to this simplistic logic, then, violence established itself as a principal means of political struggle in the United States; and during these years open confrontation replaced the ballot, first on the campus and then across the land.[69]

During the 1968-70 period, in speeches and published works of the most militant among the New Left, we find indeed an increasing absence of references to the cause, to ideology, to doctrine, even to the counterculture. Mounting emphasis is laid instead on discussions of terrorist strategy, confrontation, killing of police, and bombing. No matter where we turn on the American scene, as viewed by these writers, we find civil disobedience and sabotage, diversions, shootouts with the police, and attacks against public buildings. "Through the heartland of America," says Lawrence, "along both coasts, in every region, in all the key cities, arson, looting, snipers [and] wanton destruction" are a daily occurrence.

During the past several years, insurrectionary tactics of protesters, Lawrence continues, may be divided into four general stages, the first three of which we have already lived through. The initial phase, characteristic of the early rumblings of the New Left, he terms the conventional riot, when the targets, chosen at random, usually consisted of neighborhood stores or parked cars. The rioters were disorganized and undisciplined, and made use of the weapons at hand—bricks, stones, or bottles. In these early onslaughts, which were usually of limited duration, activity was confined to the point of origin.

In the second phase, the hyper-riot, some specific targets were selected. Police as well as passing motorists were considered fair game, and many police officers, as well as private citizens were injured. Tactics were now showing some signs of pre-planning. Although weapons at hand or those discovered at the site were still in wide use, some Molotov cocktails were also brought to the scene. The action in this phase was still limited, though at times it tended to spread beyond the point of origin.

The third phase, civil insurgency, involved a leap to a definitely higher level of popular struggle. Targets were now defined in advance and with more precision, and included selected stores, police headquarters, and firemen and their equipment. Armed rioters and sniper teams would exchange fire with the police. They would intercept or jam police broadcasts, and then attempt to single out for attack the first groups of law enforcement officers to arrive on the scene. The use of hand guns and rifles became increasingly common. At this stage the riots might have lasted several days or as much as a week, and often spread to a nonadjacent area. It was obvious now that the rioters were to some degree organized.

The last and the most advanced stage of confrontation with the Establishment Lawrence describes as urban guerrilla warfare. Though this phase is yet to be well defined, certain characteristics of this type of fighting are surfacing. Police, firemen, and government officials, as well as other symbols of the system, are now the targets. Extensive tactical planning that assumes the use of trained combatants pursuing specific political goals is in sight. To the hand guns and rifles already in use are added weapons of terror, live bombs. The attack may last for several days or more and may spread far beyond the original scene. The masses of rioters in this phase, as envisioned by Lawrence, are under the firm direction of militant groups in a number of cities and are now linked together. Easy targets such as small police stations or substations may be taken, if only for their symbolic value, and the ghettos may be declared independent of government control.[70]

Using this analysis as the basis for his conclusions, Lawrence issues the warning that if the riots continue the present rate of escalation, the seventies will be the decade of urban guerrilla warfare. In spelling out the fate in store, Lawrence explains that small groups of fighters would attack in scattered urban areas, using hit-and-run tactics and wearing down the opposition with chaos and terror. They would create the impression that the local authorities throughout the country were powerless.[71]

A somewhat similar train of thought is found in the writings and statements of other militants. Among them, writing from Peking, Robert F. Williams envisions America as being "brought to her knees in 90 days of highly organized fierce fighting, sabotage and massive fire storm."[72] Max Stanford predicts that black rioters will use "sabotage in the cities—knocking out the electrical power first, then transportation—and guerrilla warfare in the countryside . . . With the cities powerless the oppressor will be helpless."[73] Yet another writer, William Epton, vice chairman of the pro-Peking Progressive Labor Party, tells us that in order to obtain full freedom "we are going to have to kill a lot of cops, a lot of these judges, and we will have to go against the army."[74]

In essence, these sentiments and many similar ones are reminiscent of earlier statements of some hard-core militants, particularly Stokely Carmichael and Huey Newton. Carmichael minced no words when he announced that he was thinking not in terms of bricks or bottles, but of total aggressive guerrilla warfare, in the countryside and throughout the entire country.[75] Newton pointed out that since the country was largely urban, new means would have to be devised to counter the developments in technology and communications. He implied that some solutions were already at hand and that they would be imparted at the right moment.[76]

Among the militant elements of the New Left, the group calling itself the Weathermen is the most extreme in its obsession with violence. This faction apparently operates on the theory that the more advanced a society is technologically, the more vulnerable it is to urban guerrilla tactics. The highly patterned way of life throughout the land and the inability of the Establishment to distinguish friend from foe make of America, in the words of some Weathermen, an easy prey for irregular troops.[77]

In an interview with Martin Walker, a writer for the *Manchester Guardian*, an anonymous Weatherman outlined the following "scenario for chaos:"

1. A coordinated assault on the police, including assassination of officers and of their families (to deter men from joining the force) leaves the force out of order, undermanned, overstretched, and with low morale;

2. Guerrilla assaults on pipelines, fuel depots, railway lines, and bridges slow communications and foster widespread alarm;

3. Bombs or bomb threats in every international airport within the United States keep air travelers and officials constantly insecure (since the Weathermen work on a six-to-one ratio of bomb threats to actual bombs planted, every threat must be checked out by the authorities, who have to work six times as hard as the bombers);

4. Bombs or bomb threats should be used liberally in major telephone exchanges. (Manhattan, for instance, can be isolated with as many bombs as it takes to blow up or destroy only twelve bridges and tunnels.)[78]

Official sources, filled with references to riots, assassination of policemen, arson, looting, sniping, and destruction of property, are used by militants as the basis for these and similar statements. Such terms as urban guerrilla, civil insurrection, politics of terror, even civil war, recur with increasing frequency in the media and in reports of commissions. But in many instances the accounts of acts of violence fail to afford any insight into the causes and nature of such happenings. Furthermore, routine violation or unsolved crime is frequently listed in these reports under the heading of political crime.[79]

The disproportionate coverage given to individual acts of terror has often given the militant delusions of grandeur. Some of these people have been credited by their associates with acts they were not aware of having committed. And since it made good copy to attribute bombings to a particular group such as the Weathermen, for instance, many a Weatherman has been led to believe that his faction was more powerful than he might otherwise have thought. Published statistics from official sources for the fifteen months ending April 1970 would have supplied him with all the proof he needed that his group led the pack. The figures showed 4,330 incendiary bombings, with 43 killed, and property damage in excess of $21.8 million.[80] The figures showed also that nearly 1,200 U.S. policemen had protested in Washington against the assassination of twenty officers in 1970 by revolutionary Maoists, anarchists, nihilists, or other groups.

Such a record of solid accomplishment could easily convince the militant that the policy paid off: it confused and alarmed the Establishment more effectively than any open protest through conventional channels.

However, in order to pursue this total war with the system, the militant now found himself forced to carry on his day-to-day existence under the conditions usually imposed for terrorists: severe limitation of contacts, disguise, lying in hiding, constant fear of infiltration or betrayal. This led, of course, to abrupt cessation of all activities not directly connected with the tactics or logistics of terror. When some of the militants, such as Mark Rudd, Bernardine Dohrn, Rap Brown, Cathlyn Wilkerson, and Cameron David Bishop, were placed on the F.B.I.'s "Ten Most Wanted List," the complete reorganization of their lives became imperative. Approximately a thousand of the revolutionaries reported to have remained active after 1970 were forced to operate under a set of rules that made it more difficult to apprehend them. And as a last resort, they would say, "If the going gets rough, there is always Canada."

Though these conditions did toughen the fugitives, perplex the F.B.I., and ease the difficulties of staying underground, they also interfered seriously with the militants' former role as spokesmen or leaders. They were now completely cut off from physical contact with their erstwhile followers. For a dedicated terrorist, mass support is out of the question. It is simply too dangerous to be permitted.

Many of the Weathermen indicated that they did not regard this as too serious a problem because they felt they could still claim the sympathy of a majority of dissident youth. During the riots and demonstrations of the previous years many a young person had acquired a police record, which, the Weathermen insisted, branded them permanently. Even if they subsequently had a change of heart, they must eventually return to the side of the revolutionaries, because, the line continues, the Establishment would refuse to erase their past violations. In support of this position Lawrence quotes an Associated Press dispatch of April 19, 1970, headed, "Millions of Citizens in the U.S. 'Subversive files.' " According to this report millions of Americans had been placed on the subversive lists by the Federal government, the civil service, the F.B.I., and by military intelligence. The army was reported to have blacklists of names and descriptions and pictures of citizens "who might be involved in civil disturbance situations;'" while "the Secret Service has a computer with 100,000 names and 50,000 investigative dossiers on persons it calls dangerous." Finally, Lawrence contends that one Senate sub-committee revealed that Federal investigators now have access to 164 million police records, 323 million medical histories and 279 million psychiatric dossiers." He concludes, "That is a hell of a lot of crooks, sick people and psychos—especially when its number exceeds the present population of the country."[81]

In the opinion of some Weathermen, terrorist manpower, already spread thin, should for the time being concentrate on projects other than the political enlightenment of the mass of oppositionists. Rather, this should be the domain of that segment of activists which interacts between the lowest level of agitators and the most effective and most militant arm of the opposition: the terrorists themselves. Furthermore, they insist, the possible loss of supporters should not give cause for alarm. The terrorists regard the political process itself as becoming less and less attractive to the young.

Irrespective of what concessions the Establishment may be forced to make, the youth of today, whether he be a part of black America, of student America, or of dropped-out America, is completely convinced that today's rulers are bankrupting the nation in order to stay in power or to win an election. "Even the grandchildren of our grandchildren would not be able to balance the budgets of the sixties." This argument is favored by the Weathermen to back up the boast that young generations will join the revolution not because they want to but because they must.

Sweeping aside all counterarguments, this claim and others

seem to emerge from the growing confusion of political thought among the terrorists. During 1969 many of them were holding to Lenin's statement that "there is nothing easier than to push over what is already falling down." They thus predicted that the politics of ruthless terrorism would quickly disrupt American life. However, since American institutions as a whole refused to be a pushover, the whole concept had by 1971 degenerated into a neither-win-nor-lose policy. "Just as the U.S. Army feels justified in a no-win policy in Vietnam, the Weathermen must feel justified in a no-win policy in the United States," reports Martin Walker.[82]

In 1969, also, Weathermen and some pro-Maoist groups sponsored the Leninist concept that an élite faction could act and educate itself at the same time. Their calculations in this respect, however, proved particularly disappointing. Well hidden from view in order to avoid capture, at the same time they sealed themselves off from prospective cadres. They remain so well concealed today that they are completely isolated from the mainstream of political activity of the New Left.

After their initial bombings and bomb threats had been received with apparent interest and even approval, the terrorists found themselves at a loss to comprehend the mixed emotions aroused among the New Leftists by their repeated acts of ruthlessness. From the middle of 1970, most of the non-violent protesters whose support they had taken for granted in 1969 all but deserted the cause and returned en masse to seeking recourse through recognized political channels. This was the moderates' line of reasoning: "To one who is already armed with a bomb, i.e., with voting rights, no better T.N.T. is necessary;" or "If he is already a member of the Berkeley City Council, a New Leftist has no reason to kill a policeman; he can fire him." Huey Newton, in February 1972, implied that the terrorists' tactics of yesterday had solved none of the existing problems. "We have rejected the rhetorics of the gun," he said; "it got about 40 of us killed and sent hundreds to prison."[83]

At what rate will the violence so fashionable in the sixties continue to lose favor in the West? Will this decline affect only open terror or other manifestations of violence as well? What impact will "the omnipotent weapon"—the vote of the eighteen-year-old—have on the future? Which will contribute more to the needed changes and reforms—the self-serving inclination of the Establishment to make concessions or the intervention of the young who would accelerate this process? And what will be the final consequences of all the New Left protests, the demonstrations, the riots, the use of violence, and the threats of violence? These are all questions that must be left to a future study.

Except for the revival of a few old concepts of urban guerrilla—"the concrete jungle" instead of the countryside, emphasis on the young both as soldier and as general of insurrection, and the use of violent means to point up issues—we see that the New Leftists have contributed very little to the general theory of guerrilla warfare. In those cases when they did adapt guerrilla methods to their activities, there was little that could be called innovative or original in purely theoretical terms. At the same time, with all its tactical amateurishness, disorganization, and lack of planning or discipline, and in the absence of what is called a guerrilla rule-book, the movement has undeniably won many political victories, and these at a lower cost than most guerrilla movements of the past.

In broader dimensions, the principal contribution of the New Left in the West rests in the precedents and examples both good and bad it may offer to the disaffected youth in the Eastern countries. Berkeley, Columbia, Paris, Cornell, and Berlin may furnish Eastern students and young workers with a blueprint for an imaginative combination of legal and illegal means, petitions and demonstrations, as well as guerrilla and quasi-guerrilla methods aimed at shaking up and revising their outmoded systems. At this juncture it would be foolhardy to speculate on the outcome of such a turn of events. But even now it is certain that future researchers will have their work cut out for them.

## Notes

1. U.S., Congress, Senate, Committee on the Judiciary, "Introduction" to *The New Left*, by Thomas J. Dodd, 90th Congress, Second Session (Washington, D.C.: U.S. Government Printing Office, 1968), p. 1. For a fuller understanding of the nature of the New Left, see Peter L. Berger and Richard John Neuhaus, *Movement and Revolution* (Garden City, N.Y.: Doubleday, 1970); Nathan Glazer, *Remembering the Answers: Essays of the American Student Revolt* (New York: Basic Books, 1970); Sidney Hook, *Academic Freedom and Academic Anarchy* (New York: Cowles, 1970); Theodore Roszak, *The Making of a Counter Culture: Reflections on the Technocratic Society and Its Youthful Opposition* (Garden City, N.Y.: Doubleday, 1969); Joseph J. Schwab, *College Curriculum and Student Protest* (Chicago: University of Chicago Press, 1969); Philip E. Slater, *The Pursuit of Loneliness: American Culture at the Breaking Point* (Boston: Beacon Press, 1970); David L. Welsby and Richard G. Braungart, "Class and Politics in the Family Background of Student Political Activists," in *American Sociological Review*, October 1966.

2. Carl Oglesby, ed., *The New Left Reader* (New York: Grove Press, 1969), pp. 17-19.

3. Dodd, *The New Left*, p. 6.

4. *Ibid.*

5. Oglesby, *The New Left Reader*, p. 18.

6. The full text given in Oglesby, *The New Left Reader*, pp. 267-73.

7. *Ibid.*, pp. 18-19.

8. Comments and statements of Daniel Cohn-Bendit taken from his book *Obsolete Communism: The Left-Wing Alternative*, trans. Arnold Pomerans (London: Deutsch, 1968).

9. Oglesby, *The New Left Reader*, p. 18.

10. *Ibid.*, pp. 2-3.

11. *Ibid.*, p. 3.
12. *Ibid.*, p. 4.
13. *Ibid.*, pp. 4-5.
14. *Ibid.*
15. *Ibid.*, p. 6.
16. *Ibid.*
17. *Ibid.*
18. See C. Wright Mills, *The Causes of World War III* (New York: Simon and Schuster, 1960); C. Wright Mills, "Letter to the New Left," in Priscilla Long, comp., *The New Left: A Collection of Essays* (Boston: P. Sargent, 1969), pp. 14-25; and the following works by C. Wright Mills: *The Power Elite* (New York: Oxford University Press, 1956); *Power, Politics and People* (New York: Ballantine, 1963).
19. Quoted from Oglesby, *The New Left Reader*, p. 23.
20. *Ibid.*, p. 24.
21. *Ibid.*
22. *Ibid.*
23. Oglesby's comments in *ibid.*, p. 7.
24. *Ibid.*
25. *Ibid.*
26. *Ibid.*
27. For the concepts of Herbert Marcuse, see *One-Dimensional Man: Studies in the Ideology of Advanced Industrial Society* (Boston: Beacon Press, 1964); also, by the same author, *Soviet Marxism: A Critical Analysis* (New York: Columbia University Press, 1958); *Eros and Civilization: A Philosophical Inquiry into Freud* (New York: Random House, 1961); and "Repressive Tolerance," in Robert Paul Wolf, Barrington Moore, Jr., and Herbert Marcuse, *A Critique of Pure Tolerance* (Boston: Beacon Press, 1965). See also "Marcuse Defines His New Left Line," in *New York Times Magazine*, Oct. 27, 1968; James Baldwin, *The Fire Next Time* (New York: Dial Press, 1963); Stokely Carmichael and Charles V. Hamilton, *Black Power: The Politics of Liberation in America* (New York: Vintage Books, 1967); Harold R. Isaacs, *The New World of Negro Americans* (New York: John Day, 1963); Martin Luther King, Jr., *Where Do We Go From Here: Chaos or Community?* (New York: Harper and Row, 1967).
28. Oglesby's comment in *The New Left Reader*, p. 32.
29. Marcuse, *One-Dimensional Man*, pp. 252-53.
30. *Ibid.*, p. 256.
31. *Ibid.*, p. 257.
32. *Ibid.*
33. Material used in this chapter is drawn largely from the following sources: Massimo Teodori, *The New Left: A Documentary History* (Indianapolis and New York: Bobbs-Merril, 1969), pp. 55-71, 93-162; Christopher Lasch, *The New Radicalism in America 1889-1963: The Intellectual as a Social Type*, (New York: Vintage Books, 1967); Jack Newfield, *A Prophetic Minority* (New York: New American Library, 1966); Paul Jacobs and Saul Landau, *The New Radicals* (New York:

Vintage Books, 1966) Staughton Lynd, "Towards a History of the New Left," in Long, *The New Left*, pp. 1-13; Ronald Aronson and John C. Cowley, "The New Left in the United States," in the *Socialist Register* (London: Merlin Press, 1967); James Reston, "The Teach-in Could Be a Useful Tool," *New York Times*, May 17, 1968; Isidor F. Stone, *In a Time of Torment* (New York: Vintage Books, 1968); Carl Landauer and Robert Pickus, *Peace, Politics, the New Left and the Pity of It All* (Berkeley: World Without War Council Publication, 1966); Arnold M. Rose, volume ed., "The Negro Protest," *The American Negro Problem in the Context of Social Change, Annals of the American Academy of Political and Social Science* (AAPSS), Vol. 357 (Philadelphia, Jan. 1965); Edward Sagarin, ed., "Sex and the Contemporary American Scene," in *Annals of the AAPSS*, Vol. 376 (Philadelphia, March 1968); James C. Charlesworth, ed., "The Changing American People: Are We Deteriorating or Improving," in *Annals of the AAPSS* (Philadelphia, 1968); James C. Charlesworth, ed., "Ethics in America: Norms and Deviations," in *Annals of the AAPSS*, Vol. 363 (Philadelphia, Jan. 1966); Bertram M. Gross, ed., "Social Goal and Indicators for American Society," Vol. II, in *Annals of the AAPSS*, Vol. 373 (Philadelphia, Sept. 1967); Marvin E. Wolfgang, ed., "Patterns of Violence," in *Annals of the AAPSS*, Vol. 364 (Philadelphia, March 1966); and Philip G. Altback and Robert S. Laufer, eds., "Students Protest," in *Annals of the AAPSS*, Vol. 395 (Philadelphia, 1971).

34. See comments on these events published in the *Times* (London), Dec. 19, 1971; *Le Monde*, Dec. 4, 1971; and *Corriere della Sera*, Aug. 5, 1971.

35. See Leslie Fiedler, "The New Mutants," *Partisan Review*, Fall 1965.

36. *Ibid.*, p. 505.

37. *Ibid.*

38. For comments on these tendencies, see "The Philosophical Basis of the New Left," in Dodd, *The New Left*, pp. 15-20.

39. See "The Freedom to Be Idealistic," in *Youth in Turmoil* (New York: Time-Life Book, 1969), pp. 8-12.

40. Erich Fromm, *The Sane Society* (Greenwich, Conn.: Fawcett Publications, 1966), p. 241.

41. Quoted from Dodd, *The New Left*, p. 17.

42. Fiedler, "The New Mutants," p. 505.

43. For comments on Daniel Bell's concept of the post-industrial society, see Daniel Seligman, "A Special Kind of Rebellion," in *Youth in Turmoil*, pp. 25-26.

44. *Ibid.*, p. 26.

45. *Ibid.*, p. 9.

46. For further study, see Lee Baxandall, "Issues and Constituency of the New Left," *Liberation*, April 1966; Richard E. Flacks, "The Liberated Generation: An Exploration of the Roots of Student Protest," *Journal of Social Issues*, Vol. 23 (1967); G. G novese, "The American Left - Old and New," *National Guardian*, Feb. 19, 1966;

Kenneth Keniston, *Young Radicals: Notes on Committed Youth* (New York: Harcourt, Brace and World, 1968); Mitchell Cohen and Dennis Hale, eds., *The New Student Left: An Anthology* (Boston: Beacon Press, 1967); and Howard Zinn, "The Old Left and the New: Emancipation from Dogma," *The Nation*, April 4, 1966.

47. See Paul Goodman, *Compulsory Miseducation* (New York: Random House, 1962); Jonathan Kozol, *Death at an Early Age* (Boston: Houghton Mifflin, 1967); Henry Jules, *Culture Against Man* (New York: Random House, 1963); and Edgar Friedenberg, *Coming of Age in America* (New York: Random House, 1963).

48. See *Youth in Turmoil*, p. 21.

49. *Ibid.*, pp. 23-24.

50. In Serbian; an undated leaflet.

51. For further study of the beginning of the Free Speech Movement, see Hal Draper, *Berkeley: The New Student Revolt* (New York: Grove Press, 1965); Clark Kerr, *The Use of the University* (Cambridge: Harvard University Press, 1962); Seymour M. Lipset and Sheldon S. Wolin, *The Berkeley Student Revolt* (New York: Doubleday, 1965); Michael V. Miller and Susan Gilmore, *Revolution at Berkeley* (New York: Dell, 1965); The *Position of the Free Speech Movement on Speech and Political Activity* (Berkeley: Academic Free Speech Movement (A.F.S.M.) pamphlet, 1964); Steven Warshaw, *The Trouble at Berkeley*, photographic documents (Berkeley: Diablo Press, 1965); and Regents of the University of California, Special Forbes Committee, *Report on the University of California and Recommendations*, Submitted by Jerome C. Byrne, Special Counsel (Los Angeles, 1965).

52. See Jean-François Revel, *Without Marx or Jesus*, trans. J. F. Bernard (Garden City: Doubleday, 1970), pp. 182-242.

53. The following sources provide valuable material for further study of this tendency: "Problems and Perspectives," in Teodori, *The New Left*, pp. 348-75; Jesse Kornbluth, *Notes from the New Underground* (New York: Viking Press, 1968); Irwin Silber, "Playing the System's Game," *Guardian*, Aug. 17, 1968; and Carl Davidson, "Has S.D.S. Gone to Pot?" *New Left Notes*, Feb. 1967.

54. Quoted in Dodd, *The New Left*, p. 4.

55. There are several useful accounts of student movements and of campus power struggles. See Howard S. Becker, ed., *Campus Power Struggle* (Chicago: Aldine Publishing, 1970), Charles D. Bolton and Kenneth W. Kammeyer, *The University Student Behavior and Values* (New Haven: College and University Press, 1967); James A. Foley and Robert K. Foley, *The College Scene: Students Tell It Like It Is* (New York: Cowles Book, 1969); and Jacobs and Landau, *The New Radicals*.

56. For an official account of the riots, see Fact-Finding Commission on Columbia Disturbances, *Crisis at Columbia* (New York: Vintage Books, 1968); U.S. Senate, Committee on the Judiciary, "The Disturbances at Columbia University," *The New Left*, pp. 79-90; President's Commission on Campus Unrest, *Campus Unrest* (Washing-

ton, D. C.: U.S. Government Printing Office, 1970), pp. 35-41; New York State, Temporary Commission to Study the Causes of Campus Unrest, *The Academy in Turmoil, First Report* (Albany, 1970).

57. *Washington Post*, April 30, 1968.

58. Among other public and private papers and effects, the rioters burned the papers of Professor Orest A. Ranum, which represented ten years of research.

59. *National Review*, May 21, 1968.

60. *New Republic*, May 11, 1968.

61. U.S. Senate, *The New Left*, p. 80.

62. President's Commission, *Campus Unrest*, p. 36.

63. *New York Times*, April 28, 1968.

64. For an attempt at analyzing the causes of this "watch and wait policy" and the subsequent disaffection of rioters, see "The Paradox of Tactics," in President's Commission, *Campus Unrest*, pp. 41-47.

65. See *National Guardian*, May 11, 1968, p. 4.

66. President's Commission, *Campus Unrest*, p. 36.

67. *Ibid.*, p. 8; the university authorities' reaction to the riots as well as the response of law enforcement agencies is discussed in Grace W. Holmes, ed., *Student Protest and the Law* (Ann Arbor, Mich.: Institute of Continuing Legal Education, 1969); Louis Joughin, ed., *Academic Freedom and Tenure: A Handbook of the American Association of University Professors* (Madison: University of Wisconsin Press, 1967); Raymond M. Momboisse, "Tactics for Colleges Facing Student Demonstrations," *College and University Business* (May 1968); E. G. Williamson and John L. Cowan, *The American Student's Freedom of Expression: A Research Appraisal* (Minneapolis: University of Minnesota Press, 1966); David H. Bayley and Harold Mendelsohn, *Minorities and the Police: Confrontation in America* (New York: Free Press, 1969); "The Guard vs. Disorder," *National Guardsman* (June 1970); and Gary T. Marx, "Civil Disorders and the Agents of Social Control," *Journal of Social Issues* (Winter 1970).

68. Robert Lawrence, *Guerrilla Warfare in the United States* (Canoga Park, Calif.: Weiss, Day, 1970); see also Martin Oppenheimer *The Urban Guerrilla* (Chicago: Quadrangle Books, 1969).

69. Lawrence, *Guerrilla Warfare*, pp. 9-38.

70. *Ibid.*, pp. 90-92, 171.

71. *Ibid.*, p. 93.

72. The *Crusader*, Sept.-Oct. 1967.

73. Quoted from Lawrence, *Guerrilla Warfare*, p. 95.

74. *Ibid.*

75. *Ibid.*

76. Quoted from Oglesby, *The New Left Reader*, p. 237.

77. Unless otherwise specified, data on the Weathermen are based on a collection of essays on this faction: Harold Jacobs, ed., *Weatherman* (Ramparts Press, 1970).

78. *Manchester Guardian Weekly*, Nov. 14, 1970.

79. In 1970 Assistant Secretary of the Treasury Eugene T. Rossides reported according to the President's Commission, *Campus Unrest* (p. 38), that "between January 1, 1969, and April 15, 1970, almost 41,000 bombings, attempted bombings and bomb threats were recorded in the nation as a whole. Most could not be attributed to any specific cause. Of those that could be attributed to some cause, more than half—over 8,200—were attributable to 'campus disturbances and unrest.' "

80. Wade Green, "The Militants Who Play with Dynamite," *New York Times Magazine*, Oct. 1970, p. 38. See also "Killing Cops—The New Terror Tactics," *U.S. News & World Report*, Aug. 31, 1970; and "The 'War Against the Police'—Officers Tell Their Story," *U.S. News & World Report*, Oct. 26, 1970; International Association of Chiefs of Police, "Campus Disorder," *Police Yearbook 1970* (Washington, D.C., 1970), pp. 46-58.

81. Lawrence, *Guerrilla Warfare*, p. 119.

82. Martin Walker in *Manchester Guardian Weekly*, Nov. 14, 1970.

83. *National Observer*, Feb. 12, 1972.

# 5  Western Writers on Guerrilla: A School Manqué

Since the close of World War II an impressive number of studies on revolutionary guerrilla warfare have been published in the West. These contributions represent both the work of writers who have participated actively in guerrilla operations, either as combatants, as advisers; or as intelligence agents, and those who may never have set foot in the country they write about. It goes almost without saying that not all of the works have merit; but many of them do furnish valuable insight into the nature and the ideology of insurrection, as well as into the guerrilla's treatment of his ally, his foe, the neutral, and the population at large.

The display of interest in insurrectionary warfare, first evidenced among Western military figures, then among politicians and writers, coincided with the springing up of mass resistance movements in occupied countries during World War II. In their struggle against the Axis powers both London and Washington at this time sought to enlist the cooperation of these local groups. Inside Hitler's European fortress, as well as in parts of Asia conquered by the Japanese, members of underground factions were organizing acts of sabotage, diversion, assassination and ambush, and even all-out guerrilla campaigns. These groups were invaluable not only as a source of information on enemy activity, but they also played a significant role in the infiltration of allied agents, in returning downed allied flyers to fight again, in setting up and manning communications networks, and in performing countless other functions. In the Balkans and in China they liberated whole regions, forcing Axis troops to reconquer them. The whole cycle would then be repeated.

Brigadier Aubrey Dixon and Otto Heilbrunn declare that "the German armies in Russia suffered more damage from guerrillas" than from all the paraphernalia of modern warfare. "After all, they could match each Soviet weapon with similar or superior weapons of their own. But they were almost powerless against guerrillas."[1] Coupled with the passive resistance of the population of the conquered countries, the actions of the insurrectionists forced the Axis to retaliate, thus pinning down large forces that might otherwise have been moved to the main front. A more or less similar situation prevailed at various times in the Balkans, in Czechoslovakia, in Poland, and in Western Europe, as well as in China, in the Philippines, in Malaya, in Burma, and in Indochina. In several of the principal hotbeds of resistance— specifically in China, Southeast Asia, Poland, Greece, and Yugoslavia—communist guerrillas waged civil war against the domestic class enemy within the framework of an anti-fascist war. And it became obvious very soon that this struggle would continue after the war's end, in the process altering the fate of each country it touched.

The military effectiveness of the insurrectionists and their possible influence on postwar trends early impelled London and Washington to send advisers, instructors, liaison officers, and political representatives to the various guerrilla headquarters. Among their numbers were many allied officers up to the rank of general. Winston Churchill even sent his son Randolph to Tito's Partisan headquarters. In 1944, for example, the English, the Americans, and the Russians had sizable military missions assigned to Tito's headquarters, with many observers attached to individual Partisan units. At this time, the English and the Americans had missions with Draza Mihailović as well. In the same way the Western powers sent missions or liaison officers to Mao Tse-tung, to Chiang Kai-shek, to the Vietminh, to Malaya, to the Philippines, to Burma, and to virtually any fledgling Asian guerrilla movement that sprang up.

During 1941 and 1942 guerrilla activities were widely popularized in the West. Film makers, communications media, and book publishers vied with one another to give them top billing, since their plight easily captured the imagination and sympathy of Western audiences. As early as 1942, for instance, Chiang Kai-shek and Draza Mihailović were reported to be among the most popular allied military commanders.

The first films and books to trickle into the marketplace dealt primarily with the principal centers of resistance: China, the Ukraine, and Western Europe. It is not surprising, of course, that these efforts employed the either-or logic and the simplistic approach characteristic of war propaganda. The films in particular suffered from this one-sidedness. In general they presented the Axis fighter as the incarnation of evil. He was killing Jews and other innocents, women, children, and the aged. His prime weapons were jails and concentration camps, the machine gun and the torch.

The typical member of the resistance, on the other hand, was portrayed as a quiet Norwegian teacher, a Greek monk, a dedicated nurse from a Paris hospital, or a Chinese or Ukrainian peasant tending his crops. An ardent advocate of freedom and brotherhood, he was essentially disinterested in politics. Suddenly his life was torn asunder when the Germans or the Japanese overran his home town and began to spread disaster. To protect his neighbors he had to join hands with others to oppose the evil. All prewar differences among the villagers disappeared and the resistance movement was born. Although its members detested the killing of Axis fighters, they apparently had no choice. With the whole nation united and the resistance its fighting fist, one military feat followed on the heels of another.

As for the first books to be published in the United States and England during this period, they tended to approach the subject somewhat more objectively. They were written for the most part either by authors who had some foreknowledge of the area in question or who had witnessed the Axis occupation at first hand.

Though a few serious scholarly accounts did appear at this time, most writers lacked either the necessary evidence or the ability or the perspective to make a solid appraisal of the guerrilla's ideology and his postwar aims. At first, it was as though a tacit understanding existed among writers of the time that for the duration the question of the guerrilla's political persuasion should not be raised. Thus, even in the words of non-communist writers, a communist insurrectionist was by and large still represented as the tolerant democrat whose every effort was bent toward liberation of his fatherland. In order not to interfere with Allied cooperation, hard-liner authors in the United States and in England readily adopted this line. And in their writing also we find that a nationalist guerrilla, except in China or Yugoslavia, was usually "another anti-fascist comrade."

As for China and Yugoslavia, it was in the treatment of these two countries that the more or less silent conspiracy among Western authors first cracked. Here, as well as in part of Poland and in Greece, it became increasingly obvious that the communists and the nationalists were two irreconcilable foes. To the argument that Mao Tse-tung and Tito seemed more interested in the physical liquidation of the class enemy than in the military defeat of the Axis, hard-liner authors countered with assertions that Chiang Kai-shek and Draza Mihailović cooperated with the fascists in order to destroy the communists. By 1943 this polarization between the communist and the nationalist guerrilla in many parts of Europe and Asia were almost complete.

However, it seems that most Western analysts of the period, perhaps not wishing to disturb the delicate balance of inter-allied relations, preferred to leave a theoretical assessment for better days. Also, dispatches on the guerrillas filed by U.S. and British journalists accredited to various theaters of war were frequently biased, incomplete, inaccurate, unverified, or distorted. The bulk of information on European resistance movements came from British sources and reflected Churchill's shifting policies toward insurrectionists. The exclusive British control over this information was so tight, in fact, that in some cases it was only through British channels that members of the U.S. military missions attached to individual guerrilla headquarters in the Balkans could communicate with their own government.[2] Since the British monopoly had rarely been challenged by the Roosevelt administration, especially with respect to London's policy toward European guerrilla movements, it was next to impossible, short of resort to fiction, for a writer to produce anything approaching a valid account of resistance movements in Europe.

This unhappy situation was further complicated by the apparently confused policy of London toward certain of the European guerrillas. For instance, after the capitulation of the Low Countries and France, British intelligence advised the French Maquis and the Belgian and Dutch underground not to take unnecessary risks, but rather to await the appropriate moment for action, such as the Allied invasion. Guerrillas were instructed meanwhile to engage in mild harassment tactics, to organize and equip themselves, and to cooperate with Allied agents. A similar policy was followed by London in dealing with the Norwegian, Italian, Greek, and Czechoslovakian underground, but with a somewhat stronger accent on acts of sabotage and diversion carried out either under the control of or in cooperation with British commandos. In Yugoslavia, however, the policies of London had passed through three phases: first, cooperation with the nationalists only; then with both the nationalists and the communists; and finally, exclusively with the communists.

The capacity of the guerrilla to harass occupation forces from the rear and to disrupt communications contributed to the growing efforts of Western military analysts after 1945 to broaden their understanding of guerrilla techniques. Indeed, even on the basis of very sketchy details gathered during the war, they had acknowledged the ability of the irregulars to enforce their will upon a much stronger adversary. This alone represented a significant breakthrough in the military theory of the West, where the study of irregular warfare had been too long neglected. The new studies naturally emphasized the military aspects of the question. Thus the growing body of knowledge on guerrilla in the early postwar period, still composed of bits and pieces and with little or no attention given to political implications, fell far short of providing a solid base for more serious analyses of the entire phenomenon.

Finally, the necessity for this political assessment of the guerrilla became even more evident in the light of postwar events in those countries where communist partisans had played a role in the resistance movement. In Yugoslavia and Albania, after the end of World War II these partisans took the reins of national government. In Greece, the partisans in their war with their fellow Greeks demonstrated rare skill in exploiting the momentum gained during the anti-occupation struggle. From 1945 to 1949 suppression of the partisans was to engage significant British and Greek government forces, causing the population to suffer further and seriously interfering with reconstruction.

In the same period, Mao Tse-tung firmly entrenched himself in Mainland China, while communist rebels in the Philippines, in Malaya, and in Indochina began to step up their drive for power, involving these regions in protracted civil war. In the Philippines the turmoil lasted eight years, 1948-56; in Malaya, twelve, 1948-60; and in Indochina, except for brief interludes, it has endured for over a quarter of a century, from 1946 until the present. According to Robert McClintock, communist insurgents had participated in twenty-three out of a total of forty wars between 1945 and 1967, employing either purely guerrilla methods or combining these methods with operations of regular troops.[3] Encouraged by the examples of China, Yugoslavia, and Albania, communist spokesmen have been insisting that in revolutionary guerrilla warfare the Marxists from gray areas have finally acquired that magic weapon against which the West can find no defense.

Throughout the entire period the Eastern bloc stood behind the colonial rebel; but the only support for his counterguerrilla foe came from a disunited West. From 1950 to 1954, for instance, Ho Chi Minh's forces enjoyed the diplomatic and propaganda support of nearly all the communist parties of the world, as well as the military aid of Mao's China. At the same time, backing French General Navarre's forces were the weak metropolitan government, a limited segment of French public opinion, and the officially sympathetic ear and token promises of some members of the Western bloc.[4] Since promises, however, are one thing and military assistance another, the French expeditionary forces in Indochina found themselves politically isolated even before Dienbienphu. Wherever the communist insurrectionist in the gray areas took up arms, according to the Marxist propagandists, his chances for victory were virtually assured from the outset. In their words, one Dienbienphu was bound to follow upon another. The message of Che Guevara to the Second Tri-Continental Conference in 1967 calling for "one Vietnam upon another, and then many of them," was but a restatement of this conviction.

During the fifties and early sixties many colonial areas showed a definite tendency to move away from the old concept of normalcy. Guerrilla movements, whether or not inspired by the communists, became an integral part of the political life of the gray areas. In Indonesia, Cyprus, Kenya, Tunisia, Algeria, the Congo, Cuba, Colombia, Bolivia, Angola, and Mozambique, to mention only the archetypes, the insurrectionists openly threatened the foundation of the old system. In each of these instances, the colonial powers or the incumbent governments were demonstrating uncertainty or lack of resolve in suppressing the rebels. At the time, observers charged the Western regulars or their indigenous allies with inadequate military training, with political immaturity, or with weak leadership.

The counterguerrilla regular, who had been taught for years that there was no substitute for logistic superiority, now suddenly found himself in a situation where the correct political directive was more effective than a million bullets. In this type of confrontation, then, the "queen of arms" was not the conventional infantry, but the guerrilla detachment that ambushed the regulars and vanished; then attacked or threatened to attack again. Trained to destroy a flesh-and-blood enemy in the field, the counterguerrilla was forced to take aim at a foe he could not identify by conventional standards. Very often, therefore, he found himself shooting the innocent, thus incurring the hostility of even the neutrals. Nor was he capable of affording adequate protection to his local ally. To distinguish friendly forces from others, he had to place them under direct command and to outfit them in a uniform that made them conspicuous, quislings in the eyes of the local population.

As early as the beginning of the fifties, guerrillas in the gray areas achieved a certain degree of success in combining military operations with political actions. Even when the insurrection was not led by the communists, the insurgents felt they could rely on the backing of the Eastern bloc. Assistance might cover a range from propaganda to diplomatic recognition of the guerrillas and even, in some instances, to direct military intervention. In any event, it very soon became apparent that every one of these militarily limited rebellions could have limitless political repercussions within the Cold War, each constituting a glowing ember in a hotter war. One of the most significant contributions of guerrilla, perhaps, was that it "taught the world . . . how to behave in the gray area between diplomacy and military actions," how to control the process of escalation in order to avoid a full-scale confrontation between the superpowers.[5]

It is not surprising that England and France, the countries which in the post-World War II period suffered most from failure to develop counterguerrilla techniques, should have recognized the need for a serious revaluation of their former policies toward insurrectionary war. This subject now received top priority among professional soldiers and political scientists, journalists, and politicians. In other words, the ominous threat of nuclear confrontation between the superpowers made it imperative in the fifties that both the East and the West tread cautiously to control any guerrilla movement that might touch off a major conflagration.

The Marxist attitude on this subject is best summarized by Nikita Khrushchev in *Conquest Without War*, a collection of his speeches and writings.[6] On the role of guerrilla warfare he says: "Capitalism is a worn-out old mare, while socialism is new, young, and full of teaming energy." Involved in a death-bout, "our firm conviction is that sooner or later capitalism will give way to socialism. No one can hold man's forward movement, just as no one can prevent day following night." At a Kremlin reception on November 26, 1956, he made his famous boast: "Whether you like it or not, history is on our side. We will bury you." Though the U.S.S.R. delegation to the United Nations attempted on October 5, 1957, to discount this statement, insisting that Khrushchev had not meant what he said, Khrushchev himself in a speech to civil authorities in Los Angeles two years later, September 1959, spelled out just what he had meant by the words "we will bury capitalism." He had in mind not the work of ordinary gravediggers, but his outlook for the development of human society as a whole—that socialism would inevitably succeed capitalism. And throughout his own regime he had constantly reiterated this belief. He envisioned the time when the calendar would be based on the October Revolution. But the worldwide victory of communism would be marked above all by the triumph of communist ideas and of the Marxist-Leninist philosophy.

Having inherited Stalin's empire, Khrushchev subscribed also to Stalin's conviction that "in our times it is not the custom to give any consideration to the weak—consideration is given only to the strong." For that reason, he explained, the Soviet Union was building its nuclear armory. In 1960 he stated that the United States had now fallen behind the U.S.S.R. and was trying to catch up in the production of rockets. "They will naturally make every effort to raise their rocketry from the stage it is now in and reach a better position. But it would be naive to think that we are meanwhile going to sit with arms folded." Khrushchev acknowledged, however, that weak as the United States might be, he did not expect it to take the Soviet developments lying down. Capitalism was still strong, but the peoples of all countries would ultimately adopt socialism. The decision as to when and how would be made by each country. Undoubtedly, he continued, the United States with its impressive thermonuclear arsenal, missiles, atomic submarines, bases all over the world, around-the-clock alert and readiness to retaliate would not permit the U.S.S.R. to destroy it with impunity. As a matter of fact, he reasoned, the United States was still strong enough to destroy the Soviet Union twice, while the U.S.S.R., he said half in jest, was capable for the time being of destroying America only once.[7]

In Khrushchev's words, an effective means of heading off nuclear confrontation was to be found in insurrectionary guerrilla war, especially if it were waged in the colonies. Whether such operations were labeled anti-colonial, anti-imperialist, national liberation, or peoples' or agrarian reformist, according to Khrushchev, it all boiled down to the same thing: such tactics enabled Marxists to transform a zone of war, an area under Western control, into a zone of peace, an area under the control of the East. To win peacefully, he maintained, it was necessary to avoid direct action such as that in the Suez, in Iraq, in Lebanon, in Jordan, or in Cuba, in order that the Soviets could not be charged with biting off pieces of the West.[8]

This doctrine of Khrushchev led Mao Tse-tung, Ho Chi Minh, Giap, Castro, and other hard liners to subscribe to the thesis that wherever guerrilla warfare emerged in the gray area, the West was automatically put on the defensive. The West would be forced to consume vast quantities of matériel and to engage military forces. It would be using "a cannon to kill a fly," and would of course be constantly off-target. Its anti-guerrilla strategy would suffer defeat after defeat. True, guerrilla warfare was often waged by proxy; but, as Khrushchev insisted, there were too many such proxies outstanding because most areas of the globe wished to become free and were addressing themselves to the East for aid and comfort. What must happen in the end, to paraphrase Khrushchev once again, was that the West would find itself waging open war against a majority of the states from Asia, Africa, and South America; political war against the entire Eastern bloc; and political-psychological warfare against some Western-bloc partners who disagreed with the senseless policy of Washington and other "stubborn colonials," as well as against a segment of public opinion in the West. Thus, Khrushchev concludes, the West would be trapped in a maze.

This insistence of Khrushchev and other hard liners on characterizing guerrilla warfare in gray areas as "a substitute for the atomic bomb" was the last of many specious arguments about the phenomenon of guerrilla that finally forced Western theoreticians to face cold reality. With what politico-military means should one fight so insidious an opponent as the guerrilla? Is his type of warfare the unquestioned monopoly of the hard liners? How much of his success is due to his own astuteness and how much to the weakness of the non-communist body politic? Is the victory of the communist insurrectionaries inevitable or has it been aided and abetted by Western myopia? The English, for instance, helped Tito in Yugoslavia and the Americans pursued a seesaw policy in China. How could the non-Marxist insurrectionaries already involved in a struggle for liberation be prevented from falling under the communist spell? For answers to these and other questions we address ourselves in the discussion that follows to examining representative works of several Western analysts, most of them from the United States.

From 1945 on, Moscow made it clear that its two principal war aims had been to defeat Germany, Italy, and Japan and to save the world for Marxism-Leninism. With the capitulation of the Axis, whatever reasons the Kremlin may have had for subordinating its long-term political goals to the expediency of cooperating with the West disappeared abruptly. What Westerners interpreted as a sudden shift in Soviet policy was manifested again and again in international forums, in the Middle East, in Berlin, and in Czechoslovakia, as well as in other sore spots that festered in the wake of World War II.[9]

During the 1945-50 period, with England and France almost as depleted from their war efforts as if they had been on the losing side, the United States became the principal target of the Eastern world. Thus the main burden for adopting a new policy to counter the postwar communist line naturally fell to the Americans. The wartime ardor of Americans for the Soviets, which was beginning to cool substantially, forced many Western writers and political figures to make another, and this time a more realistic, appraisal of Moscow. In the course of this process the popular concept of a guerrilla, and of the communist partisan in particular, as a pure and noble patriot was to undergo a slow but radical change.

The first indications that such a shift was in the wind were given by some of the leading architects of American wartime policy, such as Edward Stettinius, James Byrnes, Dean Acheson, and Dwight Eisenhower. In much the same way as had the repentant Winston Churchill, each of these public figures attempted to convince his public, and perhaps himself, that he personally had always entertained grave doubts as to Stalin's sincerity and as to the possibility for long-range cooperation with the communists. Most American writers of war memoirs tended to present themselves, either directly or by inference, as merely the executive agents of the policies of the deceased Roosevelt. Whether they resorted to apologies or to euphemisms, they left many questions unanswered, and often confused the reader rather than enlightening him.

Many individuals who had participated in direct wartime dealings with the Soviets or with the partisans also published their own accounts. Among these figures were former war correspondents and commentators, diplomats, advisers, military and other experts, and observers or participants in the conferences at Teheran, Moscow, Yalta, and Potsdam. The contributions of these people did shed some light on inter-Allied wartime relations for the benefit of the American public and allowed a first glimpse at many wartime secrets, thus helping to bridge the information gap left by the communications media and by propaganda efforts. But rarely was any explanation offered as to the rationale for Anglo-American helpt to the Partisans. Even more rare was any reference to the naiveté of Churchill and Roosevelt in their face-to-face encounters with Stalin that bore such unfortunate consequences. These subjects, it would seem, were still far too delicate for public discussion. It was fashionable at the time to take the Soviets to task for "the betrayal of the Allied cause" and to rebuke them mildly for the "creation of distrust among the once trustworthy war partners." At the same time, more considered analyses of the basic World War II blunders of the Western Allies and of their overzealous assistance to the communist partisans were conveniently left to future historians.

Among these future historians would be American political scientists and an array of analysts, researchers, and foreign policy and military experts. On them would devolve the task in the fifties and sixties of reassessing not only the World War II role of the partisans, but also the importance of such basic subjects as the ideology and the political history of the U.S.S.R.; the roles of the Comintern and the Cominform; the activities in many countries of local communist hard liners, of Soviet agents and advisers, and of their manipulations of mass organizations such as the people's front in the thirties. The capacity of these writers would be put to the test on the one hand by the deterioration in East-West relations, and on the other by individual Western moves and reactions in the course of the Cold War. Thus, these studies and analyses would continue to proliferate up to the present day, spawning in the process an army of Kremlinologists and Sinologists.

However, rather than attempt a sketchy progress report on studies on the U.S.S.R., China, and the Eastern bloc in general, we shall here limit our discussion to that narrow segment of this research that relates to communist insurrectionary technique. American studies in this area would in time be placed on a more organized footing and would result in an unprecedented increase in the body of knowledge on insurrection, particularly communist insurrection. With the proverbial American talent for detail and systematization, for reference and cross-reference, any of these studies would become a classical collection of data, statistics, and chronologies which the serious student could not afford to neglect.[10]

By the late forties the American scholar already enjoyed much wider access to evidence on wartime guerrilla movements than had been possible during the war. He could, for instance, visit many former hotbeds of guerrilla, interview the participants, and consult the mushrooming documentation centers in the West. Here he could gather an abundance of factual material on various aspects of insurrectionary organization and on the strategy and tactics of different guerrilla groups, as well as profiles of leading participants, casualty figures, and estimates of war damage. Also, in principle, at his disposal were tons of captured Axis documents, declassified Allied records, court proceedings of war crimes trials, and materials of national institutes in countries where the partisans had acceded to power at the war's end.[11]

With all these sources available to him, an American researcher could now sort out the facts and weed out many misconceptions and wartime exaggerations. From the technical standpoint, at least, it would seem that the subject of guerrilla should have been well on its way to receiving the same scholarly treatment as that accorded many other fields by the American academician in the postwar period. However, there seem to have been several obstacles to such a development—some technical, others psychological in nature, and still others ideological-political. Taken together, all these problems, as we shall see, contributed to slowing down the progress of insurrectionary study, leaving it always just a step or two behind reality.

The first and simplest explanation for dealy in the development of the study immediately after World War II may be found in the fact that the field of guerrilla war was a theoretical no-man's land. It was at first presumed to be an integral part of the military history of the Second World War, and as such the natural domain of the soldier and of the historian. However, it was thought to belong also to the general field of political thought, since many guerrilla movements espoused a specific ideology. Then, too, in view of the substantial political and structural changes and dislocations such movements had caused on the broader scene, the general subject seemed to belong in the field of international relations. At many points, moreover, the study of insurrection touched upon other disciplines, such as economics, jurisprudence, diplomatic history, religion, public health, education, literature, journalism, and psychology. In other words, the whole field lay open to examination by experts of every discipline, but in the United States no particular group advanced to lay claim to it. If the subject was treated at all, great care was exercised to keep the discussion well within tacitly established boundary lines.

Still another stumbling-block in the path of the American researcher was that the concept of guerrilla warfare itself seemed alien to him. Once freed from his wartime obligation to lavish praise on the anti-fascist guerrilla, he was now gaining access to sources that pointed up the violence, the lawlessness, the senseless destruction of the innocent that characterized insurrectionist activity. The guerrilla fighter was losing much of his charisma in the eyes of American authors and of the American public. Even though he was not yet completely discredited, in China and in Greece the former anti-fascist was now displaying the same zeal in attacking local populations, with its utter disregard for the sufferings inflicted on the innocent, as he directed toward attacking his local nationalist foe. Since there was no way of guessing the limits of his excesses, it was feared by many that his activities could infect dissident elements in the colonies, in areas bordering on the communist countries, or even in the Western states, thus providing these elements with blueprints for the violent overthrow of the governments in power.

The American academician, often inadequately prepared both by training and by tradition to understand the background of violent upheavals in far-away places, was now faced with having to reconcile two conflicting views. How could he on the one hand glorify the previously held position of the partisan while at the same time criticizing him for now wantonly destroying everything in his path? The reasons for this reluctance went even deeper, because the American scholar seems to have been influenced to some degree by the attitude on guerrilla held by the military and by Washington officials of the time. The military tended to minimize the military role of the guerrilla, while officialdom scoffed at his political effectiveness.

As a rule, American military experts were inclined to accord but a minor role to the wartime guerrilla. They maintained that the collapse of the Axis powers had not resulted from guerrilla pressure. The Axis capitulated rather because of the combined superiority of big powers, with their mass armies on the Eastern and Western fronts, as well as because of the saturation bombardment of industrially centralized Japan and Germany. During the 1941-45 period, American generals had no occasion to confront a hostile guerrilla force, for as it turned out, all insurrectionists, including those who fought one another as communists and nationalists, had been enlisted in the Allied cause. Without compelling evidence to guide him, the American expert had no basis for speculating on the guerrilla as a future foe. Many military leaders, who regarded guerrilla as primarily a political matter, felt that any decision should best be left to civilian policy makers.[12]

In addition, this was the era of nuclear weapons, which in itself threatened to relegate the guerrilla to the archives of history. The United States emerged from the war as a superpower, relatively unscarred by the hostilities, with unparalleled industrial potential and, for the time being, with a monopoly on the means of destruction. It could boast an atomic arsenal and a strategic air force that had given an impressive account of themselves over Hiroshima and Nagasaki, as well as in the Saar and in the Ruhr. What guerrilla act of sabotage or diversion could conceivably compare? If there was to be a war, it would be a major one, it was commonly believed, once again to be waged with and decided by heavy hardware. Under such conditions what would be the role of the guerrilla in the rear? Whom could he ambush or harass? Was not the whole question academic, since even the most basic questions relating to atomic war had yet to be formulated?

Civilian policy makers, again, even less informed than the military, provided little guidance. The Civil War in China, 1945-49, did offer many indications of the mobilizing potentials of ideology and of the effectiveness of guerrilla warfare in underdeveloped countries. These problems, however, seemed to have no direct bearing on the immediate interests of the United States. By the same token, the question of relating mass technology to the decentralized industrial regions commonly selected as guerrilla targets seemed premature. This problem would not arise until the outbreak of the Korean War in 1950.

If any rational or coherent ideas on the future of insurrectionary warfare were exchanged in the corridors of Washington at the time, they remained in the background, for the most part vague or unspoken. Here and there some prominent public figure might express the opinion that in a possible showdown with the communist bloc, a freedom-loving patriot from the Eastern bloc would rise again, demonstrating the same fire and the same imagination he had displayed in fighting the Axis. In other words, he would act as the avant-garde of the Western world, since it was he who was suffering most from the communist system. But here, again, the answer bore no relation to the nature of the question. How could such a wish stand the ghost of a chance of fulfillment in an era when one atomic bomb would do the work of countless numbers of patriots? Solitary as his role must surely be, what tactical function could the Eastern anti-communist freedom fighter perform? How could his possible contribution fit within the framework of a nuclear war?

The number of unknown factors concerning the type of war that could be expected when and if the Soviets acquired a nuclear capability was so overwhelming as to preclude any meaningful discussion. In the late forties the average American was aware in a general way that his country possessed a frightful weapon, one so formidable that it might in a single stroke destroy a city of many million inhabitants, or a whole country, or many countries. It could also render a region, even an entire continent, uninhabitable for decades to come, since radiation was likely to finish what the bomb had missed.

This time, besides, American soil would be vulnerable. No American soldier would have to cross the ocean to fight as he had done in two world wars. In those cases his enemy had been a soldier from far-off lands, and battles were waged at places he had never heard of. In the past it was always a distant city that had been destroyed—Berlin or Rome, Coventry or Le Havre, Antwerp or Narvik, Leningrad or Stalingrad, Singapore or Tokyo; and with the exception of Pearl Harbor, the home soil had never been touched by war in this century. But in a future conflict any American city or village could be the target. Long-range missiles could pulverize huge areas in New Hampshire or Nevada, Alaska or Alabama. Whatever the case, never again would war be "a foreign war," involving only foreign homes, foreign museums, and foreign industry.

The recurrent theme of the day seemed to be that the United States as well as the whole of mankind had been catapulted into the nuclear era. As for suggestions regarding what should be done under the circumstances, few responsible people came forth with any rational or worthwhile ideas. Should we retain and improve the nuclear arsenal in order to be always a step ahead of the Soviets when they acquired it, or should we destroy it? Was the taxpayer to tighten his belt endlessly to pay for devices that would perhaps never be used? Should the arsenal figure only as a threat, or merely as a deterrent to the other side? If an unprovoked attack occurred in the future, should it be repelled or should the opposition be blown out of existence? Does not this type of weapon presuppose in principle the creation of an entirely new military? Meanwhile, what was to be done with the conventional forces of the military? Who was after all to be entrusted with the unleashing of this new weaponry? Or with its stockpiling? Or with the decision to abolish it? Would we have to rely on loosely organized international bodies, on quarrelsome small countries, or on the governments of the present and future nuclear powers? And if the choice were to fall to the last-named, what assurance did we have that the governments of the nuclear powers would be more apt to find a peaceful means of settling the crisis than they had on previous occasions?

The late forties marked the beginning of a frustrating search for answers to these and many other questions. The Americans experimented with solutions, tested and abandoned many plans, formulated and reformulated their political-military doctrine. These exhaustive inquiries, again a promising topic for a separate study, merely resolved themselves into a protracted exploration for solution of a puzzle that had so far stumped all the experts: how to protect the United States from nuclear attack of another superpower, and how to protect the rest of the world from the effects of a confrontation between East and West. The subject was too important to be left to generals, too intricate technically to be confided to politicians, and too shrouded in secrecy to be brought in concrete terms to the public rostrum. Besides, the government officials and military men and scientists in the know were bound to secrecy for security reasons. And the general public, just when it desperately needed enlightenment, was getting its information from uninformed or misinformed sources.

Spokesmen were legion, each seemingly with his own angle. Leftists charged the administration in Washington with many sins: with the discovery, the manufacture, and the use of the bomb; with continuing research; with unwillingness to reveal its secret to other nations, and with sinister plans to deliver the bomb against the Eastern bloc; and, from the moment when the Soviet Union became a nuclear power, with refusal to disarm unilaterally. The confirmed pacifist viewed the stockpiling of atomic weapons as murderous and suicidal. The writer of science fiction and the Hollywood playwright capitalized on the fear of a push-button disaster. The voices of the earliest of hawks and doves were also heard: the hawks hinting that the bomb should be dropped on the Soviet Union before Stalin had the capacity to attack first or to retaliate; the doves proposing that the U.S.S.R. should best be treated as though it already had a nuclear arsenal. Mindful of the American restraint during its monopoly on the bomb, the Kremlin, the doves argued, would be given the noblest of precedents to follow.[13]

In these frenzied efforts to find answers—efforts which already in the late forties involved expenditures of billions and the tapping of ever fresh human resources, American society had very little energy left for long-range planning on the possible role of the guerrilla who might spring up in the future somewhere in Asia, or in Africa, or in Latin America, or in the colonies. For military minds especially, the first concern was protection from the holocaust; then concentration on conventional means of making or averting war. The subject of guerrilla warfare, a minor threat among so many major ones, rated a very low priority in Pentagon thinking and planning. In June 1950, however, when the Korean War broke out, American strategists were handed a good many surprises. The North Koreans threw themselves into the fray with both the conventional soldier and the guerrilla, employing all those strategical and tactical patterns that many a western expert considered outdated in an atomic era.

The North Korean attack against the South had been preceded in the March-May period by an intensification of guerrilla activities in the area between Seoul and the thirty-eighth parallel. Small bands of illegals had organized acts of sabotage and diversion and had established caches, an intelligence network, and observation posts. They were harrassing frontier patrols and liquidating selected representatives of the local administrations. These actions, hardly distinguishable at first glance from many similar incidents that had been taking place in the frontier zone throught the late forties, were interpreted by the Seoul government as nothing out of the ordinary. This time, however, they were a prelude to a general offensive by North Korean regulars.

The aim of the Northern troops, according to Pyongyang, was to overthrow the puppet government of Syngman Rhee, to free their southern brothers from capitalist oppression, and to unite the two Koreas. Weak and caught off guard, South Korean troops retreated. American and U.N. forces came to their assistance; and with their material superiority in firepower and in the air quickly reversed the Northern tide. Informed by friendly sources that the U.N. forces would not invade North Korea, Chinese volunteers entered the fray. Their appearance, unexpected and in force, turned the tide once again. But before long MacArthur landed at Inchon, while the South Korean and U.N. forces launched a successful counteroffensive. Again the invaders were repulsed. Lost territory was recaptured, and before long the status quo ante had for the most part been reestablished. There now ensued a protracted series of fighting contacts, the sort of engagements the hard liner calls teeter-totter bouts. Finally, after many months of tortuous negotiations at Panmunjon, the war ended officially, leaving in its wake the seeds of future crises.

During the clash, which has been widely discussed in American political literature, the Pyongyang planners concentrated on the deployment of larger or smaller regular units searching for fighting contacts with the U.N. troops. They would shift positions and attack in depth only when all the odds seemed to be in their favor. However, when the U.N. forces demonstrated unexpected resistance, the North Koreans would abruptly call a halt and withdraw to another position. With their strong political indoctrination, the North Korean army cared very little for real estate. Only when they were tactically outmaneuvered and trapped, or when an individual outpost had obvious political or propaganda significance, did they make a serious effort to capture or defend a specific area.

Lightly armed and mobile, the larger North Korean and

later the Chinese units at times provided more targets than the U.N. troops could effectively oppose. The United States Air Force attacked them with notable success in the frontal zones and along the main communications lines. Attacks against smaller units, however, those spread throughout the desolate mountainous areas of South Korea, usually involved the expenditure of far greater resources than were warranted by any possible gains. Then, as we have mentioned, there were the guerrilla bands in the rear of the allied front: agents from the north who infiltrated the ranks of fleeing refugees; teams of saboteurs and many part-time local partisans going about their business in the daytime and fighting at night.

All of these elements had to be dealt with, but how? Targets were many, most of them invisible. Against them, of what use were the overwhelming strength and firepower of the U.N. forces? Should this mass of advanced equipment be left to rust in supply depots? Should hundreds of highly trained men fly thousands of air combat sorties and waste napalm and tons of ammunition on "plowing up mountains" or "machine-gunning grasshoppers or anthills?" The U.S. forces, whose strength lay in their hardware and whose tactical plans were based on that hardware, felt compelled to use it. As it turned out, however, the fire was often directed against anything that moved or stood in the way: a suspected partisan, a noncombatant, or even a buffalo. Quite often, though, the peasant hut concealed a bunker, a church the radio station, while partisans who had ambushed troops in the area merged with the peasants intent on cultivating their fields.

The directives in the latest American field manual offered very little help with these problems. Written for the benefit of the conventional soldier, the manual envisioned the enemy as the traditional fighting man, with uniform and insignia and openly bearing arms. According to the basic concepts set forth in the manual, a given area had to be either in enemy hands or captured or contested. In Korea, however, a new element was introduced: the guerrilla, who made every area a contested area. He might cooperate with the North Korean or with the Chinese volunteers or he might act independently. He mined the roads and cut communications lines. At night, when the U.N. troops were in bivouac, he could put the whole camp on alert with a few bullets fired in the direction of the barracks. By the time patrols had been sent out to capture him, he had disappeared. Furthermore, the guerrilla instilled fear in the local inhabitants. The simple South Korean peasant living in guerrilla-infested zones was caught in the middle: should he obey the daytime orders of the U.N. troops, who could level his village in a matter of minutes, or the night orders of raiders who were picking off his uncooperative neighbors?

In the final analysis, who would bear the responsibility of overcoming the guerrilla—the weak Seoul government or the well-armed U.N. forces who were hampered by political-legal limitations? Was the decision to be based on political or on military criteria? Military logic dictated that the guerrilla was fair game as long as he was an infiltrator from the north. If he was a native of South Korea, then he was also a political problem, for at least in theory he was subject to prosecution by the Seoul government alone. The confusion in this theoretical area was compounded by the more real problem of how to cope with an enemy who attacked only to vanish into thin air. Did the situation call for conventional military measures or for political treatment that was foreign to American military thinking? Perhaps some combination of the two was called for.

Moreover, the decision by the Pyongyang strategists to invade South Korea was based on two assumptions, neither of which made the puzzle easier to solve. First, it was assumed that the Americans would not resort to nuclear arms in the Korean theater; and secondly, it was apparent after the Washington decision not to cross the thirty-eighth parallel that the U.N. forces were there with the intention neither of winning nor losing. Pyongyang drew from these assumptions two obvious conclusions: first, an enemy who for whatever reason abjures the use of his most powerful weapon should be treated as though he did not posses that weapon; and second, the enemy's decision to fight with one hand tied behind his back was certainly not binding on both sides. This policy of the north in its turn created two problems for the Americans in Korea—one involving the role of the enlisted man sent to fight the communists, the other relating to the part assigned the general officer. The soldier would question the rationale of his participation in a neither-win-nor-lose conflict and the general his function as a military leader.

The American G.I., the marine, and the flyer were sent to Korea well-equipped and psychologically prepared to do battle with any enemy regular. At the outset they regarded it as their mission to defeat the intruders from the north, to prove to the communists that the free world would not stand idly by while communists invaded a noncommunist state, and, once their mission had been accomplished, to pack up their gear and go home. In the mind of the average fighting man, this policy would normally have meant that the northerners should be treated as every enemy had been in the past: that is, the combat should have been carried on at every level and by every means available, on the front lines, in the enemy's rear, and to ultimate victory. But suddenly his commanders were insisting that in Korea an American soldier was not involved in an actual war, but rather in a police action. Strangely enough, as it turned out, few of the officers themselves appeared to know what this term really meant. What kind of police action was it that required the presence of mass army, navy, air force, and mechanized units, that ravaged entire regions, and that forced hundreds of thousands of refugees into exile? Was this a new type of war? Or was the combat soldier facing a new type of enemy?

It did not take long for the G.I. to sense that contrary to the rules of the game his enemy was enjoying a privileged status. The foe had somehow been granted two types of sanctuary: one, North Korea and China, off limits to U.N. ground forces; the other, China, off limits for the U.S. flyer.

Soldiers began to complain that the enemy could come to the south when combat-ready, fight the U.N. troops until he had accomplished his purpose or exhausted himself, and then pull back to the sanctuary of the north to rest, regroup, or retrain. Fresh troops then took his place to continue the battle. This rotation appeared to the U.N. infantryman to be never-ending. What could have been the origin of such a double standard, where one set of rules applied for the enemy and a completely different set for the U.N. troops? Was the enemy to be destroyed or simply meted out some token punishment for encroaching upon another nation's sovereignty? Should he be killed or rebuked or forced to reform? What possible justification could be found for requiring a noncommunist soldier to sacrifice himself in such a war? Could it be possible that some of our leaders themselves believed this was not a just war? Or did they believe that this was not a war at all, rather a diplomatic maneuver carried on by force of arms?

Once again, contrary to all strategic calculations of the late forties, here was the G.I., a foreign soldier in a foreign land. At an early stage in this conflict it became painfully evident to him that he lacked adequate training to take on the Korean partisans. All Koreans looked alike to him and any one of them could have been an illegal. By what means was this illegal to be recognized or smoked out? As the G.I. was to learn through bitter experience, the partisan in South Korea could appear from any quarter and in any guise—in the person of an old man, as a boy carrying messages, as a woman with a hand grenade concealed in her baby's carriage, a refugee with a gun under his hat, an interpreter, a local priest, or a teacher. He believed himself surrounded by these enemies. Feeling let down and even betrayed, he raised the logical question: Did we come here to save them or to be killed by them? And to make matter worse, the partisan enemy relied on weapons that the G.I. knew little about— ideology, propaganda, agitation, political terror. The enlisted man was heard to ask again and again, How is it that no one taught us about these arms in boot camp? Why are most of our officers as unfamiliar with these weapons as we are? Should the enemy's ideas be challenged with bullets or with better ideas?

The confusion in the mind of the ordinary soldier found its parallel in the problem facing the top command. The generals in charge arrived on the scene fully prepared to work out overall plans, to oversee combat operations, and to treat the enemy in the same manner in which he treated the U.N. forces. Political issues, however, were to be left as usual to civilian leaders in Washington. But in Korea the general was soon given to understand that more was at stake than an ordinary military clash between two foes over a given territory. The traditional division of functions between military and civilian became clouded.

At the onset of the war Washington officialdom appeared to show little interest in tactical matters. They displayed little opposition to MacArthur's efforts to pressure the North Koreans into withdrawing above the thirty-eighth parallel by taking all the military steps he considered expedient. But the Truman administration soon became apprehensive. They seemed to fear that such a course might incite China to flex its muscles. Because some U.N. allies gave indication of similar misgivings, MacArthur was ultimately replaced. In spite of this, Chinese volunteers joined the cause of their North Korean brothers, thus placing MacArthur's successors in a new and equally ticklish situation. The American command was called upon to defeat the northern invaders, yet to avoid expanding the war in a way that might involve the Chinese, or what would be worse, the Soviet Union. To satisfy Washington's wishes for victory in the field and yet not to provoke China or Russia, U.N. troops were to defeat the North Koreans and Chinese volunteers, but not too soundly. They were to walk a tightrope and strike with a big stick, but not too hard.

The U.N. allies who participated in the Korean venture were another element that the commanding general had to contend with. Toward the end of 1950 segments of public opinion in England, France, Belgium, and Canada had already begun to charge Washington with a lack of specific goals in Korea. Many leaders in these countries as well as in other Western countries feared that the operation could drag on indefinitely, exhausting them financially and exacting a heavy toll of killed and wounded for no apparent purpose. For the United States to be waging a war against North Korea, a small communist country, at a time when Washington could not itself define its long-term policy toward the U.S.S.R. and China, its principal adversaries, seemed to many of these critics as irrational as it was self-defeating. The critics seemed to forget in some cases that their own troops as well were actively engaged in pacification actions in areas liberated from the communists. Possibly they considered it expedient to transfer the burden of guilt for alleged use of excessive force to the Americans. The U.N. counterguerrilla operations, considered over-harsh, came under fire by these critics.

The American commander in the field thus found himself in the cross-fire. His battle plans had to be reconciled first with Washington's policy not to widen the war and then with an effort to convince the world that the counterintervention in Korea was an international, not solely an American project. Any further plans had to be coordinated with the desires of his U.N. allies. Finally, it was to his advantage to avoid further irritation to Moscow or Peking. Should he demonstrate a degree of McCarthyist individualism, he risked losing his job. In other words, his centrale, Washington, believed in him only so long as he played Washington's game. The national supreme commands of his U.N. allies seemed at the same time to lack confidence in him, while all shades of leftists, as well as Peking, Moscow, and Pyongyang, accused him of engineering war crimes. The only area where his function as a fighting man seemed to bear any relation to his previous training was in the matter of tactics, but even this situation was only temporary.

It was not long before Washington officialdom left its imprint here, too. The field commanders were gradually forced to abdicate many of their traditional responsibilities to initiate or to carry on new field actions. There was now the ever-present possibility that any new action might serve as a prelude either to a fresh clash between the United States and its allies or between East and West. For this reason, the commander had to clear every contemplated action with Washington and to get the stamp of approval of civilians located on another continent.

The fear of what came to be know as the McCarthy heresy was apparently very real among career generals of the time; few of them were willingly to place their heads on the block. The commanding officer was forbidden to authorize any long-range offensive actions such as paratroop drops or infiltration of small units in the enemy's rear, or to order U.S. naval incursions into North Korean or Chinese territorial waters. The territory on which the U.N. troops should operate and the mass of weapons and the degree of force that should be used often were specified in detail. He received directives also as to when to unleash a local offensive and when to call a halt. The long process by which the American military would learn to follow tactical orders from Washington may be said to have been initiated at this juncture. The general would learn how not to exceed his individual tactical instructions, how to prosecute the war in his area of command without going overboard. Both these procedures marked the beginning of his transformation from military leader to military official. Critics charged later, in fact, that he became little more than a glamorized military clerk.

In fairness it may be said that at the time, this change in the relationship between civilian and military authority seemed sound enough. Basing its policy on the argument that the conflict in Korea was primarily political, and that the enemy was shifting and unpredictable, Washington was convinced that civilian leaders must hold the reins. No field commander, no matter how well informed, could know for certain at a given moment what was motivating his president-commander-in-chief. The American president, unofficial leader of the free world, must be presumed to have a clear view of the whole picture, while the perspective of the field commander was severely limited.

When the Korean conflict finally ended in stalemate, it was not surprising that the G.I. should expect an earnest search for solutions to the problems he had encountered in a war called a police action, a war in which conventional force had been pitted against guerrilla. This expectation was all the more reasonable because many down-to-earth Americans and returning veterans had begun to wonder aloud why the Truman and the Eisenhower administrations had been content to settle for only partial victory after demanding such sacrifices. Some criticized Washington for its conduct of operations, others for political unpreparedness to wage war with the communists, in particular, with the communist guerrilla. Many of the critics, inclined to look upon the American soldier as fiercely anti-communist, appeared at a loss to understand how some captured American soldiers and élite officers, too, had succumbed to the pressure of communist interrogators and had publicly accused their own nation of waging a criminal war. The disclosure—not too widely publicized—that a smaller group of them had even defected to Mao's China after the war's end caused many Americans to pose even more embarrassing questions.

Could our politically unarmed soldier-technician from the West be a match for his insurrectionist-ideologue foe in a guerrilla contest? Why did the communist troops, even when weaker and on the run, still seem to be tactically on the offensive when employing their guerrilla arm? Did not our enlisted men and officers alike need a thorough political indoctrination instead of the short, superficial briefing on communist insurrectionary methods they received; and if so, who was to direct the project? Was it only political literacy and knowledge of the area in question that were lacking for success in combating the guerrilla? Or was it the fact that the soldier from an affluent, civilized country possesses certain inherent traits that prevent him from putting down his often underfed guerrilla enemy? Was it his lack of individualism, his training to act as a member of a team? Or was it his inability to withstand the pressure of uncertainty and ever-present danger?

Still other very practical questions arose to plague the average enlisted man. Why did the Turks and the Greeks seem to have had more success in fighting the guerrilla in Korea than their American allies? Why was there so much emphasis on the soldier's equipment—better guns, reserve socks and underwear, toilet articles—instead of what might have been considered more relevant to this type of warfare— the development of physical toughness, iron nerves, combat imagination, and lightening of combat gear?

Who was to be entrusted with making the on-the-spot decisions called for in this war of surprise action and ambush, and of high mobility, where every move has both military and political implications? What would happen, for instance, if the squad leader out on patrol spotted a guerrilla force on the move and called for an air attack? Could he be expected to ask his men to sit it out until the complex American military-political communications system brought back the answer? Could it be that perhaps another, a new type of military, composed of politicians in uniform empowered to make decisions on the spot, might be the answer? Then again, might not this question be academic or even heretical?

In the meantime, the U.S.S.R. had acquired a nuclear arsenal, an accomplishment that forced the United States to reassess and update its strategic doctrine of the forties. With the fear of holocaust now a very real one, the problem of insurgency and counterinsurgency, which had seemed so important at the time of the Korean conflict, had to take a back seat. The Korean episode seemed to be forgotten almost overnight. If instances of guerrilla did emerge, they concerned others, the English, the French, the Dutch, the Portuguese, the countries of South America, or the gray areas in general. In these cases, the guerrilla was said to be attempting to overthrow the incumbent or to expel the colonizers or to prepare conditions for accession of the communists to power. In the United States he was viewed primarily as a foreign-policy problem. The turmoil he caused, therefore, was left to the disposition of diplomats on the spot, of intelligence men, and of those Washington officials who were involved in conducting relations with other countries. The bulk of the efforts of the U.S. military at this period, 1955-60, was concentrated on the arms race. Any remaining energy went to updating American conventional arms, to stabilizing the chains of command, and to incorporating into the system all the changes in the prerogatives of the military brought about by Korea.

Since it was not possible, however, to sidestep completely all the American experience with guerrilla in Korea, a handful of Pentagon analysts was assigned to assess the phenomenon and to prepare for the use of the military summaries on the strategy and tactics of insurrectionists. Funds for this project were in fact appropriated and the results were put into the hands of American officers, military instructors, and cadets. These manuscripts of the Pentagon analysts, which were classified and are mainly a rehash of the war in Korea and of World War II, contributed more to the codification of some of the past campaigns than to a rounding out of the conceptions of the politico-military role of the Pentagon. As for any real contribution these studies may have made to enlightening the American public, the less said the better. Any impact in the direction of broadening the knowledge of government officials was equally limited. Anyone wishing to probe deeper into the subject than would have been possible from the classified, abbreviated, and lifeless reports would have been able to gain some insight into the current thought of American officialdom only through an information leak, through the sporadic declassification of documents, or from unguarded statements of individuals in the know. Even then, whatever the general public might have been able to draw out of these sources was dated and out of context in most instances, or reflected the detailed evaluation of an isolated guerrilla action that only an expert could profit from.

It fell to the American political scientist, then, to present the general public with its first comprehensive and comprehensible picture of insurrection. The offerings from this source consist mainly of serious studies, a refreshing contrast to the encomiums heaped upon the partisan during World War II, to the apologetic autobiographies of participants, to the reports of newsmen, to the emotion-packed accounts of refugees, to the wordy descriptions of politicians, and to the secret utterances by which military men or diplomats added to the general confusion on the subject. The efforts of the political scientists are distinguished on the whole by an insistence on thorough documentation and adhere to the principle of *audiatur et altera pars*.

Because the conscientious theoretician felt that the impact of the guerrilla on the world scene in the middle fifites had been crucial, he could not agree with the military or the political leaders that the subject should be sidetracked or should continue to be treated in a one-sided, light-handed manner. Mainland China, with the guerrilla as the mainspring, had already fallen within the Eastern orbit. In Southeast Asia and then in Algeria the Viet Minh and the F.L.N. were to render serious, even mortal blows to the French colonial empire. Many British, Belgian, Dutch, Spanish, and Portuguese possessions were involved to such an extent by the anarchy of guerrilla that they seemed to be political no man's lands. In South America and the Middle East the insurrectionist was also active. As for Cuba, while U.S. officials, political scientists, and journalists were trying to decide whether Castro was a Marxist, an agrarian reformer, or a modern Robin Hood, the Monroe Doctrine had been defied and the Eastern bloc had established a base fifty miles from American shores.

American political scientists, whose findings we shall attempt to analyze in this summary, thus faced a formidable challenge. First they had to make of insurrectionary warfare a respectable topic of inquiry by overcoming the resistance of the academic community. The subject of guerrilla had up to then been denied a place in the university curriculum. In addition, in order to invest the guerrilla with the importance his past record warranted, the academic had to neutralize the inherent distaste of the American public for this "illegitimate and indecent" subject that, as many believed, did not essentially touch them. To accomplish this many a writer was obliged to go to great lengths to prove the obvious to his colleagues and to the reading public: first, that the guerrilla, threatening the status quo with such frequency and intensity, could not reasonably be separated from studies of the political process; and second, that an American forewarned is forearmed.

At this point, the researcher seems to have availed himself of two methodological novelties: the insistent use of factual presentation and the incorporation of his research efforts on guerrilla into several specialized area studies. The first process led him to pack as much data as he could between the covers of his book. This made it possible for him to adopt a detatched attitude toward the ideology of individual participants in guerrilla turmoil. To lend it an aura of the scientific, he had therefore to depoliticize purely political warfare. The second procedure, while lightening his burden, permitted him at the same time to weave the facts he had amassed into the framework of the disciplines recognized as integral parts of area studies, such as history, economics, geography, and sociology.

As we shall see, the use of these two approaches had its advantages and its disadvantages. While a writer might expand greatly the technical knowledge on an individual guerrilla movement, he might in his diligent search for objectivity often neglect to fit such a movement into the world political scene. He would thus escape, whether deliberately or not, the necessity of making value judgments.

Here, somewhat encapsulated, is the way a typical American political scientist, using the methodology we have described, might present a guerrilla movement. First of all, his position is in sharp contrast to that of the hard liner: having no cause to defend, the American researcher finds it unnecessary to insist that there are only two opinions, his own and the wrong one. He tends to consider all the participants in the clash rather than just the side he happens to be familiar with. His attitude is less paternalistic. He rarely sets out with preconceived ideas, only to follow through by selecting the evidence that would seem to uphold them. Finally, the recent work bears little resemblance to that of World War II and to earlier American accounts on guerrilla. The modern-day writer, preoccupied as he is with the discovery and checking of the evidence, rarely has either the time or the inclination for panegyrics or editorializing.

The political scientist's research is likely to demonstrate an awareness of the usual requirements of scholarly work: a conscientious effort not to overlook any possible source of material; verification of the author's findings; meticulous attention to chronology; insistence on treating the relationship between cause and effect, and on comparing the author's conclusions with those of other authors. A work of this kind is likely to contain an abundance of statistics and copious data on the sociopolitical profile of the country in question. In fact, in his zeal to supply complete background information, the political scientist may end up by seeming to give this material the main thrust rather than his text.

The author frequently expands on this detail by going on to treat the causes for the uprising. He may discuss the general ineffectiveness of the incumbent administration of such issues as corruption and nepotism. Or, in the case of the colonies, he may offer his observations on the poor contacts between the metropolis and the local rulers. Having collected all the facts he can discover, he generally leaves his broader comments to be made either by protagonists or enemies of the regime, by foreign experts, or by members of international committees of inquiry. In all fairness, however, he has made a real effort to analyze local political parties, their organizational structure and the personalities of their leaders, and the degree of their connection with foreign states. If the communists are in any way involved in an uprising, its entire range of tactics is given wide coverage. The most thought-provoking sections are usually those that examine how, when, and where the power vacuum has come into being and what specific methods the communists have used to exploit it.

The course of an insurrection tends to be described by an American analyst through the presentation of as many incontrovertible facts as possible. Announcement of the winner, however, is more than likely to be made through comments of the participants or of foreign observers; and if these are given in another language, the translations are likely to be rendered in idiomatic English. When the American writer refers to factors that may have decided the outcome of the battle, it is simply a matter of his trying to treat these considerations as briefly as possible because most of them do not easily lend themselves to footnoting.

With the sequence of events presented in this manner, the reader is gradually prepared for a victorious outcome for one side or the other. If the writer can successfully maneuver through this factual chronology and can incorporate in it all the available data on foreign diplomatic, financial, and military assistance, as well as on the reaction of the United Nations and of world opinion, the reader may lay aside the book feeling he has the complete picture. But why events took the course they did may not always be clear. Indeed, there are indications that many an American author tends to steer away from attempts to measure and to assess those indeterminate factors that assure the victory of one side or another in these conflicts. The political level of participants, self-denial and self-sacrifice, singleness of purpose, sense of timing, tactical versatility, and elasticity are among those that come to mind. Many believe that the assessment of these factors, which are too imponderable to be treated in a concrete manner, requires a degree of skill quite out of proportion to the author's apparent desire to let the facts speak for themselves.*

If revolutionary insurrectionary war is both a trade and an art, it is the analysis of the phenomenon as an art that is most often missing from the American text on guerrilla. Undoubtedly, the processes that go on in the mind of a man involved in revolution do not belong within the purview of his research. However, they also touch other fields in which the author claims no competence or which he has no desire to examine. Assume, for instance, that his subject is the 1970 Tet offensive of the Viet Cong and the North Vietnamese regulars against South Vietnam. He may record and analyze the offensive in detail, but the researcher is helpless to measure by his usual methods of analysis the fanaticism of the Viet Cong fighter or the degree of his endurance. Is his staying power generated by indoctrination or by the momentary pressure of a leader against his men? Or does it spring from the V.C.'s background? Or perhaps from the fact that the majority of Vietnamese men born between 1920 and 1950 have had to struggle against a succession of flags? Conditioned almost from birth to fusillades, sacrifice, and death, they fight as though it were an every-day affair. This the observer-author is likely to interpret as fanaticism.

Using the same research tools, the analyst may cite a sudden defection of soldiers from one side to another. If he has done his work thoroughly, he may even quote a number of the men involved, their names, and the villages they came from. As for the reasons that have led them to change sides, these in most cases are beyond his reach. Then again, one might well ask why many villagers from the fertile valleys and

---

\* This characteristic more than any other has led some students to remark that much in the same manner as the hard liner avoids stubborn realities, the American author on guerrilla shies away from expressing his own thoughts. Ostensibly, just as the hard liner avoids crowding his conclusions with too many facts, so the American writer steers clear of polluting his body of evidence with too many comments of his own.

the delta regions are likely to side with the Viet Cong, while the montagnards, the landless, and those with little to lose are prevailingly anti-communist. Is the analyst to seek the answer in geography or in the inherent stubbornness of a mountain man who rejects the city-bred rebel ordering him whom to kill and when to die? Will the answer be found in history, or in the montagnard's alleged willingness at times to die for nothing? Might not the researcher be better advised to leave these questions to the psychologist, to the sociologist, to the philosopher, or to the priest?

Though many American studies in guerrilla offer a wealth of data on the makeup of individual guerrilla movements, only a handful of them speculate on the reasons for the generally small percentage of workers among the guerrillas, or on the relatively high percentage of middle- and upper-class offspring in the class enemy's midst. Just what inspires these young people to join the communists? Can it be a suddenly acquired sense of security springing from a new acquaintance with iron discipline and an unaccustomed demand for selflessness? Do these questions perhaps belong in the domain of the analyst?

The necessity to stick to cold, dry facts and to steer clear of fields other than the author's own can easily impair the validity of a text on guerrilla warfare. Though the extent to which the work suffers is not measurable or predictable, these restrictions appear to contribute to the formalistic objectivity that is believed in academic circles to be imperative. On one side this quality may make such studies invaluable to the student, but does it really provide him with an unimpeachable source? Does it leave him with adequate material for making an independent judgment? On the other hand, given the fast pace of current affairs, has not much of the material become dated almost before it leaves the press?

Even in those few cases when an earnest effort has been made to depart from a mere cataloguing of the stages in the development of a local guerrilla movement in favor of making a broader assessment, it is only the exceptional instance in which the author has not become bogged down by his formalistic approach. Instead of finding an abundance of data on a specific case, then, we are presented in many instances with much more material than might seem necessary. Just as the author cannot describe in detail all the leaves on one tree, he fails in his attempt to picture the whole forest. If, for example, he singles out the communists as the principal instigators of insurrection in different areas, it is his precise research which impels him to observe that in no two places do they act the same. This in turn leads him inevitably to present each of these instances as a separate phenomenon. Thus the only common thread holding them together—communism—is itself cut to pieces. The fact that the guerrilla threatens the status quo the world over is made unmistakably clear. As for the political and the human makeup of this guerrilla and what it is that makes him so successful, the careful reader is likely to find himself as much in the dark after studying the textbook as before he opened it.

It seems to be the fashion in our age to charge the author not so much with not knowing all the answers as with not asking the right questions. This growing clamor for a more precise kind of information about the political and psychological aspects of insurrectionary warfare is directed at one fundamental issue: Why are our leaders and their Western colleagues constantly a step behind the insurrectionist and why does the West appear to have been defeated even when the guerrilla movement has not won?

Is it because our leaders suffer from deeply rooted provincialism? Or does it rest in their bureaucratism, or in their superficial acquaintance with Marxist philosophy, or in their apparent reluctance to probe any ideological novelty? How can one explain the lack of resourcefulness manifest in their repeating over and over again the same ill-advised and unsuccessful counterguerrilla patterns? We might ascribe this to a decline in imagination, or to an absence of competent leaders, or to the lack of a national ideology. Could the *Zeitgeist* perhaps be operating against these leaders, a possibility we have already suggested? Can it be their disregard of the wishes of the people, a rather common element of warfare? Or the natural outgrowth of indecisive policies toward the Eastern bloc and the gray areas? What sort of reasoning has led one Washington administration after another to shunt back and forth the responsibility for the struggle against the guerrilla, shifting it in turn from the military to civilian official to computer to bureaucrat and back to the military? Why does Washington, which usually drags its heels when any action is called for, strike with lightning speed only when it recalls from the battlefront someone like MacArthur or Westmoreland or John Lavelle whether or not their efforts were considered expedient?

How serious is the failure of our military to meet the guerrilla threat? Where can the blame for this failure be placed? Should we regard it as an unwarranted dependence on matériel or as an implied underestimation of the full capability of the combat soldier? Can the modern regular, especially if he has been pampered and geared to fight from nine to five forty hours a week, be considered a match for the insurrectionist, usually a volunteer who demands only more and more combat? Why are our generals compared with increasing frequency to hidebound bureaucrats or to would-be businessmen or to blisterless, tenured trade-union leaders?

How can we explain the fact that these and many similar questions continue to be asked by people who lay no claim to expertise? What makes the author-academician so reluctant to probe more deeply into these matters? Is a new thought really considered a heresy today? Or is it that fresh thoughts or original interpretations have no place in the formalistic schematic approach? Is it not one of the functions of the political scientist to determine whether the guerrilla is here to stay or a dated phenomenon? What trends in the different schools of thought on guerrilla are to prevail, those of the hard liners, which disregard sacrifice and destruction, or the concepts of the South American rebels? Or the recommendation of Nkrumah that the sword of the guerrilla should represent a threat but should be used only on rare occasions? Or the tendency of the New Leftists to replace the guerrilla's bullet with the ballot? And is it not possible in the long run that guerrilla methods will be adopted by the criminal or the modern-day pirate?

Needless to say, it is hardly realistic to expect an American writer on guerrilla to formulate all these questions or to be in a position to propose answers. He is far more likely to center his attention on what he believes to be his essential role: that of unearthing, codifying, and presenting to the serious student an ever-expanding body of knowledge on insurrection. Therefore, to combine his role of professional researcher with the ambitions of an innovator in national policy toward the guerrilla on a world or a local scale seems contrary to his credo. And this holds especially true in a country whose leaders seem to be still at sea over who should take charge of the task of either putting us a step ahead of the controversial guerrilla, or at least of bringing us abreast of him.

## Notes

1. Brigadier C. Aubrey Dixon and Otto Heilbrunn, *Communist Guerrilla Warfare* (New York: Praeger), p. 21.

2. For broader discussion of the methods used by members of the British military mission to Draza Mihailovic headquarters to sever any contact of the U.S. liaison officers with American officials, see Albert Seitz (Col. U.S.A., ret.), *Mihailovic: Hoax or Hero?* (Columbus, Ohio: Leigh House, 1953), pp. 10-14; Walter Mansfield, "Mihailovic and Tito" in *The Book on Drazaa* (*Knjiga od Drazi* [in Serbian] (Windsor, Canada: Serbian National Defense, 1956, Vol. II), pp. 345-56).

3. Robert McClintock, *The Meaning of Limited War* (Boston: Houghton Mifflin, 1967), pp. 197-8.

4. See "Requiem for the Battle of Dienbienphu," in Jules Roy, *The Battle of Dienbienphu* trans. R. Baldick (New York: Harper and Row, 1965), pp. 288-310.

5. See *The Economist*, Sept. 11, 1965.

6. *Conquest Without War*, comp. and ed. by N. H. Mager and Jacques Katel (New York: Simon and Schuster 1961) pp. 49-50, 229 and 231.

7. *Khrushchev Remembers*, Strobe Talbot, ed. (Boston: Little, Brown, 1970), p. 517. For a broad discussion of nuclear confrontation, see also in the same book: "Fidel Castro and the Caribbean Crisis" (Chapter 20, pp. 488-505), and "Defending the Socialist Paradise" (Chapter 21, pp. 506-25).

8. *Conquest Without War*, p. 327., *American Authors: Ever A Step Behind the Guerrilla?*

9. For a fuller understanding of this shift, its roots and early manifestations, see D. F. Fleming, *The Cold War and Its Origins, 1917-1960* (London: George Allen and Unwin, 1961), Vols. I and II; Hugh Seton-Watson, *The New Imperialism* (London: The Bodley Head, 1961); Hugh Seton-Watson, *Neither War Nor Peace* (New York: Praeger, 1960); Evan Luard, ed., *The Cold War* (New York: Praeger, 1964); Marshall D. Shulman, *Stalin's Foreign Policy Reappraised* (Cambridge: Harvard University Press, 1963); Ian Grey, *The First Fifty Years* (New York: Coward-McCann, 1967), pp. 305-436; Alexander Werth, *Russia at War 1941-1945* (New York: E. P. Dutton, 1964); Louis Aragon, *A History of the U.S.S.R.* (New York: David McKay, 1962), pp. 417-536; Frederick C. Barghoorn, *Soviet Foreign Propaganda* (Princeton, N. J.: Princeton University Press, 1964); Andrei J. Vyshinskii, *Problems of International Law and International Politics* (Moscow: State Publishing House of Judicial Literature, 1952 [in Russian]), pp. 5-395; *Problems of Foreign Policy of the U.S.S.R. and Contemporary International Relations* (Moscow: State Publishing House of Political Literature, 1958 [in Russian]); V. G. Truhanovskii, *Foreign Policy of England after the Second World War* (Moscow: State Publishing House of Political Literature, 1957 [in Russian]); M. A. Grechev, *Colonial Politics of the U.S.A. after the Second World War* (Moscow: Academy of Science of the U.S.S.R., 1958 [in Russian]); Val Zorin, *Monopolies and Politics of the U.S.A.* (Moscow: Institute of Foreign Relations, 1960 [in Russian]); and *History of the U.S.S.R.* (Moscow: Superior Party School of the Central Committee of the CP U.S.S.R., 1960 [in Russian]), pp. 731-91, 831-85.

10. See the suggested readings.

11. For many a Western researcher, these institutes represented sources of data of one-sided value at best. For instance, in Poland, Albania, and Yugoslavia, after 1945 he could collect information on activities of communist guerrillas, though it might be laudatory and often tailored, as well as acquaint himself with an endless series of accusations agsinst the nationalist insurgents. Data on German atrocities

were generally somewhat more reliable, though often crimes committed by the occupation troops against the civilian population were presented as though they were perpetrated exclusively against communist activists and sympathizers. In this connotation the Yugoslav Committee on War Crimes (1944-48) may serve as the most illustrative example.

12. Interestingly enough, it was the American military experts who during this period as well as in the decade to follow (1945-55) were the last to shed some light on matters of guerrilla warfare for the benefit of the general public.

13. In the serious literature on guerrilla warfare that has appeared in the United States, these conceptions remained for the most part without a representative protagonist or a published work. They surfaced mainly in sporadic statements or comments of various political figures or candidates for public office during election campaigns.

# Bibliography

Aguilar, Luis E. "Régis Debray: Where Logic Failed," *The Reporter*, December 28, 1967.

Ali, Tariq, ed. *The New Revolutionaries: A Handbook of the International Radical Left*. New York: William Morrow, 1969.

Allen, William E. D. *Guerrilla War in Abyssinia*. Middlesex, Eng.: Harmondsworth; New York: Penguin Books, 1943.

Almond, Gabriel A. *The Appeals of Communism*. Princeton, N.J.: Princeton University Press, 1954.

Altbach, Philip G., and Laufer, Robert S., eds. "Students Protest." *Annals of the American Academy of Political and Social Science* [AAPSS], Vol. 395, May 1971.

American University, Washington, D.C. Special Operations Research Office. *Case Studies in Insurgency and Revolutionary War*. 4 vols. Washington, D.C., 1963-64.

American University, Washington, D.C. Special Operations Research Office. *A Counterinsurgency Bibliography*. By D. M. Condit and others. Washington, D.C., 1963.

Andrian, Charles. "Patterns of African Socialist Thought." *African Forum*, Vol. 1, no. 3 (Winter 1966).

Aragon, Louis. *A History of the U.S.S.R. from Lenin to Khrushchev*. Translated by Patrick O'Brian. New York: David McKay, 1964.

Arendt, Hannah. *On Revolution.* New York: Viking Press, 1963.

Armstrong, John A., ed. *Soviet Partisans in World War II.* Madison: University of Wisconsin Press, 1964.

Atkinson, James D. *The Edge of War.* Chicago: Henry Regnery, 1960.

Baclagon, Uldarico S. *Philippine Campaigns.* Manila: Graphic House, 1952.

Baldwin, James. *The Fire Next Time.* New York: Dial Press, 1963.

Barghoorn, Frederick C. *Soviet Foreign Propaganda,* Princeton, N.J.: Princeton University Press, 1964.

Barker, Dudley. *Grivas: Portrait of a Terrorist.* New York: Harcourt, Brace, 1960.

Barnet, Richard J. *Intervention and Revolution: The United States in the Third World.* New York: World Publishing Co., 1968.

Barnett, Donald L., and Njama, Karari. *Mau Mau from Within: Autobiography of Kenya's Peasant Revolt.* New York: Monthly Review Press, 1966.

Barrett, David D. *Dixie Mission: The United States Army Observer Group in Yenan, 1944.* China Research Monographs, No. 6. Berkeley, Calif.: University of California, Center for Chinese Studies, 1970.

Bayley, David H., and Mendelsoh, Harold. *Minorities and the Police: Confrontation in America.* New York: Free Press, 1969. Bayo, G. A.

Bayo, G. A. *One Hundred and Fifty Questions Asked of a Guerrilla Fighter.* New York: U.S. Joint Publications Research Service, 1959.

Beals, Carleton. *Great Guerrilla Warriors.* New York: Tower Publications, 1971.

Becker, Howard S. *Campus Power Struggle.* Chicago: Aldine, 1970.

Behr, E. *The Algerian Problem.* New York: 1962.

Béjar, Hector. *Peru 1965: Notes on a Guerrilla Experience.*

Translated by William Rose. New York: Monthly Review Press. 1969.

Bell, J. Bowyer. *The Long War: Israel and the Arabs Since 1946.* Englewood Cliffs, N.J.: Prentice-Hall, 1969.

Bell, J. Bowyer, *The Myth of the Guerrilla: Revolutionary Theory and Malpractice.* New York: Alfred Knopf, 1971.

Bennett, Norman R. *Studies in East African History.* Boston: Boston University Press, 1963.

Berger, Peter L., and Neuhaus, Richard John. *Movement and Revolution.* Garden City, N.Y.: Doubleday, 1970.

Berrier, Hilaire du. *Background to Betrayal: The Tragedy of Vietnam.* Boston: Western Islands, 1965.

Black, Cyril E., and Thornton, Thomas P., eds. *Communism and Revolution: The Strategic Uses of Political Violence.* Princeton, N.J.: Princeton University Press, 1964.

Bodard, Lucien. *The Quicksand War: Prelude to Vietnam.* Translated by Patrick O'Brian. Boston: Little, Brown, 1967.

Bohannon, Paul. "Africa's Land." *Tribal and Peasant Economies: Readings in Economic Anthropology.* Edited by George Dalton. Garden City, N.Y.: Natural History Press, 1967.

Bolton, Charles D., and Kameyer, Kenneth C. W. *The University Student: A Study of Student Behavior and Values.* New Haven, Conn.: College and University Press, 1967.

Bonnet, Gabriel G. M., *Les querres insurrectionnelles et révolutionnaires de l'antiquité à nos jours.* Paris: Payot, 1958.

Bretton, Henry L. *The Rise and Fall of Kwame Nkrumah: A Study of Personal Rule in Africa.* London: Pall Mall Press, 1966; New York: Praeger, 1966.

Bromberger, Serge. *Les rebelles algériens.* Paris: Plon, 1958.

Brome, Vincent. *The International Brigades: Spain, 1936-1939.* New York: William Morrow, 1966.

Browne, Malcolm W. *The New Face of War.* Indianapolis,

Ind.: Bobbs-Merrill, 1965.

Brzezinski, Zbigniew K., ed. *Africa and the Communist World*. Stanford, Calif.: Stanford University Press, 1963.

Burchett, Wilfred G. *The Furtive War: The United States in Vietnam and Laos*. New York: International Publishers, 1963.

————— *Vietnam: Inside Story of the Guerrilla War*. New York: International Publishers, 1965.

—————. "In 'Portuguese Guinea': Seeing for Oneself." *West Africa*, 4 November 1967.

————— *Revolution in Guinea: Selected Texts*. Translated and edited by Richard Handyside. New York: Monthly Review Press, 1970.

Cameron, James. *The African Revolution*. New York: Random House, 1961.

Campbell, Arthur. *Guerrillas: A History and Analysis from Napoleon's Time to the 1960s*. New York: John Day, 1968.

Caply, Michel. *Guérrilla au Laos*. Paris: Presses de la Cité, 1966.

Carmichael, Stokely, and Hamilton, Charles V. *Black Power: The Politics of Liberation in America*. New York: Random House, 1967.

Carothers, John C. *The Psychology of Mau Mau*. Nairobi: Government Printer, 1954.

Carter, Gwendolen M. *Independence for Africa*. New York: Praeger; and London: Thames and Hudson, 1961.

—————. *The Politics of Inequality: South Africa since 1948*. 2d ed., rev. New York: Praeger, 1959.

Caute, David. *Frantz Fanon*. New York: Viking Press, 1970; and London: Fontana, 1970.

Chaliand, Gérard. *Armed Struggle in Africa: With the Guerrillas in Portuguese Guinea*. Translated by David Rattray and Robert Leonhardt. New York: Monthly Review Press, 1969.

Chamberlin, William H. *The Russian Revolution*. 2 vols. Reprint. New York: Macmillan, 1960.

Charlesworth, James C., ed. "The Changing American People: Are We Deteriorating or Improving." *Annals of the* Vol. 378, July 1968.

———. ed. "Ethics in America: Norms and Deviations." *Annals of the AAPSS*, Vol. 363, January 1966.

Chassin, Lionel M. *The Communist Conquest of China: A History of the Civil War 1945-1949.* Translated by Timothy Osato and Louis Gelas. Cambridge, Mass: Harvard University Press, 1965.

Chilcote, Ronald H. *Portuguese Africa.* Englewood Cliffs, N.J.: Prentice-Hall, 1967.

Chu Teh. *The Battle Front of the Liberated Areas.* Peking: Foreign Languages Press, 1962.

*Civil Affairs in the Cold War.* Special Study No. 151. Operations Research Office, Bethesda, Md.: Johns Hopkins University, 1961.

*Civil Affairs in Future Armed Conflicts.* Operations Research Office. Bethesda, Md.: Johns Hopkins University, 1960.

Clark, Michael K. *Algeria in Turmoil: A History of the Rebellion.* London: Thames & Hudson, 1959; and New York: Praeger, 1959.

Clausewitz, Karl von. *On War.* Translated by O. J. Matthijs Jolles. New York: Modern Library, 1943.

Cleaver, Eldridge. *Eldridge Cleaver: Post-Prison Writings and Speeches.* Edited by Robert Scheer. New York: Random House, 1969.

——— *Soul on Ice.* New York: Dell Publishing Co., 1968.

Clutterbuck, Richard L. *The Long, Long War: Counterinsurgency in Malaya and Vietnam.* New York: Praeger, 1966.

Cockburn, Alexander, and Blackburn, Robin. *Student Power.* Baltimore, Md.: Penguin Books, 1969.

Cohen, Mitchell, and Hale, Dennis, eds. *The New Student Left: An Anthology.* Boston: Beacon Press, 1966.

Cohn-Bendit, Daniel, and Cohn-Bendit, Gabriel. *Obsolete Communism: The Left-Wing Alternative.* Translated by Arnold Pomerans. London: Deutsch, 1968.

Coleman, James S. "Nationalism in Tropical Africa." *Ameri-*

can *Political Science Review*, Vol. 48, June 1954.

Coleman, James S., and Rosberg, Jr., Carl G. eds. *Political Parties and National Integration in Tropical Africa*. Berkeley: University of California Press, 1964.

Condit, D. M. *Case Study in Guerrilla War: Greece During World War II*. Washington, D.C.: Special Warfare Research Division, Special Operations Research Office, The American University, 1961.

Confino, M., and Samir, S., eds. *The U.S.S.R. and the Middle East*. New York: John Wiley & Sons, 1973.

Cornell, Richard. *Youth and Communism: An Historical Analysis of International Communist Youth Movements*. New York: Walker & Co., 1965.

Coser, Lewis A. *The Functions of Social Conflict*. Glencoe, Ill.: Free Press, 1956.

Cronkite, Walter. *Vietnam Perspective: CBS News Special Report*. New York: Pocket Books, 1965.

Cross, James E. *Conflict in the Shadows: The Nature and Politics of Guerrilla War*. Garden City, N.Y.: Doubleday.

Crozier, Brian. *The Rebels: A Study of Post-War Insurrections*. London: Chatto and Windus, 1960; and Boston: Beacon Press, 1960.

Dallin, Alexander, ed. *Diversity in International Communism: A Documentary Record, 1961-1963*. New York: Columbia University Press.

———. *German Rule in Russia, 1941-45: A Study of Occupation Policies*. London: Macmillan, 1957; and New York: St. Martin's Press, 1957.

Davidson, Basil. *The Liberation of Guiné: Aspects of an African Revolution*. London: Harmondsworth, 1969; and Baltimore, Md.: Penguin Books, 1969.

Debray, Régis. *Revolution in the Revolution? Armed Struggle and Political Struggle in Latin America*. Translated by Bobbye Ortiz. New York: Grove Press, 1967.

Delf, George. *Jomo Kenyatta: Towards Truth About "The Light of Kenya,"* Garden City, N.Y.: Doubleday, 1961.

Dimitrov, Georgi. *The United Front Against Fascism*.

Speeches delivered at the Seventh World Congress of the Communist International, 25 July - 20 August 1935. New York: New Century Publishers, 1935.

Dinerstein, Herbert S. *War and the Soviet Union: Nuclear Weapons and the Revolution in Soviet Military and Political Thinking*. New York: Praeger, 1959.

Dixon, C. Aubrey, and Heilbrunn, Otto. *Communist Guerrilla Warfare*. New York: Praeger, 1960.

Donnelly, Desmond. *Struggle for the World: The Cold War, 1917-1965*. New York: St. Martin's Press, 1965.

Dougherty, James E. "The Guerrilla War in Malaya." *U.S. Naval Institute Proceedings*, Vol. 84, No. 9, September 1958.

Doyle, Conan. *The War in South Africa: Its Cause and Conduct*. London: Smith-Elder, 1902; and New York: McClure & Phillips, 1902.

Draper, Hal. *Berkeley: The New Student Revolt*. New York: Grove Press, 1965.

Draper, Theodore. *Castro's Revolution: Myths and Realities*. New York: Praeger, 1962.

Dresher, Melvin. *Games of Strategy: Theory and Applications*. Englewood Cliffs, N.J.: Prentice-Hall, 1961.

Dumont, René. *False Start in Africa*. Translated by Phyllis Nauts Ott. New York: Praeger, 1966.

Duffy, James. *Portuguese Africa*. Cambridge, Mass.: Harvard University Press, 1959.

Duncanson, Dennis J. *Government and Revolution in Vietnam*. New York and London: Oxford University Press, 1968.

Dyer, Murray. *The Weapon on the Wall: Rethinking Psychological Warfare*. Baltimore, Md.: Johns Hopkins Press, 1958.

Eckstein, Harry. *Internal War: Problems and Approaches*. New York: Free Press of Glencoe, 1964.

Elliott-Bateman, Michael. *Defeat in the East: The Mark of Mao Tse-tung on War*. London and New York: Oxford University Press, 1967.

———— *The Role of Force in History: A Study of Bismarck's Policy of Blood and Iron.* Translated by Jack Cohen. Edited by Ernst Wangermann. New York: International Publishers, 1968.

Fage, J. D. *Ghana: A Historical Interpretation.* Madison: University of Wisconsin Press, 1959.

Fairbairn, Geoffrey. *Revolutionary Warfare and Communist Strategy: The Threat to South-east Asia.* London: Faber and Faber, 1968.

Falk, Richard A., ed. *The International Law of Civil War.* Baltimore, Md.: Johns Hoplins Press, 1971.

————, Kolko, Gabriel, and Lifton, Robert Jay, eds. *Crimes of War.* New York: Random House, 1971.

Fall, Bernard G. *Last Reflections on a War.* Garden City, N.Y.: Doubleday, 1967.

————. *Street Without Joy: Indo-China at War 1946-54.* Harrisburg, Pa.: Stackpole, 1961.

————. *The Two Viet-Nams: A Plitical and Military Analysis.* Rev. ed. London and Dunmow: Pall Mall Press. 1965.

————. *Viet-Nam Witness, 1953-66.* New York: Praeger, 1966.

Falls, Cyril B. *The Art of War: From the Age of Napoleon to the Present Day.* London and New York: Oxford University Press, 1961.

Fanon, Frantz. *Black Skin, White Masks.* Translated by Charles L. Markmann. New York: Grove Press, 1967.

————. *Studies in a Dying Colonialism.* Translated by Haakon Chevalier. New York: Monthly Review Press, 1965.

————. *Toward the African Revolution: Political Essays.* Translated by Haakon Chevalier. New York: Monthly Review Press, 1967.

————. *The Wretched of the Earth.* Translated by Constance Farrington. New York: Grove Press, 1968.

Feit, Edward. *South Africa: The Dynamics of the African National Congress.* London and New York: Oxford University Press, 1962.

Fischer, Louis. *Gandhi: His Life and Message for the World.* New York: New American Library, 1954.

Fleming, D. F. *The Cold War and Its Origins.* 2 vols. Garden City, N.Y.: Doubleday, 1961.

———, ed. *The Memoirs of General Grivas.* New York: Prager, 1965.

Foley, James A., and Foley, Robert K. *The College Scene: Students Tell It Like It Is.* New York: Cowles Book Co., 1969.

Friedenberg, Edgar Z. *Coming of Age in America: Growth and Acquiescence.* New York: Random House, 1965.

Friedland, William H., and Rosberg, Jr., Carl G., eds. *African Socialism.* Stanford, Calif.: Stanford University Press, 1964.

Friedrich, Carl J., ed. *Revolution: Yearbook.* American Society for Political and Legal Philosophy. New York: Atherton Press, 1966.

———, and Brzezinski, Zbigniew. *Totalitarian Dictatorship and Autocracy.* 2d. ed. rev. by Carl J. Friedrich. Cambridge, Mass.: Harvard University Press, 1965.

Fromm, Erich. *The Sane Society.* Greenwich, Conn.: Fawcett Publications, 1966.

Furtado, Celso. *Diagnosis of the Brazilian Crisis.* Translated by Suzette Macedo. Berkeley and Los Angeles: University of California Press, 1965.

Galula, David. *Counterinsurgency Warfare: Theory and Practice.* New York: Praeger, 1964.

Gann, Lewis H. *Guerrillas in History.* Stanford, Calif.: Hoover Institution Press, 1971.

Garthoff, Raymond L. *Soviet Military Doctrine.* Glencoe, Ill.: Free Press, 1953.

Gettleman, Marvin E., ed. *Vietnam: History, Documents and Opinions on a Major World Crisis.* Greenwich, Conn.: Fawcett Publications, 1965.

Geyer, Georgie Ann. "An Interview with Régis Debray." *Saturday Review,* Vol. 5, 24 August 1968.

Giap, Vo-Nguyen, see Vo-Nguyen-Giap.

Gillespie, Joan. *Algeria: Rebellion and Revolution.* New York: Praeger, 1961.

Gilly, Adolfo. "The Guerrilla Movement in Guatemala," *Monthly Review,* Vol. 17, Nos. 1 & 2. May and June 1965.

Ginsburg, Robert N. *U.S. Military Strategy in the Sixties.* New York: Norton, 1965.

Girling, J. L. S. *People's War: Conditions and Consequences in China and Southeast Asia.* New York: Praeger, 1969: and London: Allen & Unwin, 1969.

Glazer, Nathan. *Remembering the Answers: Essays on the American Student Revolt.* New York: Basic Books, 1970.

González, Luis J., and Sánchez Salazar, Gustavo A. *The Great Rebel: Ché Guevara in Bolivia.* Translated by Helen R. Lane. New York: Grove Press, 1969.

Goodman, Paul. *Compulsory Mis-education and the Community of Scholars.* New York: Random House, 1962; and New York: Vintage Books, 1964.

Goodwin, Richard N. *Triumph or Tragedy: Reflections on Vietnam.* New York: Vintage Books, 1966.

Green, Gil. *Terrorism—Is It Revolutionary?* New York: New Outlook Publishers, 1970.

Greene, Thomas N., ed. *The Guerrilla—And How to Fight Him.* New York: Praeger, 1962.

Grey, Ian. *The First Fifty Years: Soviet Russia, 1917-67.* New York: Coward-McCann, 1967.

Griffith, II. Samuel B., *The Chinese People's Liberation Army.* The United States and China in World Affairs Series. New York: McGraw-Hill, 1967.

————. *Peking and People's Wars.* New York: Praeger, 1966.

Griffith, William E. "Yugoslavia." *Africa and the Communist World.* Edited by Zbigniew Brzezinski. Stanford, Calif.: Stanford University Press, 1963.

Grivas, George. *General Grivas on Guerrilla Warfare.* Translated by A. A. Pallis. New York: Praeger, 1965.

_____. *The Memoirs of General Grivas*. Edited by Charles Foley. New York: Praeger, 1965.

Gross, Bertram M., ed. "Social Goal and Indicators for American Society." 2 vols. *Annals of the AAPSS*, Vol. 373, September 1967.

Guevara, Ernesto. *The Complete Bolivian Diaries of Ché Guevara and Other Captured Documents*. Edited by Daniel James. New York: Stein and Day, 1968.

_____. *Ché Guevara on Guerrilla Warfare*. New York: Praeger, 1961.

Guevara, Ernesto. *Ché Guevara on Revolution: A Documentary Overview*. Edited by Jay Mallin. Coral Gables, Fla.: University of Miami Press, 1969.

_____. *Ché Guevara Speaks: Selected Writings and Speeches*. Edited by George Lavan. New York: Merit Publishers, 1967.

_____. *Ché: Selected Works of Ernesto Guevara*. Edited by Rolando E. Bonachea and Nelson P. Valdes. Cambridge, Mass.: M.I.T. Press, 1969.

_____. *Venceremos! The Speeches and Writings of Ché Guevara*. Edited by John Gerassi. New York: Simon and Schuster, 1968.

Gurr, Ted Robert. *Why Men Rebel*. Princeton, N.J.: Princeton University Press, 1969.

Hagen, Everett E. *On the Theory of Social Change: How Economic Growth Begins*. Homewood, Ill.: Dorsey Press, 1962.

Halperin, Morton H. *Limited War in the Nuclear Age*. New York: John Wiley & Sons, 1963.

Halpern, Manfred. *The Politics of Social Change in the Middle East and North Africa*. Princeton, N.J.: Princeton University Press, 1963.

Hamilton, Michael P., ed. *The Vietnam War: Christian Perspectives*. Grand Rapids, Mich.: William B. Eerdmans Publishing Co., 1967.

Hammond, Richard J. "Economic Imperialism: Sidelights on

a Stereotype." *Journal of Economic History*, Vol. 21, December 1961.

———. *Portugal's African Problem: Some Economic Facets.* New York: Carnegie Endowment for International Peace, 1962.

Hanrahan, Gene Z. *The Communist Struggle in Malaya.* New York: International Secretariat, Institute for Pacific Relations, 1954.

Harris, Richard J. *Death of a Revolutionary: Ché Guevara's Last Mission.* New York: Norton, 1970.

Hatch, John C. *Africa Today—And Tomorrow: An Outline of Basic Facts and Major Problems.* New York: Praeger, 1960.

Hayden, Joseph R. *The Philippines: A Study in National Development.* New York: Macmillan, 1942.

Heilbrunn, Otto. *Partisan Warfare.* New York: Praeger, 1962.

———. *Warfare in the Enemy's Rear.* New York: Praeger, 1963 and London: Allen & Unwin, 1963.

Henderson, Ian, with Goodhart, Philip. *Hunt for Kimathi.* English edition, London: Hamilton, 1958, American edition entitled: *Manhunt in Kenya.* New York: Doubleday, 1958.

Hennessy, Maurice N. *The Congo: A Brief History and Appraisal.* New York: Praeger, 1962.

Hensman, C. R. *From Gandhi to Guevara: The Polemics of Revolt.* London: Allen Lane, 1969.

Herskovits, Melville J. *The Human Factor in Changing Africa.* New York: Alfred Knopf, 1962.

Herzog, Arthur. *The War-Peace Establishment.* New York: Harper & Row, 1963.

Higgens, Marguerite. *Our Vietnam Nightmare.* New York: Harper & Row, 1965.

Hobsbawn, Eric J. *Social Bandits and Primitive Rebels: Studies in the Archaic Forms of Social Movement in the Nineteenth and Twentieth Centuries.* Glencoe, Ill.: Free Press, 1960.

Ho-Chi-Minh. *On Revolution: Selected Writings 1920-66.*

Edited by Bernard B. Fall. New York: Praeger, 1967.

Holmes, Grace W., ed. *Student Protest and the Law.* Ann Arbor, Mich.: Institute of Continuing Legal Education, 1969.

Hook, Sidney. *Academic Freedom and Academic Anarchy.* New York: Cowles Book Co., 1970.

Horowitz, David, ed. *Containment and Revolution.* Boston: Beacon Press, 1969.

Horowitz, Irving L. *The Three Worlds of Development: The Theory and Practice of International Stratification.* New York: Oxford University Press, 1966.

Howell, Edgar M. *The Soviet Partisan Movement 1941-44.* Pamphlet No. 20-244. Washington, D.C.: U.S. Department of the Army, 1956.

Hoang-Van-Chi. *From Colonialism to Communism: A Case History of North Vietnam.* New York: Praeger, 1964.

Htaik, Thoung. "Encirclement Methods in Counterguerrilla Warfare." *Military Review.* June 1961. Reprinted in *Special Warfare: U.S. Army.* Washington, D.C.: Government Printing Office, 1962.

Hubatsch, Walther, ed. *Hitler's War Directives, 1939-1945.* Translated and edited by H. R. Trevor-Roper. London: Pan, 1966.

Huberman, Leo, and Sweezy, Paul M. *Cuba: Anatomy of a Revolution.* 2d ed. New York: Monthly Review Press, 1961.

––––––. eds. *Régis Debray and the Latin American Revolution.* New York: Monthly Review Press, 1968.

Humphreys, Robert A., and Lynch, John, eds. *The Origins of the Latin American Revolutions.* New York: Alfred Knopf, 1965.

Hunter, Guy. *The New Societies in Tropical Africa: A Selective Study.* London and New York: Oxford University Press, 1962; and New York: Praeger, 1964.

Hunter, Robert. *Revolution: Why, How, Where?* New York: Harper & Brothers, 1940.

Huntington, Samuel P. "Patterns of Violence in World

Politics." *Changing Patterns of Military Politics*. Edited by Samuel P. Huntington. New York: Free Press of Glencoe, 1962.

_____. "Political Development and Political Decay." *World Politics*, Vol. 17, No. 3. April 1965.

_____. *The Soldier and the State: The Theory and Politics of Civil-Military Relations*. Cambridge, Mass.: Harvard University Press, 1957.

Hunton, W. Alphaeus. *Decision in Africa: Sources of Current Conflict*. rev. ed. New York: International Publishers, 1960.

Hyde, Douglas. *The Roots of Guerrilla Warfare*. London: Bodley Head, 1968.

International Conference on the History of Resistance Movements. 1st. Liege . . . 1958. *European Resistance Movements, 1939-45*. New York: Pergamon, 1960.

Isaacs, Harold R. *The New World of Negro Americans*. New York: John Day, 1963.

Jackson, Barbara Ward. *The Rich Nations and the Poor Nations*. New York: Norton, 1962.

Jacobs, Harold, ed. *Weatherman*. Ramparts Press. 1970.

Jacobs, Paul, and Landau, Saul. *The New Radicals: A Report with Documents*. New York: Random House, 1966.

Jacobs, W. D. "Irregular Warfare and the Soviets." *Military Review*, May 1958.

James, Daniel, ed. *The Complete Bolivian Diaries of Chê Guevara and Other Captured Documents* New York: Stein and Day, 1968.

Janis, I. L. *Air War and Emotional Stress: Psychological Studies of Bombing and Civilian Defense*. New York: McGraw-Hill, 1951.

Janowitz, Morris. *The Professional Soldier: A social and Political Portrait*. New York: Free Press, 1964.

Johnson, Chalmera A. *Autopsy on People's War*. Berkeley: University of California Press, 1973.

_____. *Peasant Nationalism and Communist Power: The Emergence of Revolutionary China, 1937-1945*. Stanford,

Calif.: Stanford University Press, 1962.

———. *Revolutionary Change.* Basic Studies in Politics Series, edited by Sheldon S. Wolin. Boston: Little, Brown, 1966.

Johnson, John J., ed. *The Role of the Military in Underdeveloped Countries.* Princeton, N.J.: Princton University Press, 1962.

Joughin, George L., ed. *Academic Freedom and Tenure: A Handbook of the American Association of University Professors.* Madison: University of Wisconsin Press, 1967.

Jules, Henry. *Culture Against Man.* New York: Random House, 1963.

July, Robert W. *A History of the African People* New York: Scribner, 1970.

Kahin, George M., and Lewis, John W. *The United States in Vietnam.* New York: Dial Press. 1967.

Kai-Yu Hsu. *Chou En-Lai: China's Gray Eminence.* Garden City, New York: Doubleday, 1968.

Kaunda, Kenneth. *Zambia Shall Be Free: An Autobiography.* New York: Praeger, 1963.

Kecskemeti, Paul. *The Unexpected Revolution: Social Forces in the Hungarian Uprising.* Stanford, Calif.: Stanford University Press, 1961.

Kenniston, Kenneth. *Young Radicals: Notes on Committed Youth.* New York: Harcourt Brace & World, 1968.

Kerr, Clark. *The Uses of the University.* Cambridge, Mass.: Harvard University Press, 1963.

Khouri, Fred J. *The Arab-Israeli Dilemma.* Syracuse, N.Y.: Syracuse University Press, 1968.

Khrushchev, Nikita S. *Conquest Without War: An Analytical Anthology . . .* Compiled and edited by N. H. Mager and Jacques Katel. New York: Simon and Schuster, 1961.

———. *Khrushchev Remembers.* Translated and edited by Strobe Talbott. Boston: Little, Brown, 1970.

———. "For New Victories of the World Communist Movement," *Kommunist,* January 1961. Translated version published under the title *Khrushchev Report on*

*Moscow Conference of Representatives of Communist and Workers Parties.* Washington, D.C.: Government Printing Office, 1961.

Kimche, David. *The Afro-Asian Movement: Ideology and Foreign Policy of the Third World.* New York: John Wiley & Sons, 1973.

King, Martin Luther, Jr. *Where Do We Go From Here: Chaos or Community?* New York: Harper & Row, 1967.

Kinkead, Eugene. *In Every War But One.* New York: Norton, 1959.

Kolarz, Walter. *Communism and Colonialism: Essays.* New York: St. Martin's Press, 1964.

Kornbluth, Jesse, ed. *Notes from the New Underground: An Anthology.* New York: Viking Press, 1968.

Kozol, Jonathan. *Death at an Early Age: The Destruction of the Hearts and Minds of Negro Children in the Boston Public Schools.* Boston: Houghton Mifflin, 1967.

Kraft, Joseph. *The Struggle for Algeria.* Garden City, N.Y.: Doubleday, 1961.

Kubek, Anthony. *How the Far East Was Lost: American Policy and the Creation of Communist China, 1941-1949.* Chicago: Henry Regnery, 1963.

———. *Vietnam: Between Two Truces.* Translated by Konrad Kellen and Joel Carmichael. New York: Random House, 1966.

Landauer, Carl, and Pickus, Robert. *Peace, Politics, the New Left and the Pity of It All.* Berkeley, Calif.: World Without War Council Publication, 1966.

Langer, Paul F., and Zasloff, Joseph J. *North Vietnam and the Pathet Lao: Partners in the Struggle for Laos.* Cambridge, Mass.: Harvard University Press, 1970.

Larkin, Bruce D. *China and Africa, 1949-1970: The Foreign Policy of The People's Republic of China.* Berkeley: University of California Press, 1971.

Lasch, Christopher. *The New Radicalism in America 1889-1963: The Intellectual as a Social Type.* New York: Vintage Books, 1967.

Lavan, George., ed. *Ché Guevara Speaks: Selected Speeches and Writings.* New York: Merit Publishers, 1967.

Lawrence, Robert. *Guerrilla Warfare in the United States.* Canoga Park, Calif.: Weiss, Day, 1970.

Lawrence, T. E. *Seven Pillars of Wisdom, A Triumph.* Garden City, N.Y.: Garden City Publishing Co., 1938.

Leaky, L. S. B. *Mau Mau and the Kikuyu.* New York: Methuen, 1952.

Lederer, Ivo J., ed. *Russian Foreign Policy: Essays in Historical Perspective.* New Haven, Conn.: Yale University Press, 1962.

Lefever, Ernest. *Crisis in the Congo: A United Nations Force in Action.* Washington, D.C.: Brookings Institution, 1965.

Leigh, Ione. *In the Shadow of the Mau Mau.* London: W. H. Allen, 1955.

Leighton, Richard M., and Sanders, Ralph, eds. *Insurgency and Counterinsurgency: An Anthology.* Industrial College of the Armed Forces, Publication No. R-226. Washington, D.C.: 1962.

Lemarchand, René. *Political Awakening in the Belgian Congo.* Berkeley: University of California Press, 1964.

Le May, Curtis E. "Airpower in Guerrilla Warfare," *Air Force Information Policy Letter, Supplement for Commanders,* Vol. 107, 15 June 1962.

――――. "Counter Insurgency and the Challenge Imposed." *Airman,* Vol. 6, July 1962.

Lenczowski, George. *Russia and the West in Iran 1918-1948.* Ithaca, N.Y.: Cornell University Press, 1949.

Lenin, V. I. "Guerrilla Warfare," and "Lessons of the Moscow Uprising." *Collected Works,* vol. 11, June 1906-January 1907. Moscow: Progress Publishers, 1965.

――――. "Lessons of the Revolution." *Collected Works,* vol. 25, June-September 1917. Moscow: Progress Publishers, 1964.

――――. "The Military Programme of the Proletarian Revolution." *Selected Works: In Three Volumes,* vol. 1, 1897 to January 1917. New York: International Publishers, New

World Paperbacks. 1967.

Levy, Bert. *Guerrilla Warfare*. Boulder, Colo.: Panther Publications, 1964.

Lewis, William Arthur. *Politics in West Africa*. New York: Oxford University Press, 1965.

Lindsay, Franklin A. *"Unconventional Warfare."* *Foreign Affairs*, vol. 40, January 1962.

Linebarger, Paul M. A. *Psychological Warfare*. 2d ed. New York: Duell, Sloane and Pearce, 1960.

Lipset, Seymour M., and Wolin, Sheldon S., eds. *The Berkeley Student Revolt: Facts and Interpretations*. Garden City, N.Y.: Anchor Books, 1965.

Lomax, Louis E. *Thailand: The War That Is, the War That Will Be*. New York: Random House, 1967.

Long, Priscilla, comp., *The New Left: A Collection of Essays*. Boston: P. Sargent, 1969.

*Look*. [Magazine]. 9 April 1953.

Lovelace, Daniel D. *China and "People's War" in Thailand, 1964-1969*. China Research Monographs, No. 8. Berkeley, Calif.: Center for Chinese Studies, 1971.

Luard, Evan, ed., *The Cold War: A Re-appraisal*. New York: Praeger, 1964.

Lumumba, Patrice. *Congo, My Country*. New York: Praeger, 1962.

Lutz, William, and Brent, Harry, eds. *On Revolution*. Cambridge, Mass.: Winthrop Publishers, Inc., 1971.

Luxemburg, Rosa. *The Russian Revolution and Leninism or Marxism?* Ann Arbor: University of Michigan Press, 1961.

Lynd, Staughton. "Towards a History of the New Left." *The New Left: A Collection of Essays*. Compiled by Priscilla Long. Boston: P. Sargent, 1969.

McClintock, Robert. *The Meaning of Limited War*. Boston: Houghton Mifflin, 1967.

McCuen, John J. *The Art of Counter-Revolutionary War: The Strategy of Counter-insurgency*. London: Faber and Faber, 1966.

Mackintosh, J. M. *Strategy and Tactics of Soviet Foreign*

*Policy*. London and New York: Oxford University Press, 1962.

McNeill, William H. *Greek Dilemma: War and Aftermath*. London: Gollancz, 1947; and Philadelphia: Lippincott, 1947.

Malraux, André. *Anti-Memoirs*. Translated by Terence Kilmartin. New York: Holt, Rinehart and Winston, 1968.

"Many Africas: Continent in Turmoil." *Journal of International Affairs*, vol. 15, no. 1, 1961.

————. *On Guerrilla Warfare*, Translated by Samuel B. Griffith, II. New York: Praeger, 1961.

————. *Selected Military Writings of Mao Tse-tung*. Peking: Foreign Languages Press, 1963.

————. *Selected Works* 5 vols. New York: International Publishers, n.d.

Marcuse, Herbert. *Eros and Civilizatiion: A Philosophical Inquiry into Freud*. New York: Vintage Books, 1961.

————. *One-Dimensional Man: Studies in the Ideology of Advanced Industrial Society*. Boston: Beacon Press, 1964.

————. "Marcuse Defines his New Left Line: Interview." Edited by J. L. Ferrier and others. Translated by H. Weaver. *New York Times Magazine*, 27 October 1968.

————. "Repressive Tolerance." *A Critique of Pure Tolerance*. by Robert Paul Wolf, Barrington Moore, Jr., and Herbert Marcuse. Boston: Beacon Press, 1965.

————. *Soviet Marxism: A Critical Analysis*. New York: Columbia University Press, 1958.

————. "Minimanual of the Urban Guerrilla." *Tricontinental*, no. 16, 1970.

Martin, David. *Ally Betrayed: The Uncensored Story of Tito and Mihailovíc*. New York: Prentice-Hall, 1946.

Merriam, Alan P. *Congo, Background of Conflict*. Evanston, Ill.: Northwestern University Press, 1961.

Miller, Michael V., and Gilmore, Susan., eds. *Revolution in Berkeley: The Crisis in American Education*. New York: Dial Press, 1965.

Miller, Norman, and Aya, Roderick, eds. *National Liberation:*

*Revolution in the Third World.* New York: Free Press, 1971.

Millis, Walter, ed. *American Military Thought.* Indianapolis, Ind.: Bobbs-Merrill, 1966.

"The Military-Industrial Complex: USSR/USA." *Journal of International Affairs,* vol. 26, no. 1, 1972.

Mills, C. Wright. *The Causes of World War III.* New York: Simon and Schuster, 1960.

_____. "Letter to the New Left." *The New Left: A collection of Essays.* Edited by Priscilla Long. Boston: P. Sargent, 1969.

_____. *The Power Elite.* New York: Oxford University Press, 1956.

_____. *Power, Politics and People: The Collected Essays of C. Wright Mills.* Edited by Irving L. Horowitz. New York: Ballantine Books, 1963.

Modelski, George A. *The International Relations of Internal War.* Research Monograph No. 11 Center of International Studies, Woodrow Wilson School of Public and International Affairs. Princeton, N.J.: Princeton University Press, 1961.

Moore, Robin. *The Green Berets.* New York: Crown Publishers, 1965.

Molotov, V. M. *On Armed Forces of the United Nations on Foreign Territory.* Washington, D.C.: Embassy of the U.S.S.R., 1946.

Moreira, Adriano. *Portugal's Stand in Africa.* Translated by William Davis and others. New York: University Publishers, 1962.

Morgenthau, Hans J. *Vietnam and the United States.* Washington, D.C.: Public Affairs Press, 1965.

Mosby, John S. *Mosby's War Reminiscences and Stuart's Cavalry Campaigns.* New York: Pageant Book Co., 1960.

Napier, W. F. P. *History of the War in the Peninsula.* 6 vols. London: Frederick Warne & Co., 1842; and Philadelphia: Carey & Hart, 1842.

Nasution, Abdul Haris. *Fundamentals of Guerrilla Warfare.* New York: Praeger, 1965.

Natsinas, Alexander. *Guerrilla Warfare: The Organization and Employment of Irregulars.* Greece: U.S. Army Service Group Detachment, Intelligence Section, 1950.

Newfield, Jack. *A Prophetic Minority.* New York: New American Library, 1966.

Ney, Virgil. *Notes on Guerrilla Warfare: Principles and Practices.* Washington, D.C.: Command Publications, 1961.

Nkrumah, Kwame. *Africa Must Unite.* New York: Praeger, 1963.

––––––. *The Autobiography of Kwame Nkrumah.* New York: University Place Bookshop, 1957.

––––––. *Consciencism: Philosophy and Ideology for Decolonization and Development with Particular Reference to the African Revolution.* New York: Monthly Review Press, 1965.

––––––. *Dark Days in Ghana.* 2d ed. New York: International Publishers, 1968.

––––––. *Handbook of Revolutionary Warfare: A Guide to the Armed Phase of the African Revolution.* New York: International Publishers, 1969.

––––––. *I Speak of Freedom: A Statement of African Ideology.* New York: Praeger, 1961.

––––––. *Neo-Colonialism: The Last Stage of Imperialism.* New York: International Publishers, 1966.

North, Robert C. *Kuomintang and Chinese Communist Elites.* Elite Studies Series, No. 8. Stanford, Calif.: Stanford University Press, July 1952.

Novack, George. *Marxism versus Neo-Anarchist Terrorism.* A Merit Pamphlet. New York: Pathfinder Press, 1970.

Nowell, Charles E. *A History of Portugal.* New York: Van Nostrand, 1952.

Nyerere, Julius K. *Freedom and Socialism: Uhuru na ujamaa: A Selection from Writings and Speeches 1965-1967.* Dar es Salaam and New York: Oxford University Press, 1968.

_____. *Ujamaa: Essays on Socialism*. Nairobi and New York: Oxford University Press, 1968.

O'Ballance, Edgar. "The Algerian Struggle." *Army Quarterly*, October 1960.

_____. *The Greek Civil War 1944-1949*. New York: Praeger, 1966.

_____. *The Indo-China War, 1945-1954: A Study in Guerrilla Warfare*. London: Faber and Faber, 1964.

_____. *Malaya: The Communist Insurgent War, 1948-1960*. London: Faber and Faber, 1966.

Oksenberg, Michael. "China's Developmental Experience." *Proceedings of the Academy of Political Science*, vol. 31, no. 1, March 1973.

Ogburn, Charlton. *The Marauders*. New York: Harper, 1959.

Oglesby, Carl. ed. *The New Left Reader*. New York: Grove Press, 1969.

Oman, Charles W. C. *A History of the Peninsular War*. 5 vols. Oxford; 1914.

Oppenheimer, Martin. *The Urban Guerrilla*. Chicago: Quadrangle Books, 1969.

Osgood, Robert E. *Limited War: The Challenge to American Strategy*. Chicago: University of Chicago Press, 1957.

Osanka, Franklin M., ed. *Modern Guerrilla Warfare: Fighting Communist Guerrilla Movements 1941-1961*. New York: Free Press of Glencoe, 1962.

_____. *French Revolutionary Warfare from Indochina to Algeria: The Analysis of a Political and Military Doctrine*. New York: Praeger, 1964.

_____, and Shy, John W. *Guerrillas in the 1960's*. New York: Praeger, 1962.

Pélissier, René. "Pressures in Africa." *Geographical Magazine*, vol. 44, no. 2, November 1971.

Phillips, John F. K. *Kwame Nkrumah and the Future of Africa*. New York: Praeger, 1961.

Pike, Douglas. *Viet Cong: The Organization and Techniques of the National Liberation Front of South Vietnam*. Cambridge, Mass.: M.I.T. Press, 1967.

Pomeroy, William J. *Guerrilla and Counter-Guerrilla Warfare: Liberation and Suppression in the Present Period.* New York: International Publishers, 1964.

———. *Guerrilla Warfare and Marxism: A Collection of Writings from Karl Marx to the Present on Armed Struggles for Liberation and for Socialism.* New York: International Publishers, 1968.

Pustay, John S. *Counterinsurgency Warfare.* New York: Free Press, 1965.

Pye, Lucien W. *Guerrilla Communism in Malaya: Its Social and Political Meaning.* Princeton, N.J.: Princeton University Press, 1956.

Raskin, Marcus G., and Fall, Bernard B. *The Viet-Nam Reader: Articles and Documents on American Foreign Policy and the Viet-Nam Crisis.* New York: Vintage Books, 1965.

Reitz, D. *Commando: A Boer Journal of the Boer War.* New York: Charles Boni, 1930.

Rivkin, Arnold. "Lost Goals in Africa." *Foreign Affairs*, Vol. 40, October 1965.

Revel, Jean François. *Without Marx or Jesus: The New American Revolution Has Begun.* Translated by J. F. Bernard. Garden City, N.Y.: Doubleday, 1971.

"Revolutionary War: Western Response." *Journal of International Affairs*, vol. 25, no. 1, 1971.

Roberts, Walter R. *Tito, Mihailovic and the Allies, 1941-1945.* New Brunswick, N.J.: Rutgers University Press, 1973.

Robinson, Frank, and Kemp, Earl, eds. *The Truth about Vietnam: Report on the U.S. Senate Hearings.* San Diego, Calif.: Greenleaf Classics, 1966.

Rojo, Ricardo. *My Friend Ché.* Translated by Julian Casart. New York: Dial Press, 1968.

Rosberg, Carl G., Jr., and NOttingham, John. *The Myth of the Mau Mau Nationalism in Kenya.* New York: Praeger, 1966.

Rose, Arnold M., vol. ed. "The Negro Protest." *The*

*American Negro Problem in the Context of Social Change.* Annals of the AAPSS, vol. 357, January 1965.

Rostow, W. W. "Guerrilla Warfare in the Underdeveloped Areas," *Deaprtment of State Bulletin.* Vol. 45, 7 August 1961.

Roszak, Theodore. *The Making of a Counter Culture: Reflections on the Technocratic Society and Its Youthful Opposition.* Garden City, N.Y.: Doubleday, 1969.

Roy, Jules. *The Battle for Dienbienphu.* Translated by Robert Baldick. New York: Harber & Row, 1965.

Rusk, Dean. "Civil Affairs in the Area of Cold War." *Congressional Record,* Vol. 107, 27 June 1961.

Sagarin, Edward, ed. "Sex and the Contemporary American Scene." *Annals of the AAPSS,* vol. 376, March 1968.

Sanger, R. H. *Insurgent Era: New Patterns of Political, Economic, and Social Revolution.* Washington, D.C.: Potomac Books, 1967.

Scaff, Alvin H. *The Philippine Answer to Communism.* Stanford, Calif.: Stanford University Press, 1955.

Scalapino, Robert A., ed. *The Communist Revolution in Asia: Tactics, Goals and Achievements* Englewood Cliffs, N.J.: Prentice-Hall, 1965.

———. "Sino-Soviet Competition in Africa." Reprint Series. Department of Political Science, University of California, Berkeley. First appeared in *Foreign Affairs,* vol. 42, no. 4, July 1964.

Schoenbrun, David. *Vietnam: How We Got In, How To Get Out.* New York: Atheneum, 1968.

Schwab, Joseph J. *College Curriculum and Student Protest.* Chicago: University of Chicago Press, 1969.

Seitz, Albert. *Mihailovic: Hoax or Hero?* Columbus, Ohio: Leigh House, 1953.

Selznick, Philip. *The Organizational Weapon: A Study of Bolshevik Strategy and Tactics.* The Rand Series. New York: McGraw-Hill, 1952.

———. *Neither War Nor Peace: The Struggle for Power in the Post-War World.* New York: Praeger, 1960.

Sharabi, Hisham B. *Palestine and Israel: The Lethal Dilemma.* New York: Pegasus, 1969.

Shulman, Marshall D. *Stalin's Foreign Policy Reappraisad.* Cambridge, Mass.: Harvard University Press, 1963.

Stihole, Ndabaningi. *African Nationalism.* 2d ed. London and New York: Oxford University Press, 1968.

Skorzeny, Otto. *Secret Missions: War Memoirs of the Most Dangerous Man in Europe.* Translated by Jacques Le Clercq. New York: Dutton, 1950.

Slater, Philip E. *The Pursuit of Loneliness: American Culture at the Breaking Point.* Boston: Beacon Press, 1970.

Smedley, Agnes. *The Great Road: The Life and Times of Chu Teh.* New York: Monthly Review Press, 1956.

Speier, Hans. *German Rearmament and Atomic War: The Views of German Military and Political Leaders.* Evanston, Ill.: Row, Peterson, 1957.

Spiro, Herbert J. *Politics in Africa: Prospects South of the Sahara.* Englewood Cliffs, N.J.: Prentice-Hall, 1962.

Spykman, Nicholas J. *America's Strategy in World Politics: The United States and the Balance of Power.* New York: Harcourt, Brace and Co. No date.

Staley, Eugene. *The Future of Underdeveloped Countries: Political Implications of Economic Development.* New York: Praeger, 1961.

Stalin, Joseph. *Foundations of Leninism* New York: International Publishers, 1939.

———. *The War of National Liberation.* New York: International Publishers, 1942.

Stone, Isidor F. *In A Time of Torment.* New York: Vintage Books, 1968.

Strausz-Hupé, Robert; Kintner, William R.; Dougherty, James E.; and Cottrell, Alvin J. *Protracted Conflict.* New York: Harper & Brothers, 1959.

Sully, François. *Age of the Guerrilla.* New York: Avon Books, 1968.

Sun Tzu, 6th cent. B.C. *The Art of War.* Translated by Samuel B. Griffith, II. UNESCO Collection of Representative Works: Chinese Series. Oxford: Clarendon Press, 1963.

Taber, Robert. *The War of the Flea: A Study of Guerrilla Theory and Practice.* New York: L. Stuart., 1965.

Tanham, George K. *Communist Revolutionary Warfare: The Vietminh in Indochina.* New York: Praeger, 1961.

Taylor, Maxwell D. *The Uncertain Trumpet.* New York: Harper & Row, 1960.

Teodori, Massimo, ed. *The New Left: A Documentary History.* Indianapolis and New York: Bobbs Merrill, 1969.

Thayer, Charles W. *Guerrilla.* New York: Harper & Row, 1963.

Thomas, Hugh. *The Spanish Civil War.* New York: Harper & Row, 1961.

Thompson, Robert. *Defeating Communist Insurgency: The Lessons of Malaya and Vietnam.* New York: Praeger, 1966.

––––––. *No Exit From Vietnam.* New York: McKay, 1969.

––––––. *Revolutionary War in World Strategy, 1945-1969.* New York: Taplinger Publishing Co., 1970.

Toynbee, Arnold J. *American and the World Revolution.* New York: Oxford University Press, 1962.

Trinquier, Rober. *Modern Warfare: A French View of Counterinsurgency.* Translated by Daniel Lee. New York: Praeger, 1964.

Trotsky, Leon. *Military Writings.* New York: Merit Publishers, 1969.

––––––. *Problems of Civil War.* New York: Pathfinder Press, a Merit Pamphlet, 1970.

––––––. *Terrorism and Communism: A Reply to Karl Kautsky.* Ann Arbor: University of Michigan Press, 1961.

Truong Chinh. *Primer for Revolt: The Communist Takeover in Viet-Nam.* New York: Praeger, 1963.

*The United States in Africa.* American Assembly Papers. New York: 1958.

U.S. Congress. "Civil Affairs in the Area of Cold War," by Dean Rusk. *Congressional Record,* 87th Cong. 1st sess., Vol. 107, 27 June 1961.

U.S. Congress. House, Committee on Foreign Affairs. *Castro-*

*Communist Subversion in the Western Hemisphere.* Hearings before the Subcommittee on Inter-American Affairs on H.R.55. 88th Cong. 1st sess., 1963.

U.S. Congress. Senate, Committee on Foreign Relations, "Economic, Social, and Political Change in the Underdeveloped Countries and Its Implications for United States Policies," in *United States Foreign Policy*, by Center for International Studies, Mass. Inst. of Tech. 86th Cong., 2nd sess., 1962.

U.S. Congress. Senate, Committee on Foreign Relations. "Ideology and Foreign Affairs," *United States Foreign Policy.* 86th Cong., 2nd sess., 1962.

U.S. Congress. Senate, Committee on Foreign Relations, *Punta del Este Conference, January, 1962.* Report of Senators Wayne Morse and Bourke Hickenlooper. 87th Cong., 2nd sess., 1962.

U.S. Congress. Senate, Committee on Foreign Relations. "Some Observations on the Operation of the Alliance for Progress: The First Six Months." *United States -Latin American Relations.* A study prepared for Subcommittee on American Republics Affairs. 87th Cong., 2nd sess., 1962.

————. Congress. Senate. Committee on the Judiciary. *Analysis of the Khrushchev Speech of January 6, 1961.* Hearings, 87th Cong., 2nd sess. Washington: Government Printing Office, 1961.

U.S. Congress. Senate, Committee on the Judiciary. *The New Left*, by Thomas J. Dodd. 90th Cong., 2nd sess., 1968.

U.S. Congress. Senate, Special Committee to Study the Foreign Aid Program. "Foreign Assistance Activities of the Communist Bloc and Their Implications for the United States." *Foreign Air Program*, no. 8, 85th Cong., 1st sess., 1957.

U.S. Department of the Air Force. *Air Force Information Policy Letter, Supplement for Commanders.* "Airpower in Guerrilla Warfare," by C. E. Le May, Vol. 107, 15 June 1962.

U.S. Department of the Air Force. *USAF Airborne Operations: World War II and Korean War.* Washington: USAF Historical Division Liaison Office, 1962.

————. Air Research and Development Command. *The Role of Airpower in Partisan Warfare.* Maxwell Air Force Base, Alabama: Human Resources Research Institute, December 1954.

————. Air University. *Communist Attempts at Discrediting Americans.* Maxwell Air Force Base, Alabama: Research Studies Institute, 1962.

————. Air University. *Strategic Briefs.* Maxwell Air Force Base, Alabama: Research Studies Institute, 1961.

————. Air University. *U.S.A.F. Counterinsurgency Course Text: Selected Readings.* Maxwell Air Force Base, Alabama: Air University, 9162.

U.S. Army Special Warfare School. *Readings in Counter-guerrilla Operations* Fort Bragg, N.C.: Special Warfare Center, 1961.

U.S. Department of the Army. *Field Service Regulations; Doctrinal Guidance.* Field Manual 100-1. Washington, D.C.: Government Printing Office, 1959.

————. *Field Service Regulations, Operations.* Field Manual 100-5. Chapters 10, 11, and 12. Washington, D.C.: Government Printing Office, 1962.

————. *Format for a Psychological Warfare Country Plan.* Washington, D.C.: Government Printing Office, 1954.

————. *German Anti-Guerrilla Operations in the Balkans (1941-1944).* Pamphlet 2-243. Washington, D.C.: U.S. Department of the Army, 1954.

————. *Guerrilla and Counterguerrilla Warfare in Greece, 1941-1945.* Manuscript. Office of the Chief of Military History. Washington, D.C.: Government Printing Office, 1961.

————. *Guerrilla Warfare and Special Forces Operations.* Field Manual 31-21. Washington, D.C.: Government Printing Office, 1958.

————. *Operations Against Irregular Forces.* Field Manual

31-15. Washington, D.C.: Government Printing Office, 1961.

———. *The Soviet Partisan Movement, 1941-1944*. By Edgar M. Howell. Pamphlet 20-244. Washington, D.C.: Government Printing Office, 1956.

———. Office of the Chief of Civil Affairs. *Report of Civil Action Team for Guatemala*. Washington, D.C.: U.S. Department of the Army, 1961.

——— Department of State. *Cuba*. U.S. Department of State Publication 7171. Washington: Government Printing Office, April 1961.

U.S. Department of State. *The Lesson of Cuba*. Department of State Publication 7185. Washington, D.C.: Government Printing Office, 1961.

U.S. Department of State. *A Threat to the Peace*. Department of State Publication 7308. Washington, D.C.: Government Printing Office, 1961.

U.S. Department of State. *Viet-nam: Free World Challenge in Southeast Asia*, by George W. Ball. Department of State Publication 7388. Washington, D.C.: Government Printing Office, 1962.

U.S. War Department. Historical Division. *Merrill's Marauders: February to May 1944*. Washington, D.C.: Government Printing Office, 1945.

Valeriano, Napoleon D., and Bohannan, Charles T. R. *Counter-Guerrilla Operations: The Philippine Experience*. New York: Praeger, 1962.

Vatcher, William Henry. *White Laager: The Rise of Afrikaner Nationalism*. New York: Praeger, 1965.

———. *Banner of People's War: The Party's Military Line*. New York: Praeger, 1970.

———. *People's War, People's Army*. Hanoi: Foreign Languages Publishing House, 1961.

Vyshinskii, Andrei Y. *For the Peace and Friendship of Nations Against the Instigators of a New War*. Washington, D.C.: Embassy of the U.S.S.R., 1947.

Wallbank, T. Walter, ed. *Documents on Modern Africa*.

Princeton, N.J.: Van Nostrand, 1964.

Wallerstein, Immanuel. *Africa: The Politics of Independence: An Interpretation of Modern African History.* New York: Vintage Books, 1961.

Walter, Eugene V. *Terror and Resistance: A Study of Political Violence with Case Studies of Some Primitive African Communities.* New York: Oxford University Press, 1969.

Warshaw, Steven. *The Trouble in Berkeley: The Complete History, in Text and Pictures.* Berkeley, Calif.: Diablo Press, 1965.

Welsby, David L., and Braungart, Richard G. "Class and Politics in the Family Background of Student Political Activists." *American Sociological Review*, October 1966.

Werth, Alexander. *Russia at War: 1941-1945.* New York: Dutton, 1964.

Weyl, Nathaniel. *Red Star Over Cuba: The Russian Assault on the Western Hemisphere.* New York: Hillman Books, 1961.

Williamson, Edmund G., and Cowan, John L. *The American Student's Freedom of Expression: A Research Appraisal.* Minneapolis: University of Minnesota Press, 1966.

Wolf, Robert P.; Moore, Barrington, Jr.; and Marcuse, Herbert. *A Critique of Pure Tolerance.* Boston: Beacon Press, 1965.

Wolfert, Ira. *American Guerrilla in the Philippines.* New York: Simon and Schuster, 1945.

Wolfgang, Marvin E., ed. "Patterns of Violence." *Annals of the AAPSS*, vol. 364, March 1966.

Woodhouse, Christopher M. *Apple of Discord: A Survey of Recent Greek Politics in Their International Setting.* London and New York: Hutchinson, 1948.

Worsley, Peter. *The Third World.* Chicago: University of Chicago Press, 1964.

Wright, Quincy. *A Study of War.* 2d ed. Chicago: University of Chicago Press, 1965.

*Youth in Turmoil.* "The Freedom to be Idealistic," New York: Time-Life Book, 1969.

Zasloff, Joseph J. *The Role of the Sanctuary in Insurgency: Communist China's Support of the Viet Minh, 1946-54.* RM-4618-PR. Santa Monica, Calif.: Rand Corporation, 1967.

# Index

Sierra Maestra Mountains, Cuba, 49, 85, 86
Siglo II, Bolivia, 56-57
Silent Generation, 181
Sindicato Nacional dos Empregados do Comércio e da Indústria, 130
Sino-Soviet bloc, 6, 60. *See also* Eastern bloc
sit-in, 223
socialism, 21, 176-85 *passim*; Latin America and, 60, 69, 87; Africa and, 102-3, 106, 114-15, 118, 131, 146, 151, 156-57, 159-60; Khrushchev on, 257-58
Somali Republic, 158
Sorbonne, the, *see* Paris revolution (1968)
South Africa, 156, 160
South America, 3, 47, 279, 281, 288; Guevara on, 62-63; Debray on, 84-85; and Khrushchev, 156, 259. *See also by country*
Southeast Asia, 190, 204, 209-10, 250, 281. *See also* Vietnam
Soviets, *see* U.S.S.R.
Spanish colonialism, 29, 107, 148, 281
"Special Kind of Rebellion, A," 201
Sport and Recreation Association, Guinea, 130
Stalin, Joseph, 22, 27, 32,

35, 41, 152-56, 177, 180, 185; United States and, 181, 258, 261
Stanford, Max, 235-36
Stettinius, Edward, 261
strategic hamlets, 142
strategy and tactics; Marxist hard liners and, 7, 12-13, 177; in Latin America, 7, 75, 76, 80, 94; Mao Tse-tung on, 19, 25, 37-40; in Africa, 106, 122, 145, 157-58; New Left and, 177, 199, 212, 230, 234-35; mentioned, 280
strikes, 19, 116, 192, 230; in Guinea, 124, 130, 132, 133
students: Chinese, 31, 34, 40, 40, 45; schooled abroad, 31, 45, 145-50; African, 106, 132, 145-50; in New Left movement, 177-78, 188, 194, 200-204, 212, 239; French, 205-6; Eastern, 206-7; dissent among, 208-12, 215-22, 224-25, 230; mentioned, 4, 71. *See also* university
Students for a Democratic Society (SDS), 193, 224, 225
subversion, 104, 112, 133
Sudan, the, 158
Suez, the, 259
Sumadija Partisan Detach-